Y0-BCS-346

A KENOTIC CHRISTOLOGY

In the Humanity of Jesus The Christ, The Compassion of Our God

Lucien J. Richard, O.M.I.

UNIVERSITY
PRESS OF
AMERICA

University Press of America, Inc.™
P.O. Box 19101, Washington, D.C. 20036

Printed in the United States of America

ISBN: 0-8191-2200-9 (Perfect)
0-8191-2199-1 (Case)

Library of Congress Number: 81-40915

DEDICATION

In memory of my father and
of a friend, Henry Lemaire.
Both lived the kenotic way.

ACKNOWLEDGMENTS

I am thankful for the financial support that I received through an ATS grant, and to Weston School of Theology. I am grateful to Richard Martin who corrected my grammar, to Eleanor Morrissey who typed the final manuscript, to Joanna Carroll for the index, and to Mary Purcell for her proofreading.

TABLE OF CONTENTS

INTRODUCTION

"When he came to the territory of Caesarea Philippi, Jesus asked his disciples: 'Who do men say that the Son of Man is?' They answered, 'Some say John the Baptist, others Elijah, others Jeremiah or one of the prophets.' 'And you,' he asked, 'who do you say I am?'" (Mt. 16:10-17, cf. also Mark 8:27). Jesus put his question to his disciples shortly before he went to Jerusalem to suffer his passion. Two thousand years later, we are being asked the same question, and, just as then, we are given a variety of answers. /1/ While the answers are of interest, what is most important in Christology is the manner in which the question has been posed through two thousand years of Christianity. Initially, it was a two-part question: it was asked about the people - "Who do they say the Son of Man is?" - and it was asked directly of the disciples - "Who do you say the Son of Man is?" Today, the question is asked of believers and of those outside the circle of faith. While their answers are not, and need not be, the same, they cannot be unrelated and in contradiction.

From within the circle of faith it is Christology's task to show what is really meant by the profession that "Jesus is the Christ." Christology must establish the intrinsic foundation of that profession in the person of Jesus. It must attempt to answer how, why, and with what justice Jesus the proclaimer became Christ the proclaimed. And it must attempt to answer how that historically unique Jesus of Nazareth related to universal claims about the Christ. /2/ For the title "Christ" has never been used by faith merely to say his universal significance. And it is only through such an investigation that we can exclude both a unilateral kerygmatic and dogmatic Christology as well as a Christology directed solely to the historical Jesus.

There is a two-fold hermeneutic operative /3/ here: one which concerns the origins and foundations of Christianity's proclamation that Jesus is the Christ; the other, concerning the consequences of such a proclamation. Both interpretations must be made from within the circle of contemporary faith. The contemporary Christian must have an answer to Jesus' question. But a simple recitation of what others have said in response is not sufficient. Today's Christian must be concerned with the here and now - "Who do *you* say I am?" Today. To you.

Christology must be an attempt to trace the way from Jesus of Nazareth to the Christ of Christian belief. For while the theologian has to tell a story that is not only his or her story but the story of Jesus of Nazareth, he or she must tell it in a different way in every generation. The retracing of the way from Jesus of Nazareth to our proclaimed and confessed Christ can only be accomplished in the contemporaneity of faith.

In retracing this path, proper relationship must be maintained between the present Christ and the historical Jesus. Christology must constantly and simultaneously move in both directions. It must be both critical and practical. This is possible only if we take part in the past event. We must understand more clearly than ever that the message of the New Testament is a legacy, a text to be interpreted. And we must bridge the distance in time between the past event of revelation and the present reality of our own faith, for the truth of the Christian message is rooted in the historical nature of our relationship to primitive Christianity. Understanding the past Christ-event and self-interpretation are inseparable.

In a real sense, the function of Christology is to clarify what we can say *about* Jesus as well as *to* him, to clarify our "logos" about Jesus and to Jesus. Christology in the deepest sense is not simply an academic matter requiring only a familiarity with and a remembrance of things past. It requires reflection upon our contemporary encounter with the living Christ. I can only interpret the history of salvation in relation to the living interpretation that I give of myself as an historical being situated in a particular tradition and culture. Christology seeks understanding through the "interplay of the movement of tradition and the movement of the interpreter." The process of understanding is circular. But as H. Gadamer writes, this circular movement is not simply methodological; it represents "...an ontological structural element in understanding." /4/

INTRODUCTION

The process of understanding is directed by the hermeneutical circle, which Paul Ricoeur, following Augustine, formulates as follows: "We must understand in order to believe, but we must believe in order to understand." /5/ Understanding is not carried out from afar but from within the very meaning that is to be interpreted. Indeed, unless the interpreter is already involved in the meaning of the symbol, he cannot know where nor how to begin. Again, according to Ricoeur, "Never, in fact, does the interpreter get near what his texts say unless he lives in the aura of the meaning he is inquiring after." /6/

In the hermeneutical process, it is impossible to separate oneself from the object of investigation. On the contrary, it is necessary to enter into the object. What is needed, in Gadamer's and Ricoeur's terms, is a conversation with the text, with the tradition. This conversation is construed with the dialectic of question and answer. Understanding is something that occurs in the conversation itself; it is imposed by neither the interpreter nor the text. Understanding is a happening; it is not simply an accomplishment. As an event, understanding involves the correlation of theory and practice. It involves response to the "history." As P. Hodgson writes: "Response and practice belong to the essence of the hermeneutical enterprise. They do not merely follow from understanding but enable it: truth is won only by engagement." /7/ In a real sense truth is realized only in doing as we read in the epistle of James:

> Only be sure that you act on the message and do not merely listen; for that would be to mislead yourselves. A man who listens to the message but never acts upon it is like one who looks in a mirror at the face nature gave him. He glances at himself and goes away, and at once forgets what he looked like. But the man who looks closely into the perfect law, the law that makes us free, and who lives in its company, does not forget what he hears, but acts upon it; and that is the man who by acting will find happiness. /8/

That is an echo of Jesus' statement in the Gospel of John: "Whoever has the will to do the will of God shall know whether my teaching comes from him or is merely my own." /9/ The meaning of faith is formally found not simply in the comprehension of the content of a confession, but in the act of confessing itself. The content of faith can only be known in the exercise of faith. There can be no separation of action and meaning, no escape of faith to the realm of pure subjectivity and inwardness. There can be no dichotomy between subject and object, between being and consciousness.

It should not be surprising if this is difficult for modern people to accept. Descartes so effectively separated subject and object that they seemed destined never to be brought together again. The impact of Descartes' bifurcation of selfhood in the _res cogitans_ and the _res extensa_ was mediated through the transformation it received at the hands of Kant. Kant engineered a Copernican revolution in epistemology by conceiving the human subject as the active constructor of his universe of meaning rather than as one upon whom a universe of meaning is imposed. He centered the world around the knower instead of the knower around the world. Yet while Kant saw the knower as an active agent, he emptied him of flesh and individuality in an attempt to give a totally "objective" account of reality. The conscious personality who knows the reality was purposefully excluded.

Kantian epistemology led to an epistemological model that would dominate in the following century: i.e., the model of autonomous rationality. In this scenario, the individual constitutes his own universe of meaning; he is the free being who creates his own world. The knower and the category of freedom is primary. The focus is primarily upon the individual rather than the social being, upon the achievement of the inner self. The Kantian model leaves us with a split between subject and object, between the self-defining and the self-defined subject and the objective world with which the autonomous subject must reconcile himself/herself. No valid hermeneutical process is possible within this split since there exists an unbridgeable gap between object and subject.

This position has been severely criticized by John Macmurray, who suggests that it leads to the understanding that: "The art of thinking is constituted by a purely theoretical intention. It involves a withdrawal from action and so from all positive, practical relation with the Other." /10/ The self is not simply an observer, not purely subjective, totally uninvolved and withdrawn. In criticizing Kant's and Descartes' adoption of the "I think" as the starting point of philosophical reflection, J. Macmurray writes: "... thought is inherently private; and any philosophy which takes its stand on the primacy of thought, which defines the self as thinker, is committed formally to an extreme logical individualism. It is necessarily egocentric." /11/ According to John Macmurray, the thinking must start with action. Action is primary. Macmurray advocates the substitution of the "I do" for the "I think" as the center of reference.

When the self is understood as agent, it is part of the world in which it acts, since action is causally effective. Macmurray writes that as subject, the self "...stands 'over against' the world, which is its object. The self as subject then is not part of the world it knows, but withdrawn from it, and so, in conception, outside it, as other than its objective." /12/ A theoretical model of the self must avoid becoming confused with its own methodological process. The problem occurs when we define our own being as that of the thinker. Then according to Macmurray, "...we transform this methodological solipsism into an existential one," /13/ and are then determined to explain knowledge without any reference to action.

The kind of knowledge essential to Christology is personal knowledge, involving a fundamental relation of "doing" to "knowing." Michael Polanyi in his book Personal Knowledge has called our attention to that fundamental relation. For Polanyi, knowledge always means coming to grips with reality within a framework of personal commitment. When we assert the truth of something, we assert that it bears on reality. In his preface to Personal Knowledge, Polanyi writes:

> Personal knowledge is an intellectual commitment, and as such inherently hazardous...into every act of knowing there enters a passionate contribution of the person knowing what is being known,

> and...this co-efficient is no mere imperfection but a vital component of his knowledge. /14/

There are some truths which we only know not by detached observation but by dwelling in them. /15/ Personal knowledge is not private knowledge; rather, it is knowledge which we as members of a community accredit together in the give and take of life. Passion, personal intuition, and collective sentiment can make cognitive claims. /16/

Knowledge for Polanyi implies opening to wider contact with reality which makes the knower more like an explorer than an architect. Discovery is the paradigm case of knowledge. Personal knowledge requires not an abstract, empty apprehension of the self, but an apprehension of the self in its relations with the world outside of itself. Self-consciousness is not a primary but a secondary movement. The self must first immerse itself in the world and only then, through reflection, will it be found again in its fullness. The self realizes itself in its activity, in a sense losing itself in the world. It is only through knowledge of the world that anything significant is learned about the self. Human identity is not simply achieved through a process of internal discovery, but by coming to terms with an exterior context which defines the human subject and which must be internalized and overcome. Identity is achieved through a process of reconciliation to and transformation of external reality.

Karl Rahner writes, "As existing in an interpersonal world, a person arrives concretely at his own self-interpretation, however much it comes from within and enters within, only within the self-interpretation of his interpersonal world, and by participating in and receiving from the tradition of the historical self-interpretation of those people who form his interpersonal world from out of the past and through the present into the future. A person always forms his own secular self-understanding only within a community of persons in the experience of a history which he never makes alone, in dialogue and in experience which reproduces the productive self-interpretation of other people." /17/

Here, instead of conceiving the individual as constituting his universe of meaning, an individual's consciousness arises in a situation where meaning has already been constituted. The question of human identity is put in a social context; it is achieved in relationship to others. Rahner advocates dialogue as the only possible approach to the subject/object relationship.

True dialogue does not invade; it does not manipulate. For there can be no such thing as dialogical manipulation. The primary dimension of true dialogue is intersubjectivity, or intercommunication, which cannot be reduced to a simple relation between a knowing subject and a knowable object. Just as there is no such thing as an isolated human being, there is also no such thing as isolated thinking.

According to P. Freire, "The thinking subject cannot think alone. In the act of thinking about the object, he/she cannot think without the co-operation of another subject. There is no longer an "I think" but a "we think." It is the "we think" which establishes the "I think" and not the contrary. /18/ Dialogue is simply the co-participation of persons in the very act of thinking and speaking. In this dialogue the object is not simply the goal of the act of thinking, but the mediator of communication. Dialogue achieves a communion of horizons which leads to self-disclosure and self-understanding.

In this encounter, some of one's horizons are negated and others affirmed. Some elements in the object's horizon recede and others come forward. Both object and subject have been called into question in terms of the answer they have given to the questionableness of existence. All knowledge that is a real understanding is linked to the self-formative process of the knowing subject. According to Palmer, "...every true hermeneutical experience is a new creation, a new disclosure of being, it stands in a firm relationship to the present and historically could not have happened before." /19/

Here human activity is located not primarily in the realm of contemplation, in the realm of the <u>cogitare</u>, but in the realm of action, in the realm of praxis. We must penetrate the object in communion with it; we must respond to the object as though we must change - respondeo etsi mutabor. Indeed, we are ready to listen even if we must change. As C. H. Long writes: "The interpreter as he moves from symbolism to rationality will find that he must make another movement back into the shadows of his ego and history for he discovers that his being is mirrored in the reality of life and history and simultaneously created by him in the moment of comprehension." /20/

To respond to the object in dialogue is not simply an invitation to self-transformation; it is also an invitation to change and transform the other. If a person is incapable of changing reality, he simply adjusts himself/herself to reality. As P. Freire writes, "...the adaptive person is person as object, adaptation representating at most a weak form of self-defense." /21/

Given this understanding of knowledge and hermeneutics, our Christology will be expressed in what has been termed a transformation model. /22/ The main purpose for such a Christology is the search for personal and social transformation in the light of the teaching and the person of Jesus. The presupposition here is that that transformation is possible; that one's interest lies explicitly in being altered. There can be no intention of imposing on the "text" my own subjectivity so as to avoid my own transformation. But there can also be no avoidance of interestedness in the object - my transformation is at stake. Basically a transformational model implies action; in the case of Christology, discipleship.

For J. Moltmann the only way to elaborate a Christology is in and through the following of Jesus. "Christian existence is a practice. It is the following of the crucified one that transforms man in himself and his situation. In that sense the theology of the cross is a practical theology." /23/ Again according to Jon Sobrino: "The only way to get to know Jesus is to follow after him in one's own real life; to try to identify oneself with his own historical concern; and to try to fashion his Kingdom in our midst. In other words, only through Christian praxis is it possible for us to draw close to Jesus. Following Jesus is the precondition for knowing Jesus." /24/ Praxis is a constitutive element in the systematic elaboration of Christology.

Only an authentic religious, moral, intellectual, and social praxis can ground an authentic theology, and overcome the dualism between the believing subject and history, between subject and object. Within this epistemological perception there is a commitment to begin with the human, to attempt to think through and express the meaning of Christological assertions in terms of human self-understanding. Christology must be seen as the self-reflexive and thematic expression of faith that has its original and proper locus in human self-understanding. There is a conviction here that we can find and fashion ways of understanding Jesus only if we attentively re-evaluate the nature of humanity itself. Christology needs to stand on the solid and concrete grounds of anthropology. The theologian must first study and understand the mystery of the human in order to learn something about God, about Christ. Without understanding the human condition the theologian could hardly say anything meaningful about God, about Christ, the God-man. No matter what the range of our intellect or imagination, we must always make a relation to direct experience. Faith and religion must have their ground and starting point in human experience. And when religion transcends the limits of human experience, it must do so because of what it perceives in human experience that demands such a transcending. As J. Macmurray writes: "It is one thing to realize that the world in which we live is wider and deeper than we know, and that there may be whole reaches of it and aspects of it which are hidden from our normal consciousness. It is quite another thing to hold that there is another world which is not this world at all." /25/

The basic question to be asked then is what is there in human experience which can lead to a transcendence, to a possible religious valuation. Macmurray writes: "We are looking...for a complex of elements in human experience which no one would deny, which are obvious and direct facts, and which provide the material which is transformed by the religious attitude into what we call religious experience." /26/ The point of departure for religious experience must be from the range of experience that is universal and common to all men and women. In a sense, the field of religion is fundamentally and originally a field of common, universal, and largely uninterpreted human experience. While all the facts of experience can prove to be data for religious consciousness, certain special areas of human experience are more conducive to religious interpretation. The selection of these areas of human experience involves the process of valuation which is primarily a process of action and not simply of thought and reflection. For it is in action that we have to relate ourselves to others. But the process of valuation is reciprocal and mutual. Real valuation then demands the entering into fellowship, into the realm of history, into an historical community. The starting point of Christology is the historical and communal experience of Jesus as the Christ, as the Lord, expressed in texts, tradition, and common human experience.

Jesus Christ was experienced as disclosive of ultimacy within the realm of history. The paschal mystery in all of its symbolic dimensions was an attempt to express this disclosure. As symbolic, the paschal mystery has been interpreted by various generations as illuminating and explicating the common, ordinary existence in the world. Conversely, the paschal mystery is not simply encountered by a totally un-illuminated and un-explicated human experience. Even common human experience possesses an initial horizon that focuses concerns and searchings, and heightens sensitivities to certain meanings. The paschal mystery further enlarges and transforms these initial horizons; and they also give meaning to the paschal mystery as it encounters us individually. What is essential in this encounter is the willingness on the individual's part to allow the paschal mystery to interpret him/her. As with all authentic encounters, critical freedom and receptivity are of equal importance. This is especially true in the encounter of the self with the paschal mystery, in the elaboration of a transformative Christology. What is at stake here is the claim that in the paschal mystery God encounters the self and defines it. The disclosure of God in Jesus Christ is also a disclosure of the self. The fundamental question for Christology is the adequacy of the symbolic dimension of the Paschal Mystery to express the disclosure of God and the adequacy of a contemporary expression of that same mystery. Since the encounter is of "ultimate" concern, the adequacy of the symbol and of the contemporary expression can only be relative. The Paschal Mystery as symbol was an attempt to bring to expression the manifestation of God in Jesus Christ. As symbol, it neither originated out of a situational vacuum nor did it speak in a situational vacuum. Hence the symbol itself is relative - doubly relative because of the reality that it expresses, God in our midst, and because of the particular situation out of which it originates.

Form criticism and redaction criticism have underlined the incredible diversity in the understanding of the Paschal Mystery. Both methods recognize that in the New Testament there are a number of Christologies and that these are the results of competing Christological traditions each with a different point of departure (Early Palestinian, Judaeo-Hellenistic, Gentile, Markan, Pauline, Johannine, etc.) and a different emphasis. The same diversity is true of our own situations, of our experiences, questions, meanings.

In this context the relative adequacy of the expression and statement of our encounter with God in the Christ-event does not demand that every single expression of the original encounter be taken into consideration, nor that every dimension of our human experience be addressed. Relative adequacy can only be judged after a study of the New Testament and of its historical interpretation and of the more fundamental structures of common human experience. Only the whole of the New Testament expressions will disclose with relative adequacy the whole of the event of Jesus Christ. Similarly, only the search for the most fundamental dimensions of our human experience in its particular contemporary situation can lead to a relatively adequate contemporary expression of the event of Jesus Christ.

It is my contention that an emphasis on the Cross and on the common human experience of suffering can lead to such an expression of the Christ-event.

A KENOTIC CHRISTOLOGY

I am proposing a kenotic Christology as an attempt to enlighten, thematize, and make intelligible the common human experience and "limit situation" of human suffering. I also contend that there is a transcending dimension to human suffering that gives meaning to the Christ-event today.

According to St. Paul, the preaching of the kenotic Christ is a folly for the world. It is a folly, according to Paul Ricoeur, in the sense that such preaching does not correspond to experience. It appears as an eruption into our culture from the totally other side. However, it does correspond to one facet of the human experience - our own experience of suffering. And it is this experience that provides the ground for a preaching of the kenotic Christ.

A kenotic Christology is necessarily a transformative Christology. For an attempt to correlate human experience and religious symbols must be done within a context in which one understands that all meaning and knowledge is acquired in action, and that ultimately all meaningful action is for the sake of human solidarity, and in most cases emancipatory solidarity. Essential to the meaning of the major religious symbols is their embodiment in action. As L. Gilkey writes, "... Christian proclamation does not enter this quest (man's search for himself) only to make itself understandable and to adjust its own tradition to the present. It enters it for the sake of liberation... Hermeneutic is then not simply the 'art of understanding' written expressions of life, but of understanding all historical expressions of life within this political context." /27/

The religious symbols, such as the Cross and the Resurrection, are intrinsically related to the specific dimensions of our concrete existence and the various aspects of our actions. As L. Gilkey writes of the religious symbols, "...they promise illumination, a new understanding, they challenge the way we concretely are, they call for a new way of being, a new attitude to ourselves and to others, new forms of our actual relations in community, a new kind of action in the world...every fundamental theological symbol means a critical stance toward past and present forms of existence and order in the social world, and the call to historical and social action on behalf of a new earth." /28/ In any valid Christology what is needed first of all is a contact with the reality before reflecting theologically or otherwise on it. In a sense, it is the real following of Jesus which permits knowledge of the reality of Jesus. A kenotic Christology is credible and viable only if it does not remain simply a theory. In fact, the theory itself is only possible if it emerges out of a practice.

A KENOTIC CHRISTOLOGY

NOTES

1. Cf. M. Martin, Jesus Now (New York: E. P. Dutton, 1973).

2. Cf. C. Davis, Christ and the World Religions (New York: Herder, 1971).

3. For a history of hermeneutics: cf. Richard Palmer, Hermeneutics: Interpretation Theory in Schleiermacher, Dilthey, Heidegger, and Gadamer (Evanston, IL: Northwestern University Press, 1969).

4. H. G. Gadamer, Truth and Method (New York: Seabury Press, 1975) p. 261.

5. P. Ricoeur, The Symbolism of Evil (Boston: Beacon Press, 1967) p. 351.

6. Ibid.

7. P. C. Hodgson, Jesus--Word and Presence: An Essay in Christology (Philadelphia: Fortress, 1971) p. 39. See also M. Lamb, "The Theory--Praxis Relationship in Contemporary Christian Theologies," CTSA Proceedings Vol. 31 (1976) pp. 149-179.

8. James 1:22-28. All Scriptural quotes are taken from The New English Bible, Oxford University Press/Cambridge University Press, 1970.

9. John 7:17.

10. J. Macmurray, Persons in Relation (London: Faber and Faber, 1961) p. 20.

11. J. Macmurray, The Self as Agent (London: Faber and Faber, 1957) p. 71.

12. Ibid., p. 91.

13. J. Macmurray, Persons in Relation, p. 26.

14. M. Polanyi, Personal Knowledge: Towards a Post-Critical Philosophy (New York: Harper, 1964) p. xiv; H. Kuhn, "Personal Knowledge and the Crisis of the Philosophical Tradition," Intellect and Hope, eds. T. Langford and William H. Poteat (Durham: Duke University Press, 1968) pp. 111-135.

15. Cf. R. Gelwick, The Way of Discovery (New York: Oxford University Press, 1977); J. A. Pczynski, Doers of the Word (Missoula: Scholars Press, 1977).

16. Cf. M. Polanyi, Knowing and Being (Chicago: University of Chicago Press, 1969) p. 134.

17. K. Rahner, Foundations of Christian Faith (New York: Seabury, 1978) p. 160.

18. P. Freire, Education for Critical Consciousness (New York: Seabury, 1973) p. 137.

19. R. E. Palmer, Hermeneutics (Evanston: Northwestern University Press, 1969) p. 244.

20. C. H. Long, "Archaism and Hermeneutics," The History of Religions, ed. J. M. Kitigawa (Chicago: University of Chicago Press, 1967) pp. 86-87.

21. P. Freire, op. cit., p. 4.

22. For an analysis of transformation models cf. D. Browning, Generative Man (Philadelphia: Westminster, 1974).

23. Moltmann, The Crucified God (New York: Harper & Row, 1973) p. 30.

24. J. Sobrino, Christology at the Crossroads (New York: Orbis, 1978) p. xiii. Cf. also S. Hauerwas, "Jesus: The Story of the Kingdom," Theology Digest 26:4 (1978) pp. 303-325.

25. J. Macmurray, The Structure of Religious Experience (New Haven: Yale University Press, 1936) p. 3.

26. Ibid.

27. L. Gilkey, Naming the Whirlwind: The Renewal of God-Language (New York: Bobbs-Merrill, 1969) p. 250.

28. Ibid., pp. 375-376.

CHAPTER 1

JESUS CHRIST IN A TECHNOLOGICAL AGE

A. Introduction - A Secular Culture

Each generation has attempted to retrace the way from Jesus to the Christ from within the context of its own concerns and anxieties. Similarly, contemporary Christology can only discover its own truth in dialogue with its cultural setting. It is important, then, to discern the distinctive concerns of our contemporary situation.

Hence, the major task of Christology becomes one of translation. This culture, as other cultures, has certain basic characteristics, a mood or a mind. To speak about the "mood" or "mind" of our culture is, according to L. Gilkey, to "refer to that deep, preconceptual attitude toward an understanding of existence which dominates and forms the cultural life of any epoch, the way men of a given time characteristically apprehend the world they live in and their place within it; their fundamental self-understanding of their being in the world." /1/ But it must do so without totally capitulating to it. For while modernity is the norm, it is not necessary nor may it even be possible to translate the Christian tradition in conformity to it. As we said, theology must interpret and communicate the Christian message to a people of a specific time and space. However, there is no *a priori* guarantee that such an interpretation is possible - nor that it will succeed. The spirit and mind of a culture can be so totally in contradiction to the Christian message, that there is no point of insertion or contact. In that case, theology can be but a proclamation, an attempt at counter-culture.

To characterize the mood and spirit of a specific culture does not imply that every participant is determined by such characteristics. /2/ Yet, since the culture generally operates at a preconceptual level, its characteristics determine the general background of most cultural creations of an era. These characteristics determine the fundamental attitude of a whole group towards reality, truth, and values, and, therefore, even towards religion.

The whole of modern culture is concerned with

"the making of the human." There is an ongoing debate about humanization and dehumanization. Modern man is searching for a new image of humanity at the level of human identity and meaning. The question he is asking at the most fundamental level is: What is humanity? How should man and woman imagine himself/herself? He/she is searching for an image of authentic personal existence. While the problem of humanization has always been a central concern, it now takes on the character of an inescapable preoccupation. For we now know that dehumanization is not only a real possibility, it is an historical fact. And it is not surprising that dehumanization should be a central concern of our culture.

The general consensus today is that "the secular spirit" represents the "mind" of our culture. /3/ Innumerable writers have speculated on the nature of secularity. The following passage from the writings of Peter Berger contains the essential characteristics.

> By secularization we mean the process by which sectors of society and culture are removed from the domination of religious institutions and symbols. When we speak of society and institutions in modern Western history, of course, secularization manifests itself in the evacuation by the Christian churches of areas previously under their control or influence - as in the separation of church and state, or in the expropriation of church lands, or in the emancipation of education from ecclesial authority. When we speak of culture and symbols, however, we imply that secularization is more than a social-structural process. It affects the totality of cultural life and ideation and may be observed in the decline of religious contents in the arts, in philosophy, in literature, and, most important of all, in the rise of science as an autonomous, thoroughly secular perspective on the world. Moreover, it is implied here that the process of secularization has a subjective side as well. As there is secularization of society and culture, so there is a

> secularization of consciousness. Put simply, this means that the modern West has produced an increasing number of individuals who look upon the world and their own lives without benefit of religious interpretation. /4/

The major characteristic of secularity as it relates to religion is the absence of any reference to transcendence. P. Berger writes: "The reality of ordinary life is increasingly posited as the only reality. Or, if you will, the common sense world becomes a world without windows." /5/ Secularity involves a qualitative change in human consciousness, particularly in regard to man's self-concept and the nature of his relations with others. It leads, at this level of consciousness, to a radical change in the understanding of what it means to be human. /6/

Gilkey has underlined four major characteristics of secularity: contingency, relativity, temporality, and autonomy. He sees the last as the most important. /7/ In his essay "Aspects of a Religious Analysis of Culture" Paul Tillich has identified a fundamental relationship between secularity and the industrial society. /8/

B. A Technological Age

The predominant force at work in the industrial society is technology. According to P. Berger, the transformation brought about by technology "has had economic, social, and political dimensions, all immense in scope. It has also brought on a revolution on the level of human consciousness, fundamentally uprooting beliefs, values, and even the emotional texture of life." /9/

P. Tillich enumerates two primary elements in technology:

> The first...is the concentration of man's activities upon the methodical investigation and technical transformation of his world, including himself, and the consequent loss of the dimension of depth in his encounter with reality. Reality has

> lost its inner transcendence...God has become superfluous and the universe left to man as its master. /10/

The second characteristic of man in the industrial society is that

> ...in order to fulfill his destiny, man must be in possession of creative powers, analagous to those previously attributed to God... The conflict between what man essentially is and what he actually is, his estrangement, or in traditional terms his fallen state, is disregarded... He is pictured in a position of progressive fulfillment of his potentialities. /11/

Tillich sees technology as a thrust toward the transformation of the world and self through the progressive acquisition of power. This process of transformation is accompanied by the belief in continous upward progress. There is a built-in move to indefinite progress in technology, because it is its natural tendency not to simply fit means to ends, but to bring about new ends. There can be indefinite progress because there is always something new and better to find.

While many definitions of the technological mentality are available, the one given by Robert Nisbet provides a good starting point: "What is central to technology is the application of rational principles to the control or reordering of space, matter, and human beings." /12/ Technology is the rational ordering of processes in view of definite goals. All reality is reduced to a calculable quantity, to units. All units are brought into a design and are subjected to a predesigned control. The power of technology is founded in the capacity to extend the horizon of calculability. The reduction of all reality to a calculable quantity is undergirded by what Ferkiss has called a new materialism "which asserts that man is in fact part of nature rather than something apart from it..." /13/

Nature is not understood as rigid and determined but as a dynamic process, a constant becoming, for the technological mind is aware of the interconnection of all realities. Reality, in fact, is understood in terms of componentiality. That is, its components are self-contained units which are apprehended and manipulated atomistically. These components are interdependent; none are meaningful outside of the whole and none can be defined or understood save in relation to the whole.

Jacques Ellul argues that the operational model of technology is extended to every field of human endeavor. He writes:

> Techniques in the translation into action of man's concern to master things by means of reason, to account for what is subconscious, make quantitative what is qualitative, make clear and precise the outlines of nature, take hold of chaos and put order into it. /14/

Underlying the rise of technology is an important epistemological shift that began with Descartes. It is a basic conviction that scientific knowledge signifies the domination of all reality. We have moved from understanding truth as metaphysical, (_verum quia ens_), to truth as historical, (_verum quia factum_), to truth as a technique, (_verum quia faciendum_). Truth is found in the making, the practice. It is centered on future and action. From being concerned about the eternal - that which never changes - to the past - the factual - the contemporary man directs his attention to the future - or what he himself can create.

Man's/woman's faculty of knowledge is an instrument of power. Human knowledge signifies a seizure of power over all reality; everything becomes predictable and seizable. As the possessor of knowledge, man/woman is capable of projecting his/her world in advance. Technological man/woman is one who is in control of his/her own development. He/she is geared for manipulation of self and environment; the orientation is to action, change, and control. Hannah Arendt predicts that technological man/woman will not accept that life is a given but will grasp existence as "something he has made for himself." /15/ According to Sam Keen "the image of _homo faber_ is the key to contemporary identity." /16/

Elevating _homo faber_ to the essential characteristic of being human also implies elevating "power" to the position of man's/woman's dominant and intermediate goal. According to Hans Jonas: "To become ever more masters of the world, to advance from power to power, even if only collectively and perhaps no longer by choice, can now be seen to be the chief vocation of mankind." /17/

Both Marcuse and Heidegger have affirmed that the "logic" of technology is that of domination. In Heidegger's mind there is a fateful metaphysical decision of the will for the boundless power over the world of things. Nietzsche's anticipated "superman" is technological man/woman *par excellence*. Nietzsche had proclaimed the will to power as the key to human behavior. /18/ In his "The Genealogy of Morals" (1887), Nietzsche develops the theme that all that proceeds from power is good and all that springs from weakness is bad. /19/

But the will to power occurs within the framework of Kant's revolutionary discovery of the phenomenon of subjectivity. According to Kant, the human subject is an active generator of the universe of meaning. It is not imposed upon the subject. Kant's series of "*a priori*" categories was postulated in order to ground this subjectivity. These "*a priori*" categories are present to the mind before any experience has occurred and account for experience itself. Kant's epistemology led to a specific cognitive mode or epistemological model, namely, autonomous rationality. This model emphasizes the autonomy and freedom of the subject in constituting his/her universe of meaning. The autonomous, free individual subject is predominant. As such, the Kantian man/woman is one who is in charge of his/her own destiny, who constructs his/her own reality. For Kant this reality was primarily the inner self; in our technological age, this reality is also the external world. Rudolf Bultmann, commenting on Martin Heidegger's affirmation that the twentieth century is centered on subjectivity, writes about our age as "the era in which the world conceived as object is subjected to the planning which is controlled by the values which man himself establishes." /20/

L. Gilkey describes autonomy as man's "...innate capacity to know his own truth, to decide upon his own existence, to create his own meaning, and to establish his own values." /21/ This concept of autonomy is forcefully perceived and expressed in Sartre's *Being* and Nothingness. For Sartre, man/woman is being-for-itself, "in which consciousness and freedom are totally independent and completely autonomous. Every person is a law unto himself/herself." /22/ Technology enhances this sense of autonomy. The individual who experiences technological might feels equipped with power and influence enough even to conquer the biological conditions of existence. To be master of all is the goal of the technological mind.

The essence of technology is a will to power which is never satisfied and always demands more and more power. Technological developments have progressed to such a point that it is now possible to control our environment sufficiently to alleviate human needs. But the will to power drives individuals far beyond the point where any alleviation is effected. Paradoxically, freedom over one's destiny accompanied by the power of technology can lead to the destruction of autonomy and freedom. Technology demonstrates a tendency to dominate and violate reality, to master other people and nature.

Thus, when B. F. Skinner announced that we could no longer afford freedom for man, he merely drew attention to what was implicit in technology itself. In his book Beyond Freedom and Dignity he advocates the delegation and control of the population to specialists. Skinner believes that freedom and dignity are harmful ideas that have created all kinds of social problems. Skinner's approach is utopian, and he believes fully in human perfectability./23/ He writes: "Almost all the best changes in our culture which we now regard as worth while can be traced to perfectionistic philosophies." /24/ Man/woman can, through science, control his/her world and in so doing, he/she has the opportunity finally to achieve control of himself/herself. Skinner has a boundless confidence in the efficacy of science. He believes implicitly in the ability of man/woman to unlock all mysteries of the universe. His intention is to place man/woman in his/her true relation to the rest of nature, even at the risk of removing him/her from the center of the universe.

As C. E. Wollner writes about Skinner, he has "...pressed a soaring optimism for the prospects of modern man in that he is confident that the ascendancy of science and technology so far from besetting, if not overwhelming man, as more than one humanist has suggested it has done, is an occasion for rejoicing." /25/ Wollner considers that for Skinner "the modern movement of the proliferation of technology based on science, therefore, portends not disaster, but hope, as man at last possesses in science the optimal vehicle, the most efficacious tool for logical, quick and resourceful change." /26/ Yet B. F. Skinner's doctrine calls for the wholesale manipulation of human beings, willy-nilly, for their own good, or rather for the survival of the species. Skinner believes that the science of behaviorism has dispelled the illusion that a human being is the initiator of his own behavior. His design for a new culture is founded in an empiricism so patent that it absolutely excludes any possibility of explanation beyond material reality.

Behavioral technology has been defined as a "... developing science that aims to change the environment rather than people, that seeks to alter actions rather than feelings, and that shifts the customary psychological emphasis on the world inside men to the world outside them." /27/ Skinner conceives of culture as a social environment that patterns the behavior of its constituents. Insofar as the environment, both physical and cultural, is man-made it can be altered on a scientific basis to serve men and women. Skinner sees everything as the product of conditioning and control. /28/ But the form of control advocated by Skinner is really a form of manipulation. Manipulation can indicate the most beneficial achievements of man's skill and power over things; but it can also indicate the use of the most debasing and insidious means for the degradation of life and the overpowering of one's fellowmen. /29/ Manipulation can refer to an acceptable and beneficial planned change of nature. In the process of education towards liberty, for example, some forms of conditioning or manipulation are necessary. The question is always whether these forms of conditioning or manipulation in practical terms will eliminate the use of freedom. /30/ The fields of behavior-modification and genetic engineering are not grounded in a theory of essential human values. Inexorably driven by a desire for success, they ask whether "it works." /31/

There is no doubt that Skinner is, in a certain sense, a humanist. He believes that the progress of science allows mankind to abandon most adversive conditioning: whether it is truly operant. The operant conditionings can be concealed from or remain unknown to the persons being manipulated. The manipulator knows what kind of conditionings will be effective, and he alone decides what kind of behavior he wants to produce or reinforce. The justification is in humanitarian values: animals and persons are to be conditioned by reinforcers in a way that fosters their survival. Skinner is the perfect example of technological man. In him we see the characteristics of technology, its ambiguities and contradictions.

C. Technology and Domination

There is an ongoing presupposition that technology is ideologically neutral and that the crisis of technology is simply in terms of its usage. The crisis lies within the realities, social, political, or economic which use or exploit technology. Change the political, economic, or social system and the crisis of technology would be solved. It is the contention of many that technology is only a tool to be used for good or ill as the user chooses. In itself it is scrupulously neutral. But with technology we are no longer simply speaking about tools or automation or new discoveries. We are dealing with a methodology, a version of man/woman and the world, with a culture. Technology embodies a cognitive style of its own, and this cognitive style is transferable to other areas of life. It is possible for an individual to look upon his/her own psychological life with the same attitude with which an engineer contemplates the workings of a machine. Elements of consciousness that are intrinsic to technological production are transposed to areas of social life.

There seems to be an independent dynamism inherent to technology. Technology possesses its own autonomy and has its own distinctive world view, its own ideological system. As such, it is not neutral. Technology, by its very nature, leads to domination. According to certain authors such as H. Marcuse, science and technology have helped to create the present system of social domination. According to this author:

> Today, domination perpetuates and extends itself not only through technology but _as_ technology, and the latter provides the great legitimation of the expanding political

> power, which absorbs all spheres of culture. /32/

Domination is not easily democratized. There is endemic to it the very important question of who dominates and who is being dominated, the powerful and the powerless. Perfection lies in domination; those who are in a dominating position have best achieved the goals of humanhood. Technological man/woman is independent, completely master of his/her life. Nietzsche wrote about the men who command and rule: "They are unaccountable: they like destiny, without rhyme or reason, ruthlessly, bare of pretext, being natural organizers. These men know nothing of guilt, responsibility, consideration." /33/

D. Narcissism

In his book The Culture of Narcissism, Christopher Lasch writes: "Every society reproduces its culture - its norms, its underlying assumptions, its modes of organizing experience - in the individual, in the form of personality." /34/ The technological culture has given rise to the narcissistic personality. Narcissism has even been recognized as an important element in contemporary character disorders. So the age of technology has developed its own peculiar form of pathology. C. Lash writes: "Modern capitalist society not only elevates narcissists to prominence, it elicits and reinforces narcissistic traits in everyone." /35/

Narcissism is not simply cultural as Lash recognizes. /36/ Ernest Becker claims that narcissism is inescapable since it has a biological basis in human nature. /37/ Each person as an organism has an inbuilt tendency to incorporate and expand and protect himself against the world. Sociobiology is not suggesting that we are genetically selfish. The sociobiologists are affirming that we are genetically predisposed to be nice to people in proportion to how closely related they are. In biology, the crucial test for altruism is reproductive success. The important thing in evolution is not the good of the species but the good of the individual (or the gene). As Dawkins writes in his book The Selfish Gene, "...the predominant quality to be expected in a successful gene is ruthless selfishness. This gene selfishness will usually give rise to selfishness in individual behavior." /38/ The author warns his reader that in the building of a society "in which individuals cooperate generously and unselfishly towards a common good, you can expect little help from biological nature. Let us try to _teach_ generosity and altruism, because we are born selfish. Let us understand what our own selfish genes are up to, because we may then at least have the chance to upset their designs, something which no other species has ever aspired to." /39/ Sociobiology suggests that much of our behavior has a calculating, selfish, deceitful quality. Elaborate religious, social, and linguistic networks are erected to mark underlying manipulative motivations.

The dominant modern psychologies explain all human behavior in terms of individual pleasure and pain, individual positive and negative valence, individual needs and drives. /40/ In social psychology many authors explain all social interaction in self-serving terms. /41/ Psychologists and psychiatrists almost invariably side with self-gratification over traditional restraint. /42/ Phillip Rieff in his _Triumph of the Therapeutic_ /43/ underlines the fact that contemporary culture proposes a permissive ethic of self-realization in which the well-being of the individual is of the highest value.

Many Western philosophies see "the other" not in its full otherness but as an occasion for one's own self-discovery or self-realization. They invariably make other people into valuable investments which will pay off eventually in the dividend of one's own self-realization. In a person such as E. Fromm, who has emphasized the importance of the "other," we still encounter an emphasis on "self-realization." For him the ideal is "any aim which furthers the growth, freedom, and happiness of the self." He writes in his _Man for Himself_:

> The character structure of the mature and integrated personality, the productive character, constitutes the source and the basis of virtue... "Vice," in the last analysis, is indifference to one's own self and self-mutilation. Not self-renunciation nor selfishness but self-love, not the negation of the individual but the affirmation of his truly human self, are the

> supreme values of humanistic ethics. If man is to have confidence in values, he must know himself and the capacity of his nature for goodness and productiveness. /44/

Fromm makes self-realization the goal of any growth, and relation to others simply the means to that goal.

Psychology and psychiatry not only describe man as selfishly motivated but implicitly or explicitly teach that he ought to be so. Sociobiology holds repression and inhibition of individual impulse to be undesirable and all guilt as dysfunctional neurosis created by cruel child-rearing and a needlessly repressive society.

The contemporary climate is therapeutic. People hunger not for personal salvation, but for the feeling of personal well-being, health, and psychic security. In this therapeutic context, love and meaning are defined simply as the fulfillment of the patient's emotional requirements. A person is never encouraged to subordinate his needs and interests to others or to some cause outside himself/herself. The self-sacrifice and self-abasement of the old concept of love are seen as oppressive, offensive to common sense, and injurious to personal health and well-being. To "liberate" humanity from such outmoded ideas as "love" and "duty" has become the mission of the post-Freudian therapies and particularly of their converts and popularizers for whom mental health means the overthrow of "inhibitions" and the elevation of the self.

It is not surprising, then, that a retreat to purely personal satisfaction was one of the main themes of the Seventies. There was a revival of the cult of expanded consciousness, health, and personal growth. To live for the moment was the prevailing code - to live for oneself, not for humanity. Survival became the catchword of the Seventies and "collective narcissism" the dominant disposition. /45/

In the past few years there has been a proliferation of books concerning the promotion of the individual. /46/ While these books differ in the kind of self-love they appeal to, they share a certain value: the major concern and most important objective in life is the happiness of the individual. Guilt is always purely subjective and always bad. The dominant influence in these books is Assertiveness Therapy which contends that since people are usually trying to push you around you should push them first. The underlying philosophy is that self-interest is the supreme value.

E. False Optimism

While a technological age nurtures our narcissistic natures it also brings about an explosive situation. For while technology makes life more interdependent, it alienates men and women by objectifying and controlling them in their relationships to one another and to nature. The alienating character of technology lies precisely in its constant attempt at reducing realities to calculable quantities. Human beings resent being reduced to calculable units. But the dream of being independent and completely masters of our lives has been battered by the traumatic recognition that, through technology, our thoughts, feelings, and talents are being manipulated. A radical experience of alienation and hopelessness is inevitable. Alienation springs from the reaction of men and women to being reduced to calculable entities; hopelessness, from the anonymity of the manipulators. /47/

As Ruben Alves writes:

> One can change at will those who seem to be in power and shift from one party to another. It makes no difference. Because those who seem to be in charge are not really in charge. They are nothing more than transistors in a network of power, executives plugged into a system. And ultimately it is the system that programs the course of operations. Individuals are expendable, disposable. /48/

There is a growing feeling of helplessness and hopelessness among people who perceive their lives as being dominated by anonymous forces. Hannah Arendt calls it "rule of Nobody." Hope must be associated with names, not numbers. Helplessness increases in direct proportion to numbering mechanisms. Men and women feel helpless before a fluid, inhuman, incommunicable force. Reality has no meaning. As Paul

A KENOTIC CHRISTOLOGY

Tillich writes:

> The protest is directed against the position of man in the system of production and consumption of our society. Man is supposed to be master of his world and of himself. But actually he has become a part of the reality he has created,...a cog within a universal machine to which he must adapt himself in order not to be smashed by it. But this adaptation makes him a means for ends which are means themselves, and in which an ultimate end is lacking. Out of this predicament of man in the industrial society, the experience of emptiness and meaninglessness, of dehumanization and estrangement have resulted. Man has ceased to encounter reality as meaningful. /49/

It is a small step from alienation and despair to rage and violent self-assertion. The violent assertion of individuals against the "System" is not simply a revolt against the anonymity of a technological society, but it is also deeply rooted in the autonomy, subjectivity, and narcissism that characterize that society.

The optimistic technological mentality must be qualified in the context of this turn toward the self and its realization, in an atmosphere of selfishness and narcissism. There should be no illusion about discovering an easy way of achieving a harmony between self-interest and the welfare of others. Consistent optimism in this area leads to false security and the underestimation of anarchy and loss of freedom. There can no longer be any illusions about conflict that exists between self-interest and the public good. The Marxist dream of harmony between individual and society is also an illusion. As Niebuhr writes, "The error is partly the consequence of the Marxist belief that the tendency toward domination is caused by the class structure of human society and will disappear with the revolution which destroys the class system." /50/

The optimism of our technological society has not

been without opposition. Existentialism in its various forms has challenged quite radically the spirit of our culture. /51/ Existentialism has underlined the finitude of man and the ultimacy of death. It sees anxiety as a basic and irremovable ingredient of personal existence. Indeed, it belongs to existence itself. Existence is not a positive state, not even simply neutral, but a state that negates possibilities. Ultimately, existence is for death. While suffering is inherent to human existence, it consists in more than poverty, war, violence, illness; it is a suffering which occurs in the depths of the human spirit. As E. Becker writes:

> Once admit that you are a defecating creature and you invite the primeval ocean of creature anxiety to flood over you. But it is more than creature anxiety, it is also man's anxiety, the anxiety that results from the human paradox that man is an animal who is conscious of his animal limitation. Anxiety is the result of the perception of the truth of one's condition. What does it mean to be a <u>self-conscious animal</u>? The idea is ludicrous, if it is not monstrous. It means to know that one is food for worms. This is the terror: to have emerged from nothing, to have a name, consciousness of self, deep inner feelings, an excruciating inner yearning for life and self-expression - and with all this yet to die. /52/

One dimension of sin is the refusal on the part of man to accept his own identity as a biological creature. The human creature belongs to the biosphere; he/she participates in the same necessities and possibilities as all other creatures. In sin, the rejection of this condition is that man identifies his essence as that which he/she has least in common with nature. E. Becker has strongly reminded us of our limits. The human person cannot evolve beyond his/her character and limits; he/she cannot get rid of his/her limits. Becker asks how can a self-conscious creature change the dilemma of his/her existence? There is simply no way to transcend the limits of the human condition or to change the psychological structural condition that makes humanity possible. /53/ In a pessimistic tone, he writes:

> ...Creation is a nightmare spectacular taking place on a planet that has been soaked for hundreds of millions of years in the blood of all its creatures. The soberest conclusion that we could make about what has actually been taking place on the planet for about three billion years is that it is being turned into a vast pit of fertilizer. /54/

In some of its forms, existentialism can lead to perceiving existence as purely absurd. /55/ Existence has neither meaning nor value. The ultimate goal and relief of existence is death. In his philosophical writings, Sartre laid out the basis for nihilism. Although the individual stands alone as a moral universe unto himself, no matter what action he/she takes, the result is uselessness and hopelessness. Here, consensus and commitment become impossible. People tend to act to get whatever they can for themselves.

Existentialism in its various forms has indicated clearly enough that humankind's situation is such that it cannot be cured by any progress in technology. While it offers little hope for the future, at least it gives an honest appraisal of our situation. As G. Hall writes: "The only physician who can be trusted to heal is one who has been thorough and honest in his diagnosis." /56/ Existentialism, while not providing us with easy answers, has warned against false answers. Realism is necessary; and whatever technology will achieve for man, it must in the words of Becker be done in the lived truth of creation, of the grotesque, of the rumble of panic underneath everything. Otherwise it is false." /57/ Too much energy and effort have been given to the task of keeping from ourselves the truth of our condition.

While our technological culture has led to an overwhelmingly positive expectation, our experiences have been increasingly negative. The events of this century have exceeded our capacity to comprehend them on the basis of the categories of modern thought. As R. Niebuhr writes: "The history of mankind exhibits no more ironic experiences than the contrast between the sanguine hopes of recent centuries and the bitter experience of modern man." /58/ This dilemma is even more accentuated on the North American continent because, as George Grant writes: "North Americans have no history before the denial of progress and therefore the denial of progress appears especially foreign to us." /59/ The repressive approach to negation, as a totally assimilated one, can only be a temporary way of dealing with the experience of negation and evil. We must discover ways to face our negative experience without falling into a permanently enervating despair. We must find a frame of reference where negation can be affirmed and not repressed, without losing hope.

Within the framework of our technological world view, there is no opening through which one can view and understand our increasingly negative experiences. This culture provides no frame of reference, no mythos for the experience of negation. For an individual or even groups of individuals to challenge the premise of our technological society is to enter a very lonely road. As G. Grant writes: "So pervasive and deep-rooted is the faith that all human problems will be solved by unlimited technological development that it is a terrible moment for the individual when he crosses the rubicon and puts that faith into question... One can thereafter only approach modern society with fear and perhaps trembling and, above all, caution." /60/

The fundamental question to be asked is how can human freedom prevail against the determinism man and woman have created for themselves? The question is that of the possible chances of unselfish insight in the arena of selfish, self-seeking powers. Are we to let the technocratic image of man/woman govern our future or have we a credible alternative that can challenge it to the root? In what way can we establish a frame of reference to deal with the experience of negation in an officially optimistic society?

F. A Christian Response

Has Christianity any role to play in the answering of these questions? Can it provide our contemporary culture with a model of human and theological anthropology that is willing to enter into the bleakest and most empty reaches of negation, a theology that will not back away from negation and evil as deep threats to individuals and society? /61/

A KENOTIC CHRISTOLOGY

Christianity proclaims that in Christ the human ideal has been attained, in history and in fact, and that unless one is human as Christ was human, one cannot be human at all. The Constitution of Vatican II, "The Church in the Modern World," affirms this in many ways:

> The truth is that only in the mystery of the Incarnate Word does the mystery of man take on light. For Adam, the first man, was a figure of him who was to come, namely, Christ the Lord. Christ, the final Adam, by the revelation of the mystery of the Father and his love, fully reveals man to man himself and makes his supreme calling clear... Again, whoever follows after Christ the perfect man becomes himself more of a man. /62/

Over the centuries and expressed in various forms, Christians have understood that authentic humanity has been revealed in the figure of Jesus Christ and made possible to all mankind. What is being claimed by Vatican II is that in Jesus Christ what is implicitly true of every man becomes explicitly true. In a real way, Christianity may be called a humanism, a Christological humanism. In its Constitution "Gaudium et Spes" the Church associates itself with a new humanism. The divine is not forgotten; it is understood as being implicit in man's growing responsibility for his brothers and for history. The question about God has become a question about God's presence in human life as creator and redeemer. Man's personal history is the "locus of the supernatural."

In the ongoing debate about humanization and dehumanization in the search for an image of authentic humanhood, Christianity puts forth the person of Jesus Christ. While the history of Jesus Christ does not provide a completely and radically new point of departure to answer the question about humanization, it does, according to Christianity's claim, "transform the already existing reality of man and his historical question about himself." /63/

Christianity proclaims that it has in Jesus Christ a model of the human, an image of the human. Can it also provide a frame of reference for the experience of negation?

While Christianity in North America has preoccupied itself with the negative, it has done so in view of its transformative power. The ongoing goal is the rendering positive of life's negatives. North American Christianity has even involved a denial of the Cross, through a false emphasis on the Resurrection. The Resurrection is understood as a once-and-for-all conquest in which the Cross simply becomes an event of the past. The Cross becomes the symbol of an evil that has no longer any power over us, that no longer needs to be taken seriously. The impact of the "already here" has blocked out the cutting edge of the "not yet."

Within the context of the Christian faith, there has been an ongoing tendency to see the Gospel from a triumphalistic perspective. There is a constant attempt - conscious or unconscious - to give the Christian message the last word. The Gospel is presented as the source of the solution to every human problem. There is a tendency to forget the Gospel's own modesty, since there is always a "not yet." Christianity in North America replaces the "already/not yet" with a straightforward "already." According to G. Hall: "It produces a Gospel that consists primarily in the overcoming of the experience of evil and negation, a Gospel where 'yes' disqualifies the 'no' of human existence." /64/ This attitude makes it very difficult to take seriously the evil that is so visibly present in our existence. If evil has already been overcome, then history is trivialized and human responsibility for the future is set aside.

The Christian vision that is part of our American heritage is fundamentally positive. This vision has not prepared us to encounter the more negative dimension of our existence as it progressively becomes apparent to larger numbers of humans. According to G. Hall, Christianity is "so thoroughly indentified with the official optimism of the culture that it is constitutionally incapable of entertaining the affliction with which man in our time is really afflicted./65/ Christianity, for a few people, serves to ward off the full effects of the experience of negation. It has functioned as a sanctuary against the harsh realities of evil in our world, against the darkness of experience, in an apparently thoroughly victorious way, easily explaining away negation, evil, death. It has too early given a positive core of meaning to a very negative experience.

But while the Gospel presents the activity of God in Jesus as creating a new reality and making the fullness of life available to humans, he accomplishes this in <u>kenosis</u>, a self-emptying. The hymn in Philippians presents Jesus as recognizing that being equal with God means most profoundly to be "not grasping." The self-emptying of Jesus unto death - and death on the Cross - is the revelation that to be God is to be unselfishness itself. H. Urs von Balthasar underlined this when he wrote: "It is precisely in the kenosis of Christ (and nowhere else) that the inner majesty of God's love appears, of God who 'is love' (I John 4:8) and a 'Trinity.'" /66/

A theology based on the kenosis will be a theology "from below" rooted in the suffering humanity of Jesus and unafraid to affirm the passion of God, his entering into the depths of human reality. The image of man that it will create will oppose the contemporary image of man as master. It will underline man's poverty - man, the receiver. It will stand in stark opposition to our culture based on domination and mastery, hopefully challenging and modifying it through an understanding of man based on self-emptying.

Such a theology will focus on the Cross. A theology of the Cross proceeds from the fundamental assumption that any authentic optimism and hope has limits. According to Hall: "The Gospel of the Cross tries to interpret the meaning of the experience of limits, and to seek through that experience the possibilities that may be inherent in it, or may emerge out of it." /67/

The Cross cannot be the last word; Jesus was raised by God. But neither is the Resurrection the last word on history. In his victory, Christ remains with us in the agony and failure of our humanity. The Resurrection cannot become the primary theological foundation for a false optimism, or for the negation of negativity. The salvation brought about in the death and Resurrection of Jesus is not simply the alleviation and removal of the experience of negation.

JESUS CHRIST IN A TECHNOLOGICAL AGE

In reconstituting the image of the human in terms of theology of the Cross, it is necessary to say something about the image of humankind embodied in the person and life of Jesus Christ. The image of the human necessary in our culture must be established from the vantage point of Christology. This Christology needs to be directly and compellingly explicated in the midst of the multiple experiences of negation in contemporary culture.

This is not a theology the world wants. But any other theology would be a deception. This theology is based on a view of man that many will consider unrealistic and idealistic. Yet if one really considers the facts, an alternative image of man based on self-limitation and self-emptying may be very realistic. It is becoming more evident from day to day that man is not master. The evidence no longer supports such a claim. The question is: What is realism today? Paul Ehrlich writes:

> Perhaps the major necessary ingredient that has been missing from a solution to the problem of both the United States and the rest of the world is a goal, a vision of the kind of Spaceship Earth that ought to be and the kind of crew that should man her. Society has always had its visionaries who talked of love, beauty, peace and plenty. But somehow the "practical" men have always been there just to praise the smog as a sign of progress, to preach "just" wars, and to restrict love while giving hate free rein. It must be one of the greatest ironies of the history of _homo sapiens_ that the only salvation for the practical men now lies in what they think of as the dreams of idealists. The question now is: can the "realists" be persuaded to face reality in time? /68/

Some "realists" are facing the facts. E. F. Schumacher, who is an economist and also a radical humanist, demands a radical change in his book _Small Is Beautiful_. /69/ The need for profound human change emerges as a condition for the very survival of the human race. E. Fromm writes: "In fact for the first time in history the physical survival of the human race depends on a radical change of the human heart." /70/

Within the past few years, many books have been written, pleading for the subordination of economy to the real needs of people. These authors are in agreement that increases in material consumption do not necessarily mean increases in well-being. A new attitude toward nature is demanded, a restraint in the use of technology, its subordination to real human needs. These authors have understood the need for characteriological and spiritual changes in order for social changes to occur. /71/

Materialism, an attitude which seeks fulfillment in the single-minded pursuit of wealth, does not contain within itself a limiting principle. But the earth does. So the idea, as E. F. Schumacher writes, of "unlimited economic growth, more and more until everybody is saturated with wealth, needs to be seriously questioned on at least two counts: the availability of basic resources and elementary or additionally the capacity of the environment to cope with the degree of interference implied." /72/ According to Schumacher, "If human vices such as greed and envy are systematically cultivated, the inevitable result is nothing less than a collapse of intelligence. A man driven by greed and envy loses the power of seeing things as they really are." /73/

The principle of unlimited consumption as the goal of living can only lead to disharmony and, ultimately, war. In a limited world, unlimited consumption implies the deprivation of some amidst unlimited egotism. According to G. Hall, "What chiefly fires this epochal transformation is the awareness that in the last analysis the civilization the modern era wanted to bequeath is dangerous and destructive. It is <u>no</u> civilization, in fact. There is a growing recognition that the image of man/woman elaborated by the greatest minds in the past three or four centuries, man/woman as master, is ultimately annihilating. The mastery of nature must inevitably mean the mastery of human nature, the subjugation of man's/woman's own being, to the manipulative technique he has applied to everything else." /74/ The image of man/woman as Master is not redeemable; the logic of mastery leads directly to the death of the spirit, the death of man. As G. Hall writes: "Unless man turns from mastering to servicing, from grasping to receiving, from independence to interdependence, we will simply not last very long on the face of the earth." /75/

There is evidence of a desire for change. As Richard Falk writes:

> The human species may be better prepared for transition to a new system of world order than is generally evident, especially to those accustomed to thinking about change in the short-time horizons of power wielders. Teilhard de Chardin and Sri Aurobindo, among others, have discerned a shift in human sentiment toward solidarity and altruism, and we believe that this shift is one significant feature of our generally bleak modern situation. Just as the collapse of colonialism was comprehensible only after it happened, so might the collapse or displacement of the state system become visible only when we get a chance to look backward. The call for a world order more responsive to bioethical requirements - species survival, including habitability of the planet - represents a new impulse in human history, itself a hopeful sign. /76/

But the technocrat's image of man is not only explicit in our institutions, values, and goals. It is also embedded deeply in our minds, in our ways of thinking and doing, in our spirit. In attempting to change our understanding, we are still influenced by it in the very depths of our spirits. Only a fundamental and radical conversion of the spirit, a total about-face can really bring about a change. Economic and political changes are possible only if there are fundamental changes in the values and attitudes of individuals. As E. Fromm writes:

> ...a new society is possible only if, in the process of developing it, a new human being also develops, or, in more modest terms, if a fundamental change occurs in contemporary Man's character structure. /77/

The idea of self-emptying presents a clear

alternative to narcissism. It is different from both the non-self religion and the self-realization of contemporary Western culture. According to Heidegger, in order to counteract the effects of our technological culture, there must occur a "releasement" (a term Heidegger borrowed from Meister Eckhart) of the human being from the will to power. Such a "releasement" would make it possible to live in this world not as Master but as Servant - as a Servant capable of letting created reality, in its manifold expressions, simply be. Freedom from the will to power can only be achieved if reality is no longer perceived as something to be controlled. Freedom here is the person's opening, submitting in attentive awareness to the given reality.

It is this freedom that the Gospel advocates. It is a freedom based on self-emptying. Self-emptying is neither self-effacement nor servility but letting go. /78/ Self-emptying does not mean withdrawing from the other, but giving oneself up to the other. But self-emptying is not obviously a strategy designed to win much favor today.

We are faced with the necessary acceptance of our limits. No theology of glory is capable of addressing itself to this problem. But the theology of the Cross is explicitly directed to it. It is at its most basic level a theology of limits. What it rejects and militates against above all is that human superbia which feeds upon the delusion of mastery. We are not masters. We <u>are</u> beggars. The theology of the Cross does not rejoice in limits. To seek suffering, whether for oneself or for others, is not the counsel of the theology of the Cross. But in the midst of limits and suffering, the theology of the Cross tries to discern the presence of meaning. It tries to interpret the meaning of these limits as they are experienced and to relate them to the possibilities that may be inherent in them or may emerge out of them.

We must present the Paschal Mystery in all of its dimensions, with the Cross at its center - even in a time when we instinctively shy away from the negative aspects of life.

It is worth noting that amidst all the variety of models of authentic humanity that proliferate in our culture, when the most thoughtful of our secular intellectuals offer us an image of authentic manhood, and try to picture the mature human, they are in surprising agreement. For almost all, the model of human excellence is that of free self-determination from within, motivated and shaped by love for others. It is in the outgoing love for others that human nature fulfills itself. We find ourselves when, like Christ, we can lose ourselves for others. Strangely, it is the Lord on the Cross who gives to the world which put him there the only model for its own fulfillment. If we are Christians, the Lord on the Cross becomes our Lord, and we seek to incarnate his freedom, his poverty, his availability for others.

A KENOTIC CHRISTOLOGY

NOTES

1. L. Gilkey, Naming the Whirlwind: The Renewal of God-Language, (Indianapolis: Bobbs-Merrill, 1969) p. 33.

2. In characterizing a culture, there is always the danger of forgetting the manifold variety and complexity of a culture. Also, every age has its blind spots.

3. L. Gilkey, op. cit., p. 34.

4. P. Berger, The Sacred Canopy, (New York: Doubleday, 1967) pp. 107-108.

5. P. Berger, "For a World with Windows," Against the World for the World, eds. P. Berger and R. J. Neuhaus, (New York: Seabury Press, 1976) p. 10.

6. The Holocaust, Hiroshima, and the war in Vietnam have revealed human bestiality.

7. L. Gilkey, op. cit., pp. 37-73.

8. P. Tillich, Theology of Culture, (Oxford: Oxford University Press, 1959) p. 43.

9. P. Berger, Facing Up to Modernity, (New York: Basic Books, 1977) p. 70.

10. P. Tillich, Theology of Culture, op. cit., pp. 43-44.

11. Ibid., p. 45.

12. R. Nisbet, "The Impact of Technology and Ethical Decision Making," The Technological Threat, ed. J. D. Douglas (Englewood Cliffs, N.J.: Prentice-Hall, 1971) p. 41.

13. Victor C. Ferkiss, Technological Man: The Myth and the Reality, (New York: George Braziller, 1969) p. 250.

14. J. Ellul, The Technological Society, (New York: Alfred A. Knopf, 1964) p. 43.

15. Hannah Arendt, The Human Condition, (Garden City, New York: Doubleday, 1955) p. 3.

16. S. Keen, Apology for Wonder, (New York: Harper & Row, 1967) p. 117.

17. Hans Jonas, "Toward a Philosophy of Technology," Hastings Center Report, (February, 1970) p. 38.

18. F. Nietzsche, "Thus Spake Zarathustra," The Philosophy of Nietzsche, (New York: Modern Library Press, N.D.) p. LXXII.

19. F. Nietzsche, The Birth of Tragedy and the Genealogy of Morals, (Garden City, N.Y.: Doubleday, 1965) pp. 149-188.

20. R. Bultmann, "The Idea of God in Modern Man," in Theology into the Modern Age, ed. Robert W. Funk (New York: Harper & Row, 1965) p. 96.

21. L. Gilkey, op. cit., p. 58.

22. Jean-Paul Sartre, Being and Nothingness, trans. H. Barnes, (New York: Philosophical Library, 1956) pp. 47-70, 73-218.

23. B. F. Skinner, Beyond Freedom and Dignity, (New York: Bantam/Vintage Books, 1971).

24. B. F. Skinner, Cumulative Record, Third ed., (New York: Appleton, 1972) p. 3.

25. Craig E. Wollner, "Behaviorism and Humanism: B. F. Skinner and the Western Intellectual Tradition," review in Existential Psychology and Psychiatry, Vol. XIV, #3 (1975-1976) p. 158.

According to W. Thompson: "Liberals like Zbigniew Brzezinski and Herman Kahn believe we can eliminate the tragic flaw in man: following Brzezinski, we can replace the chaos of politics with the system of management; following Kahn, we can hook up the brain to computers to create an electronic superman." W. Thompson, Evil and the World Order, (New York: New York, 1976) p. 2. For these men, faith in progress is so complete that they cannot help but believe that some technological miracle will deliver us from any impending disaster.

26. Ibid., p. 159

27. Time, 20 September 1971.

28. B. F. Skinner, Science and Human Behavior, (New York: The Free Press, 1953) p. 119.

29. Heinz Otto Luthe, "What Is Manipulation?" Concilium, Vol. 63, (New York: Herder & Herder, 1971) pp. 12-26.

30. Y. Leslie Gould, The Manipulators, (New York: David McKay, 1966).

31. J. M. R. Delgado, Physical Control of the Mind, (New York: Harper & Row, 1971).

32. H. Marcuse, One-Dimensional Man (Boston: Beacon Press, 1965) p. 158.

33. F. Nietzsche, The Birth of Tragedy, op. cit., p. 210.

34. Christopher Lasch, The Culture of Narcissism, (New York: W. W. Norton, 1978) p. 34.

    Cf. also Shirley Sugarman, Sin and Madness: Studies in Narcissism, (Philadelphia: Westminster Press, 1978).

35. C. Lasch, op, cit., p. 232.

36. Ibid., p. 43.

37. Ernest Becker, The Denial of Death, (New York: Free Press, 1973).

38. R. Dawkins, The Selfish Gene, (New York: Oxford University Press, 1976) p. 2.

39. Ibid., p. 3.

40. For more details, see R. Hogan's "Theoretical Egocentricism and the Problem of Compliance," American Psychologist 5 (1975) pp. 533-540; and

Personality Theory: The Personological Tradition, (Englewood Cliffs, New Jersey: Prentice-Hall, 1976).

41. J. W. Thibault and H. H. Kelley, *The Social Psychology of Groups*, (New York: John Wiley and Sons, 1959).

    G. C. Homans, *Social Behavior: Its Elementary Forms*, (New York: Harcourt, Brace & World, 1961).

42. D. Bakan, *Sigmund Freud and the Jewish Mystical Tradition*, (Princeton: Van Nostrand Co., 1958).

43. P. Rieff, *The Triumph of the Therapeutic: The Uses of Faith After Freud*, (New York: Harper & Row, 1966).

44. E. Fromm, *Man for Himself: An Inquiry into the Psychology of Ethics*, (New York: Rinehart & Co., 1947) p. 7.

45. G. Nathan Adler, *The Underground Stream: New Life Styles and the Antinomious Personality*, (New York: Harper Torchbooks, 1971).

    J. Hougan, *Decadence: Radical Nostalgia, and Decline in the Seventies*, (New York: William Morrow, 1977).

46. R. Ringer, *Looking Out for Number One*, (New York: Funk and Wagnall's, 1978).

    B. N. Kaufman, *To Love Is to Be Happy With*, (New York: Coward, McCann & Geoghegan, 1978).

    M. Newman & B. Berkowitz, *How to Take Charge of Your Life*, (New York: Harcourt, 1978).

47. Y. R. Schacht, *Alienation*, (London: George Allen and Unwin, Ltd., 1971).

48. Ruben Alves, *Tomorrow's Child*, (New York: Harper & Row, 1972) p. 20

49. Paul Tillich, *Theology of Culture*, (Oxford: Oxford University Press, 1959) p. 46.

50. R. Niebuhr, *The Children of Light and the Children of Darkness*, (New York: Charles Scribner's Sons, 1944) p. 59.

51. M. Friedman, *To Deny Our Nothingness: Contemporary Images of Man*, (New York: Delta Books, 1967) pp. 243-309.

52. E. Becker, *The Denial of Death*, (New York: The Free Press, 1973) p. 87.

53. Ibid., pp. 276-277.

54. Ibid., p. 283.

55. M. Friedman, op. cit., pp. 309-354.

56. Douglas John Hall, *Lighten Our Darkness: Toward an Indigenous Theology of the Cross*, (Philadelphia: The Westminster Press, 1976) p. 168.

57. E. Becker, op. cit., p. 284.

58. R. Niebuhr, *Faith and History: A Comparison of Christian and Modern Views of History*, (New York: Charles Scribner's Sons, 1949) p. 9.

59. George Grant, *Philosophy in the Mass Age*, (Toronto: Capp Clark Publishing, 1966) p. 23.

60. Ibid., pp. vii-viii.

61. B. J. Callopy, "Theology and the Darkness of Death," Theological Studies, Vol. 39, #1 (1978) p. 48.

62. Pastoral Constitution, "Gaudium et Spes," in W. Abbott, *The Documents of Vatican II*, (New York: America Press, 1966) p. 220.

63. W. Pannenberg, "The Christological Foundations of Christian Anthropology," *Concilium*, Vol. 6, #9, (London: Burns & Oates, 1973) p. 100.

64. D. G. Hall, op. cit., p. 57.

65. Ibid.

66. U. von Balthasar, Love Alone, (New York: Herder & Herder, 1969) p. 15.

67. D. G. Hall, op. cit., p. 200.

68. Paul and Ann Ehrlich, Population, Environment: Issues in Human Ecology, (New York: W. H. Freeman Co., 1970) p. 324.

69. E. F. Schumacher, Small Is Beautiful: Economics as If People Mattered, (New York: Harper & Row, 1973).

70. E. Fromm, To Have or to Be, (New York: Harper & Row, 1976) p. 10

71. G. F. and J. R. Feibleman, Understanding Human Nature, (New York: Horizon Press, 1978).

    M. Stanley, The Technological Conscience: Survival and Dignity in an Age of Expertise, (New Haven: Yale University Press, 1978).

72. E. F. Schumacher, op. cit., p. 30.

73. Ibid., p. 31.

74. D. G. Hall, op. cit., p. 159.

75. Ibid., p. 183.

76. R. A. Falk, On the Creation of a Just World Order, ed. S. Mendlovitz, (New York: The Free Press, 1975) p. 220.

77. E. Fromm, op. cit., p. 9.

78. H. R. Niebuhr, The Children of Light and the Children of Darkness, op. cit., p. 19.

    According to E. F. Schumacher, the Sermon on the Mount outlines the general direction for contemporary society:

    > It may seem daring to connect these beatitudes with matters of technology and economics. But may it not be that we are in trouble precisely because we have failed for so long to make

this connection? It is not difficult to discern what these beatitudes may mean for us today:

- We are poor, not demigods.
- We have plenty to be sorrowful about, and are not emerging into a golden age.
- We need a gentle approach, a non-violent spirit, and small is beautiful.
- We must concern ourselves with justice and see right prevail.
- An all this, only this, can enable us to become peacemakers.

op. cit., pp. 157-158.

CHAPTER 2

THE JESUS OF HISTORY: THE CHRIST OF FAITH

A. Introduction

To be adequate, Christology, or, for that matter, any theology, must be a translation. Yet it needs also to be an interpretation. /1/ While the story of Jesus of Nazareth has to be told in a different way in every generation, it _is_ the story of Jesus of Nazareth, a specific history with a specific life and destiny. Christology must ask questions about Jesus of Nazareth, his message, his behavior. Access to this story is through the scriptures of the New Testament. These, as we have come to realize more and more, are testimonies of faith. The only way to Jesus of Nazareth is through the faith of the first Christian churches. The only trace left by Jesus was the faith of his disciples, and he has taken root in history by virtue of that faith. But contemporary faith that refers only to the faith of Jesus' disciples becomes, ultimately, faith in a kerygma-bearing church.

For the Scriptures affirm that the reality of God is manifested in Jesus as the Christ. The Christological reality also has the dimension of an historical fact. The manifestation of God in Jesus the Christ and the salvation promised and effected in Him are tied up with a specific historical event. They have their grounding in something that is presumed to have actually happened in the course of human history. As Norman Pittenger wrote in his book _The Word Incarnate_, "... the Incarnation of God in Christ and the Atonement wrought by him, on the one hand, are not outside history and, on the other, are not true of _all_ history. They are concerned with what Christians believe was done _in_ history and through the factuality of _particular_ historical happenings." /2/

According to the faith of the Church, salvation itself takes place precisely as history, the history of God's action upon man. Here arises the question of how God the eternal is related to that history in which his will to save achieves its historical manifestation. It is assumed that if God acts in history the distinctions to be drawn within his action are not based merely upon the different reactions of individuals to it. It is peculiar to Christianity to be a religion rooted in the life of an historical person and in historical events. A contemporary Christology cannot ignore the historical nature of its primary and normative ground, Jesus Christ. It is theologically relevant to establish that Christology - the Church's confession of Jesus as the Christ - rests firmly on his life, message, and actual conflict.

In order to avoid any form of Gnosticism, one must reaffirm that Christian faith has an essential relationship to a past historical event, that in Christology one cannot cut the cord between faith and the man Jesus of Nazareth. Christianity teaches and has taught that the Word became flesh, at one time, at one place, in one human personality. So theology and Christology cannot dispense with history or with the process of reflection upon history. Historical research into the gospels must be seen as a permanent and necessary feature of any contemporary Christology. /3/

Any form of historically minded and oriented Christology poses various problems - that of confronting the challenges of the historical-critical method - that of taking seriously the quest for the historical Jesus - and that of determining the origins of Christology and of coming to terms with the evidence of continuity and discontinuity between past and present. These questions raised by the historical dimension of the Christian faith are neither mere sophistries nor in any way external and irrelevant to a systematic Christology. The questions raised by the Enlightenment and modern criticism have not yet been resolved and have not vanished. Disrespect on the part of the systematic theologian for the historical dimension of his sources can only give free recourse to speculation of the most diverse kinds.

B. The Historical-Critical Method and Christology

The historical-critical method describes the attempt to understand the meaning of a text in its specific and original historical context, the endeavor to recover, so far as possible, the meaning intended by the author and understood by the first readers or hearers. The historical-critical method seeks to recognize and describe the meaning the Scriptural texts have had in the context of the history of early Christianity. Its goal is to present a body of ascertained facts that can answer the question: What actually happened and why?"

The introduction of historical criticism to the Biblical texts tended to seek freedom from authority and criticism of tradition. It treated Biblical material in a different manner than theological thought had done for centuries and, in the process, questioned the validity of the classical theological method. The writings of Ernst Troeltsch /3/ in particular evoke the problems created for theology by the use of the historical-critical method. The issue with which he wrestled throughout the greater part of his life was the significance of the historical-critical method for traditional Christian belief and theology. A commitment to truth and impartiality became characteristic of the historical-critical method and the presuppositions of that method, Troeltsch concluded, were basically incompatible with traditional Christian faith since it is ultimately based on supernaturalistic metaphysics. The problem was not, as so many theologians believed, that the Biblical critics emerged from their libraries with results disturbing to their believers, but that the method which led to those results was based on assumptions quite incompatible with traditional belief.

While the theologian regards the Scriptures as supernaturally inspired, the historian assumes that the Bible is intelligible only in terms of its historical context and is subject to the same principles of interpretation and criticism that are applied to other ancient literature. While the theologian believes that the events of the Bible are the results of the supernatural intervention of God, the historian regards such an explanation as a hindrance to true historical understanding. While the theologian believes that the events upon which Christianity rests are unique, the historian assumes that those events, like all events, are analogous to those in the present, and that it is only in this assumption that statements about them can be assessed at all. But if analogous to contemporary events, what is then the uniqueness of these foundational events? While the theologian believes on faith that certain events occurred, the historian regards all historical claims as having only a greater or lesser degree of probability, and he regards the attachment of faith to these claims as a corruption of historical judgment.

A KENOTIC CHRISTOLOGY

Troeltsch saw that the historical-critical method could not be regarded as a neutral thing. It could not be appropriated by the Church with only a bit of adapting here and there. "Once the historical method is applied to Biblical Science and Church history, it is a leaven that alters everything and finally bursts apart the entire structure of theological method employed until the present." /6/ On the basis of the principle of correlation, Troeltsch argued that no event or text can be understood unless it is seen in terms of its historical context. This meant that no critical historian could make use of supernatural intervention as a principle of historical explanation because this shattered the continuity of the causal nexus. Criticism makes every individual event uncertain. Only events that stand within a relationship to other events having an effect on the present are certain. Christianity loses its uniqueness for it can be understood only in relation to the whole of history. History is no place for absolute religions and absolute personalities. In his essay on the significance of the historicity of Jesus for Christian faith, Troeltsch understood Jesus' centrality simply as fulfilling the necessary requirement for the development of any tradition. Troeltsch saw Christianity as historically relative and conditioned - just as any other tradition. Christianity is a purely historical phenomenon with all the conditionedness of an individual historical phenomenon.

When the methods of historical criticism were accepted by Protestant theologians, the marriage of theology and criticism did not turn out to be a peaceful one. Liberal theology, for example, welcomed the methods of historical criticism and used them in order to establish its own theological position, only to be unsettled by the further development of the same method. /7/ The nineteenth century liberal "quest" for a life of Jesus was an attempt to make contact with the humanity of Jesus as the Christ in historical rather than metaphysical categories. The Christ of dogma and traditional ecclesiastical language seemed abstract and lifeless. The "life of Jesus" movement was an attempt to re-establish contact with the real humanity of Jesus. The search for the historical Jesus was an attempt to fix him in time and place in order to cut back the luxurious growth of ecclesiastical Christianity. Christianity would be reconstructed on the basis of the Jesus of history, and in the process, drastically simplified and clarified.

According to E. Käsemann: "It was the Enlightenment which, for the first time in the history of the Church, discovered the problem of the historical Jesus as a problem and, withdrawing from the jurisdiction of the Chalcedonian didache made it the measure of Christology." /8/ Here historical criticism served the purpose of liberating the earthly Jesus from the ecclesiastical and dogmatic elaborations which had already begun in the New Testament. The picture of the Jesus of history which liberal theologians believed had been secured by sound historical methods came under severe attack by historians using the same critical method; first by Albert Schweitzer and then by proponents of form criticism. Dialectical theology sought to achieve its _modus vivendi_ with historical criticism by neutralizing it, by insisting that Christian faith did not depend on the changing and relative results of historical inquiry. /9/ Van A. Harvey wrote: "Karl Barth, E. Brunner, Rudolph Bultmann and Paul Tillich saw in the collapse of the old quest of the historical Jesus a chance to be once again both Biblical in spirit and historically honest - Biblical in spirit because the kerygma as proclaimed by Paul and the author of the fourth Gospel was not at all concerned with the religious personality of Jesus, historically honest because statements about the personality and life of Jesus could find no justification in the historical sources. The kerygma in the New Testament was about God's identification with mankind in the full ambiguity of human history. Jesus was the bearer, the incarnation of God's Word. But, from a historical point of view, his life and personality were as ambiguous as that of any other human. Only faith perceives the divine incognito in the man Jesus." /10/

Bultmann attempted to face the crisis introduced in theology through the development and introduction of historical-critical methods and by returning to his own Lutheran tradition. Bultmann saw a restatement of the nature of faith itself as the abandonment of all securities in the "crisis" provoked by the historical-critical method. As faith lets go of any needs for human verification, it becomes invulnerable to historical criticism. Bultmann introduced a radical separation between the order of faith and scientific inquiry. The message of the Gospel is simply accidentally tied to images and representations that are in themselves mythological and culturally bound. There can be no comparison between the understanding of human existence predicated by the Gospels and the means through which that understanding is expressed and represented. The kerygma is never to be identified with its conceptualization. Bultmann's constant goal is to express faith as it attempts to represent itself. Historical criticism makes it possible to distinguish permanent truth of faith from the relative forms in which this truth is expressed. This emphasizes the incompleteness of every doctrinal proposition and the impossibility of tying faith down to any single proposition, making the task of constant reformulation essential. /12/

Thus, for Bultmann "there can be no normative Christian dogmatics; in other words, it is impossible to accomplish the theological task once for all - the task which consists of unfolding that understanding of God, and hence of the world and of man, which arises from faith, for this task permits only ever-repeated solutions or attempts at solution, each in its particular historical situation. Theology's continuing through the centuries consists not in holding fast to once-formulated propositions but in the constant reality with which faith, fed by its original understanding, masters its constantly new historical situation." /13/

Christology, according to Bultmann, is not interested in the personality of Jesus; we really know very little about that from history. It is essentially interested in the message. Jesus never spoke about himself but totally absorbed himself in his own task. /14/ Here the Church plays a very important role. There cannot be faith in Christ which "would not also be faith in the Church as the bearer of the kerygma; that is,...faith in the Holy Ghost." /15/ Now by "Church," Bultmann means not the institution but an exchatological event. E. Käsemann has criticized Bultmann on his concept of faith in the Church as the bearer of the kerygma. Bultmann sees the Church, not as an institution, but as an eschatological happening; not as the guarantor of faith, but as an object of faith. /16/ Kasemann writes:

> "Can there be an eschatological happening without a substratum, without embodiment and even without institu-

> tional forms, if it is really to occur on earth and not to remain suspended between heaven and earth? Can we really talk of the Church like this? Is there not a dualism evident here, even more profound than that of the subject-object scheme, and does it not finally become evident at the same time that for Bultmann nothing historical really has any theological substance or meaning? Do we not see instantaneously, as though the whole thing were illuminated by a flash of lightning, why the historical Jesus cannot possibly on the basic presupposition of this thinking, derive any independent significance whatever?" /17/

Relative to the question of Jesus' divinity, for example, Bultmann insists that one must consider the system of thought in which the affirmation is made. In the New Testament, the declarations made about Jesus' divinity are not intended to relate to his nature but to the significance and importance of his message. /18/ When the formulae of the New Testament are properly understood, they all carry the same meaning, they all witness to a faith in Jesus Christ as the eschatological event in which the encounter between God and man occurs. This event can only be grasped in and through a faith which has its own logic. The Councils of the early Church, as they attempted to grasp the implications of this event, were unable to express it correctly. /19/ The problematic inserted in the Council's formula, "true God, true man," is a false one because it stressed the static dimension of being which the New Testament itself affirms in dynamic categories of event and history. /20/

It is as God's Word that Jesus is God. /21/ The Word is essentially an event and a request - an invitation to faith. In the New Testament, God confronts man through his Word and calls him to self-understanding and authentic existence. Faith is the decision made in response to that call. Faith is not dependent on historical knowledge. Criticism can be ruthlessly practiced because it makes the nature of faith clear. But Bultmann's program tends to undervalue the singularity of past events; his existential canon makes the conceptual work of the interpreter the criterion of truth in the Scriptures. It walks on the edge of interiorizing and psychoanalyzing history. Indeed Bultmann's history does not need the past. /22/

Even if one ignores for the moment the possibility of historical knowledge about Jesus, it is difficult to see how one could hold, as a dialectical theologian would, that the Biblical kerygma is an object of faith and at the same time insist that faith is absolutely independent of all historical inquiry. How would one even know what the kerygma is except by an act of historical understanding?

To discern more fully the import of the historical-critical method on contemporary theology it is necessary to take a closer look at the various forms the historical method took as applied to the study of the New Testament. The use of form criticism and redaction criticism have given rise to serious theological issues. For in the usage of these methods, historical and theological issues are inextricably intertwined. /23/ Both methods have highlighted the fact that the Gospels offer direct information about the theology of the early Church but very little about the teaching of the historical Jesus. Both methods have seriously questioned the traditional view of the historical Jesus as the privileged locus of Revelation. Instead these methods have emphasized the role of the experience of the Risen Lord in the process of Revelation. The early Church re-interpreted the Jesus material to fit the needs of new situations and even treated the material with great freedom because of its conviction that the Lord who spoke is the Lord who speaks. In a sense the central, generating experience of Christianity is not Jesus' own experience but the Church's experience of Jesus as the Christ.

Form criticism and redaction criticism indicate a shift in the focus of concern. Christology is now seen not so much as a product of reflection upon the past event of Jesus but upon the present "experience" of Christians. The Church's developing conviction with regard to the resurrection, her consciousness of herself as the eschatological community, the necessity for an apologetic to Judaism, the delay of the parousia, the physical facts of movement from Palestine to Greece and from a Jewish to a predominantly Gentile environment, these are all the kinds of things upon which we must focus our attention as we seek to delineate and to understand the origins and developments of the varying Christological patterns reflected in the New Testament texts. According to Norman Perrin: "...the first step in Christology is a post-Easter step taken in response to a factor at work in earliest Christianity. It is not directly a response to the message or ministry of the historical Jesus, for these only took on Christological emphases when they were interpreted in light of the Resurrection and when Christological emphases which had developed in early Christianity were read back into them." /24/

Form criticism and redaction criticism have uncovered the incredible diversity of Christian symbolism, doctrine, belief, and moral practice. They have shattered any naive conceptions of the unity which was the Bible's presupposed appeal as a norm for belief and practice. As E. Käsemann writes: "The Canon does not present a unity of content. Because it represents the result of a late ecclesiastical process of selection and its limits were for a long time fluid, it is the precipitate of a highly-complicated development, beginning with apocalyptic Judaism and ending with early Catholicism and affected in its course by profound crisis." /25/

Both methods recognize that in the New Testament there are a number of Christologies and that these are the results of competing and coalescing Christological traditions, each with a different point of departure and a different emphasis. This approach also recognizes that there is no such thing in New Testament times as the Early Church but only the early churches with different backgrounds developing different theological emphases and concerns and, therefore, different Christological traditions.

These two methods pose, in a critical way, the problem of relating the developing Christological tradition of the early churches to the teaching of the historical Jesus - a problem which brings with it all the difficulties of determining what the historical Jesus did, in fact, teach and identifying the vital function of the early churches' faith experiences in formulating their Christologies.

Such an insight, because it recognizes that history continues and that every period and cultural experience is different from those of the past, demands an awakened sensitivity to the hermeneutical question and the problem of the reinterpretation of dogma. Because of these methods, we understand more clearly that the message of the New Testament is itself a legacy, a text to be interpreted. Form and redaction criticm emphasize that the hermeneutical exigency comes from a double distance in time which needs to be bridged, not only the distance between the past event of revelation and our own present culture, but also the distance between the Scriptural accounts and the historical events. Hermeneutics is the very demand of the faith, inasmuch as revealed truth is not a dead truth but a living truth which is always transmitted in an historical medium and which needs to be constantly made present. As Käsemann writes, "Primitive Christian Christology and soteriology do not present themselves in the form of a self-contained unity, but rather fall apart into a multiplicity of divergent conceptions which can only reflect the changed historical situation of the community. Of course, the communities of each age desire to describe the being and work of the one Jesus Christ. But it does this always with new means which are offered to it by its spiritual, religious and cultural environment. It is bound to this if only because otherwise its proclamation would be utterly incomprehensible to its contemporaries. It is bound to do it even more because it is itself subject to historical change in which continuity and discontinuity are interwoven." /26/ In various ways these historical methods have shown that the Christian community in its essence must be a hearing community and that, therefore, it is in constant pilgrimage. The Word it bears witness to cannot be bound to a sacred time, place, or institution, for the community is in constant exodus, called away from traditional ties to a promised future.

While the historical methods in their applications to the New Testament have made much clearer the hermeneutical dimensions of any Christology, they have also posed an ongoing problem for every generation of believers - the basic and important question of continuity and discontinuity with the past. The historical-critical method in its various forms has called upon contemporary Christology to radically re-evaluate its sources and foundations. The historical-critical research on the origins of New Testament Christology have dissolved the supposed link between the doctrine and the Scriptural text it was to interpret. At the same time that the dogmatic theologian is stressing the centrality of Jesus for Christology, critical studies of the New Testament have so reduced the amount of material available for a look at the historical person of Jesus, that they seem to be undermining the base for sustaining Christology. Prior to the use of the modern historical-critical method, no theologian saw a problem in the relationship between Christology and New Testament study. Today this area is one of great concern for any contemporary Christology. In the past the doctrine of the Church saw a consistent and simple relationship between the earthly Jesus and the Christ of faith. They were the same. This tradition of faith and doctrine were irrevocably shattered with the advent of modern research, above all in the historical sciences. For now the "historical" Jesus is a problem. This is a concept which would never have occurred to any of the Fathers of our Church.

The question of the historical Jesus and the Christ of faith came into focus in the rise of the historical sciences which had as a goal the discovery of "what actually happened." An attempt was made to ground faith and dogma on what the objective historians could perceive as the real course of historical events, or what could be learned about the "real" pattern of Jesus' life. This emphasis on history, crucial to Christology, unfortunately led to a form of historicism where the objective historian proceeded unaware of the number of prejudices and presuppositions which molded his interpretation. Historical study of the New Testament left a theology supported either by an a-historical dogmatic (Karl Barth) or by an historical skeptic (R. Bultmann). With the introduction of the split between fact and significance came the danger of reducing Jesus the Christ to the level of a symbol of eternal truths. The application of the historical method to the study of the New Testament has emphasized questions about the uniqueness and finality of Jesus as the Christ. It has focused attention on the question of our relationship between the historical individual Jesus of Nazareth and the absolute - truth claims made in reference to the Christ of faith. This is the reason for the continued relevance of Hegel in contemporary Christologies. /27/ One of Hegel's major theological interests concerned the connection between Christ and the historical process. For Hegel, the Christian symbols provide a comprehensive interpretation of the whole scope of historical development. Hegel made no attempt to provide a secure shelter for religious truth outside of space and time. He saw no final end for created reality that is not in continuity with the present, but rather emphasized here the intimate relation between culture and religion. In affirming Christ as the supreme appearance of the unity between man and God, Hegel advocated a universal dimension to Christianity which emphasized the difficulty of keeping together the Jesus of history and the Christ of faith, challenging the long Christological tradition stemming from Chalcedon that affirmed that in Jesus we have him who is truly God, truly man, and truly one.

While Hegel did not devalue history, many Hegelians have played down the value of the historical and the particular in their own Christologies. Certain forms of Hegelianism lead to the swallowing up of history in timeless truths and of the particular and concrete in the universal and abstract. This is the basic reason for the renewal of Logos Christology. /28/ Now Logos Christology is in danger of placing little value in the historical humanity of Jesus and of reducing Christ to a symbol of some timeless truths and, therefore, of trivializing his historicity and his uniqueness. Jesus and the event of salvation history become mere symbols of a wider universal truth about God, rather than a once-and-for-all unique manifestation of God otherwise unknowable.

According to Karl Rahner: "The post-Easter Christological teaching of the New Testament and _a fortiori_ that of the later church, cannot be simply a religious idea projected onto Jesus nor can we accept that the post-Easter Jesus expressed and formulated a Christology defining the significance of his own Resurrection... Catholic theology still cannot dispense with the truth that the pre-Easter Jesus recognized and stated so much about his own union and function in saving history that this, when confronted by and combined with the experience of his definitive fate of having been delivered by God, provided the starting point for that Christology which is already present in Paul and John, and then extends further to the Christological dogma of the Church." /29/

Again according to Rahner, "Catholic faith and its dogmatics as they have been understood up to now,... remain indissolubly bound up not only with the historical existence of Jesus of Nazareth but also with the historical events of a specific kind which took place during his life." /30/ A theologian, then, as he faces a reinterpretation of Christology must accept certain parameters. Again K. Rahner writes, "The exponent of Catholic fundamental theology and dogmatics, therefore, must hold firm to the fact that there was a Jesus of Nazareth who, in his own understanding of himself even at the pre-Easter stage, had something to do with what Christian faith believes and proclaims of Jesus Christ, the risen Lord. Otherwise, the life of Jesus and his death would not have constituted a saving event. The post-Easter faith would, in itself and taken in isolation, be the saving event and in the last analysis would have no necessary connection with Jesus himself, or with his death." /31/

Of course we must recognize the discontinuity at the very beginning of the Christian tradition when the followers of Jesus make Jesus himself an object of faith as their Lord, since it is clear enough that he was not explicitly trying to declare himself such an object. But even in admitting this, the basic problem of New Testament scholarship accorded to post-Bultmannians is establishing continuity of the Christian faith with the faith of Jesus. It is still a challenge to find the origin of the Christian faith in the event of a real historical person.

C. The "New Quest" for the Historical Jesus

More recent treatments of the problem attempt to avoid placing a one-sided emphasis on either the historical Jesus or the kerygma of the early community, through efforts to define the correlation between them. However, despite the many variations they have developed, the problem of continuity remains. Obviously what is involved here is not a merely historical continuity, and least of all a legitimation of the post-Resurrection kerygma discovered by the aid of history. Rather what is involved is the continuity in content, concerning the extent to which Jesus' own history and proclamation establish, require, and already imply the early Christian kerygma.

In 1954, Ernst Käsemann, a disciple of Bultmann, initiated what has been called the "new" quest for the historical Jesus. What was new about this quest was that it was undertaken, not in bypassing the kerygma, but through the medium of the primitive Christian message. Käsemann writes:

> "For if primitive Christianity identifies the humiliated with the exalted Lord, in so doing it is confessing that, in its presentation of history, it is incapable of abstracting from its faith. At the same time, however, it is also making clear that it is not minded to allow myth to take the place of history nor a heavenly being to take the place of the Man of Nazareth." /32/

According to Käsemann, interpretation and tradition are fundamentally inseparable. Therefore, it is not simply a question of interpreting the kerygma or even of reducing the Gospel to historical facts about Jesus. For history cannot simply be pressed into the service of the legitimization of the kerygma. It is not possible to understand Jesus Christ except in light of the Church's belief. But that belief must be interpreted in light of the historical Jesus. As Käsemann writes:

> "The historical Jesus meets us in the New Testament, our only real and original documentation of him, not as he was in himself, not as an isolated individual but as the Lord of the community which believes in him. The significance of this Jesus for faith was so profound that even in the very earliest days it almost entirely swallowed up his earthly history. The living experience of him which later generations enjoyed made the facts of his earthly life simply irrelevent, except insofar as they might serve to reflect on the permanent experience... So we only make contact with the life history of Jesus through the kerygma of the community. The community

neither could nor would separate this life history from its own history." /33/

The quest for the historical Jesus has increased our awareness that before there was a Christian Church, Jesus lived and died within the social context of the first century. /34/ Yet our knowledge of Jesus remains dependent upon the memory of his disciples. The traditions were shaped by the experiences, practices, and needs of the early Church, but the memory of Jesus was one of the contributing factors which shaped the life of the community that emerged after his death.

Whatever direction the quest may go, we cannot safely by-pass the question of whether Jesus made claims for himself or whether they were made about him by the Church. We have to ask if the claims made about Jesus are valid interpretations of his significance, and consequently, we cannot opt out of the debate about the authenticity of what is said about Jesus in the Gospels.

An attempt to interpret the significance of Christ can only hope to succeed if the appropriation of the tradition conveys something of the power of the historical figure which so forcefully shaped the religious consciousness of the first disciples. While it is not possible to reconstruct an unbroken development from the historical Jesus to later Christology, most New Testament scholars today agree that the New Testament has *de facto* a basis in Jesus himself. There is a recognition that Jesus' earthly ministry contributed a great deal to the formation of post-Easter Christology. /35/ But the Easter event cannot be the only point of departure for Christology. As L. Hurtado writes: "The assertion that resurrection appearances alone would have caused the early disciples to see Jesus as a messianic figure even though (so it is further asserted) Jesus in his earthly ministry scrupulously avoided any hint that he was to be so identified, seems to me more and more dogmatically motivated and less and less credible." /36/ Despite all these difficulties we can uphold the historical possibility and the theological legitimacy of a recourse to the Jesus of history. The primitive Christian proclamation of Christ could have emerged, and can be understood, only in the light of the history of Jesus.

Historical study of Jesus is extremely important for it gives a concrete content to faith; but it can never be a verification of the faith. As E. Schillebeeckx writes: "If one can show that the Christian kerygma is in direct line with Jesus' self-understanding as that appears from his whole ministry and from his attitude to the death which in the end he saw to be inevitable, this still proves nothing about the validity of Christian faith. Jesus' saying and way of life have no absolute self-warranting validity except for someone who is a believer." /37/

The lived reality and fullness of Christian faith always transcends what the historian can perceive of past events; critical history is simply inadequate to bear the full weight of Christian tradition. Jesus as the Christ is more than an objectively perceived figure of the past. He is for the Christian community the continuing active source of life in the Church. In a real sense, it is only from within the circle of faith, from the actual faith experience of the Church, that proper apprehension of history can take place. Even the text of Scripture as a literary presentation of the historical events in the early Church cannot simply be identified with this living tradition. The historical influence of Jesus inaugurated a tradition of devotion and adoration which Christian literature neither exhausts nor fully represents, even when closest to its source. The full reality of tradition is more than a deposit of truths stated once and for all in the apostolic period; through the continuous encounter with Jesus as the Christ, truths are formulated which re-express the living reality of apostolic faith without being explicitly linked to the Scriptural testimony. Within this perspective, it becomes evident that one cannot avoid the distinction between the Jesus of history and the Christ of faith. /38/ And it seems impossible to justify the full reality of the Christ of faith as transmitted through the ages on purely historical grounds. The historical evidence is not capable of justifying the kinds of absolute claims attached to Jesus as the Christ. /39/

Here, N. Perrin's distinction of the three different kinds of knowledge about Jesus becomes very useful. /40/ The first kind of knowledge is a descriptive historical knowledge, the kind of knowledge that seeks the facts and that can be achieved with appropriate hermeneutical methodology. Perrin describes this knowledge as "basic knowledge, by which we mean that it exists independently of any specific interest in it or usefulness to be ascribed to it, as, indeed, independent of any lack of interest in it or even danger found to be inherent in it." /41/ Such a knowledge cannot lay claims to absoluteness. It is a knowledge that is subject to correction and change on the basis of further research or discovery.

The second type of knowledge N. Perrin calls historic. It is a knowledge which makes an impact on its recipient, causing him to change his mind or self-understanding. While dependent on historical knowledge, it is a knowledge that is "significant." Again, according to Perrin, "...such significance will depend upon the establishment of some point of contact between that knowledge from the past and the situation of the man in the present." /42/ Historical knowledge becomes historic insofar as it speaks to our condition, insofar as it has a direct point of contact with us. /43/

The third form of knowledge is faith knowledge, that is, "knowledge of Jesus of Nazareth which is significant only in the context of specifically Christian faith,...knowledge of him of a kind dependent upon the acknowledgement of him as Lord and Christ." /44/ The significance of faith knowledge has a value beyond that given to any other object of historical knowledge. While historic knowledge can be drastically affected by change in knowledge of historical facts, faith knowledge to some extent can remain untouched by the vicissitudes of historical factuality.

According to Perrin:

> "Empirical historical knowledge is a special kind of knowledge and the question of its existence, factuality or truth should always be kept separate from that of its significance. 'Historic' or significant knowledge from the past should always be subject to the tests of demonstration that it is, indeed, historical knowledge and that the avenue, channel, or point of contact between it and the man from whom it became significant in the present can be defined. Religious or faith knowledge, on the other

> hand, should be subject to quite different tests; namely, the understanding of ultimate reality it mediates, the kind of religious experience it inspires, the quality of personal and communal life it makes possible and so on." /45/

While historic knowledge is dependent on historical knowledge, faith knowledge is not necessarily dependent on it. While the origin of the historical Jesus is dependent upon historical research, the faith knowledge of Jesus is dependent upon Christian proclamation and its object is a faith-image of Jesus. /46/ According to Perrin, historical research is not a determing factor in the establishment of this figure. "... like the Christ of the Gospels, the Jesus of one's faith-image is a mixture of historical reminiscence, at a somewhat distant remove, and myth, legend, and idealism." /47/ The validity of this faith-image is directly related to its origins in religious experience and, in fact, can even mediate religious experience. While historical knowledge of Jesus does contribute to the formation of the faith-image, its main source is "the proclamation of the Church, a proclamation arising out of a Christian experience of the risen Lord." /48/

While faith-knowledge and faith-images are not necessarily grounded in historical knowledge, in the case of the Christ-image, what is the relationship of this image to the historical Jesus? According to Perrin, historical knowledge contributes to the formation of the faith-image and helps to distinguish the true faith-image from the false. "The true kerygmatic Christ, the justifiable faith-image, is that consistent with the historical Jesus. The significance of the historical Jesus for Christian faith is that knowledge of this Jesus may be used as a means of testing the claims of the Church presented in the competing kerygmata to the Jesus Christ. To this limited extent, our historical knowledge of Jesus validates the Christian kerygma; it does not validate as <u>kerygma</u>, but it validates as Christian." /49/

At the core of the Synoptic tradition, and the key to its understanding, is "...the complete and absolute identification by the early Christian of the earthly Jesus of Nazareth and the risen Lord of Christian experience. /50/ While that equation leads to a great freedom in ascribing to the earthly Jesus sayings that originate out of the Christian experience of the risen Lord, yet we are justified in view of our historical knowledge of Jesus and because of the equation made by the early Christian Church between the earthly Jesus and risen Christ, to test "the validity of claims made in the name of Jesus Christ." /51/

Käsemann has highlighted the fact that the New Testament itself invites us to look more deeply into the problematic of the Jesus of history and the Christ of faith. He writes:

> "...the New Testament itself justifies us to this extent in asking the question, inasmuch as it is to the earthly Jesus that the Gospels ascribe their kerygma, wherever it actually originated, and thus they invest him unmistakably with preeminent authority. However strangely their conceptions of the history of Jesus may differ, however much the real life history of Jesus may be buried under their own proclamation, it is inherent in their history which we have to thank both for their genesis and for their form." /52/

The problem of the historical Jesus touches on the very nature of the theological method; indeed, on the very nature of faith. The return to the historical Jesus assures us of the primacy of that which founds the faith. But it does not found faith in history, as Bultmann feared so much, but helps discern the legitimate message from that which is not legitimate. In fact, the controversies of the first centuries and the metaphysical language used, were an attempt to deal with this problem. What we maintain in insisting on the historical Jesus is the irreducible singularity of what has happened in his manifestation. This represents a kairos in relation to the history of the world and that of each believer. Easter did not render this experience superfluous; on the contrary, it confirmed it - out of the once came the once and for all. Käsemann writes, "They want, if I may so express it to show that the 'extra nos' of salvation is given to faith - to cleave firmly to history is one way of giving expression to the 'extra nos' of salvation." /53/

Only the Jesus of history in his anteriority and primacy relative to the kerygma announcing it, permits this kerygma from being filled by another content. While there is clearly a difference between the "once and for all" claim about Jesus and the "once" of his ministry, Christology cannot survive in the context of a total discontinuity between the two. Christology is irreversibly grounded in a specific history and in a unique life and destiny. It has to preserve a real and actual story and bear testimony to it. Christology has to ask: "Who was Jesus of Nazareth? What did he want? What were his mission and message, his behavior, his destiny and cause?"

D. Conclusion

Christology must constantly attempt to bridge the way between Jesus of Nazareth to the Christ of Christian belief, and between the one who proclaimed not himself but the imminent Kingdom of God to the proclaimed and believed-in Christ. A vital Christology must maintain the tension between the present responsibility of faith, as it attempts to express the Christ-event, and the historical dimension and grounds of that event in the Jesus of Nazareth anew and for its day. Christology must maintain a sense of historical distance between past and present continuity with it. And it must do this within a living tradition often maintained through a most radical discontinuity. Käsemann perceives this paradox very forcefully:

> "Even the history which is recounted in the pages of the New Testament has become to us, who live nearly two thousand years later, mere history. In other words, we have no longer any immediate access to it even if we adopt the most accurate circumstantial conspectus possible. Compared to those who were contemporary with it, we speak another language, we think in other categories, we face other situations and decisions. In relation to it, we experience with peculiar force the sense that all history is conditioned by the fact of dying, and, as generation succeeds to generation, this sense emerges as discontinuity. Thus, if we desire knowledge of past history, we fall back on what was narrated. History is only

> accessible to us through tradition and only comprehensible to us through interpretation." /54/

To be in relation with the past always implies a dimension of discontinuity. One moves backward at times only by moving forward. /55/

Continuity with the past is not simply assured once and for all, for there is always the risk and chance of re-establishing it through a new, creative interpretation. Insistence on the discontinuity of history permits us to put into value the contingency of revelation and the work of salvation. Käsemann writes:

> "A primary concern of the Gospel's is unmistakably the particularity with which the eschatological event is bound to this man from Nazareth, to the arena of Palestine and to a concrete time with its special circumstances. For this eschatological event is not a new idea, nor is it the culminating point of a process of development, the significance of which can be explained by its causal connections and effects. Revelation ceases to be God's revelation once it has been brought within a causal nexus. It is what it is only when it is seen as an unconditional happening...that particularity of revelation which is manifested in its unbreakable link with a concrete life history, reflects the freedom of the Lord who acts and is the ground of our having a possibility of decision." /56/

The Christological construct of any Christian generation must be founded at every point by the historical-critical representation of Jesus. But it must go beyond it, because it introduces hermeneutical categories to establish the coherence and meaning of the figure of Jesus Christ for human existence today. And it does so in a more explicit, comprehensive way than a strictly historical image of Jesus. The Christological construct relies not only on what can be learned from historical study but also on the experience of the Christian faith community in its ongoing encounter with Jesus. It seeks to be faithful to the intention of early Christian kerygma in proclaiming Jesus to be the Messiah of God.

THE JESUS OF HISTORY: THE CHRIST OF FAITH

NOTES

1. D. Tracy defines hermeneutics as "the discipline capable of explicating the referent as distinct from either the sense of the text or the historical reconstruction of the text." Blessed Rage for Order: The New Pluralism in Theology, (New York: Seabury, 1975) p. 52.

2. N. Pittenger, The Word Incarnate, (New York: Nisbet, and Harper & Row, 1959) pp. 39-40.

3. W. Kasper, Jesus the Christ, (New York: Paulist Press, 1976) pp. 26-41.

4. E. Krentz, The Historical-Critical Method, (Philadelphia: Fortress, 1975).

5. Ernst Troeltsch is discussed by Walter Bodenstein, Neige zum Historismos, (Gutersloh: Gerd Mohn, 1959) and Van A. Harvey, The Historian and the Believer, (New York: Macmillan, 1966) pp. 3-6, 14-160.

6. E. Troeltsch, Gesammelte II Schriften, (Tubingen, 1913) p. 730. According to Troeltsch, the historical method has three principles: 1) The principle of criticism as methodological doubt implies that history only achieves probability. 2) The principle of analogy makes criticism possible. Present experience and occurrence become the criteria of probability in the past. This almighty power of analogy implies that all events are in principle similar. 3) The principle of correlation (or mutual interdependence) implies that all historical phenomena are so interrelated that a change in one phenomenon necessitates a change in the causes leading to it and the effects it has. Historical explanation rests on this chancy cause and effect. This principle rules out miracles and salvation history. E. Troeltsch: 1. "Uber Historische und Dogmatische Methode in der Theologie," Zur Religiosen Lage, Religionsphilosophie und Ethik (2. Aufl., Gesammelte II Schriften II Schriften, Aalen: Scientia Verlag, 1962=1922) pp. 729-753, and Die Bedeutung der Geschichtlichkeit Jesus fur den Glauben, (Tubingen: J. C. B. Mohr-Paul Siebeck, 1911).

7. For good surveys and bibliographies on the topic, see H. Conzelmann, Jesus (Philadelphia: Fortress, 1973); N. Perrin, _Rediscovering the Teaching of Jesus_, (New York: Harper & Row, 1976) pp. 207-249.

8. E. Käsemann, _New Testament Questions of Today_, (London: SCM, 1969) p. 33.

9. M. F. Palmer, "Can the Historian Invalidate Gospel Statements? Some Notes on Dialectical Theology," _Downside Review_ 95, 1 (1977) pp. 11-18.

10. Van A. Harvey, op. cit., p. 11.

11. R. Bultmann, _Faith and Understanding_, (New York: Harper & Row, 1969) pp. 145-165.

12. Within Roman Catholicism, this task had already been pointed out by Alfred Loisy in his work _L'Evangile and L'Eglise_ (1902). In this work, Loisy made two main points, the historical relativity of the Bible and the historical relativity of dogmatic statements. Cf. G. MacRae, "The Gospel and the Church," _Theology Digest_ 24 (4, 107) pp. 338-348.

13. R. Bultmann, _Theology of the New Testament_, (New York: Scribner's, 1955) p. 237.

14. R. Bultmann, _Faith and Understanding_, pp. 262-286.

15. R. Bultmann, "New Testament and Mythology," _Kerygma and Myth_, Vol. I, ed. Hans Werner Bartsch, trans. R. Fuller, (London: SPCK, 1965) pp. 1-44.

16. R. Bultmann, "The Primitive Christian Kerygma and the Historical Jesus," in _The Historical Jesus and the Kerygmatic Christ_, ed. Carl E. Braaten, (Nashville: Abingdon Press, 1965) p. 17.

17. E. Käsemann, _New Testament Questions of Today_, p. 56.

18. R. Bultmann, _Faith and Understanding_, p. 248.

19. Ibid., p. 257.

20. Ibid., p. 258.

21. Ibid., p. 261.

22. G. C. Brown, ed., *History, Criticism and Faith: Four Exploratory Studies*, (London: Downers Grove, 1976).

23. E. V. McKnight, *What Is Form Criticism?* (Philadelphia: Fortress Press, 1969); N. Perrin, *What Is Redaction Criticism?* (Philadelphia: Fortress Press, 1969).

24. N. Perrin, *A Modern Pilgrimage in New Testament Christology*, (Philadelphia: Fortress Press, 1974) p. 55.

25. E. Käsemann, *Essays on New Testament Themes*, (London: SCM, 1960) p. 56.

26. Ibid., p. 18.

27. Cf. O. Fitzer, "Hegel and the Incarnation: A Response to Hans Kung," *Journal of Religion* 52, (1972).

28. Cf. M. Ogden, *Christ without Myth*, (New York: Harper Bros., 1961).

29. K. Rahner, "The Position of Christology in the Church between Exegesis and Dogmatics," in *Theological Investigations XI*, (New York: Seabury Press, 1974) p. 188.

30. K. Rahner, "Remarks on the Importance of the History of Jesus for Catholic Dogmatics," in *Theological Investigations XIII*, (New York: Seabury Press, 1974) p. 201.

31. K. Rahner, "The Position of Christology...," op. cit., p. 187.

32. E. Käsemann, *Essays on New Testament Themes*, op. cit., p. 25.

33. Ibid., p. 23.

34. Cf. Vermes, *Jesus the Jew*, (London: Collins, 1973).

35. Cf. E. Käsemann, New Testament Questions of Today, op. cit., pp. 42-43;

C. F. D. Moule, The Origin of Christology, (Cambridge: Cambridge University Press, 1977).

36. L. Hurtado, "New Testament: A critique of Bousset's Influence," Theological Studies 40:2 (1979) p. 317.

37. E. Schillebeeckx, Jesus, An Experiment in Christology, (New York: Seabury Press, 1979) p. 74.

38. Cf. D. Cuppit, "One Jesus, Many Christs?" in Christ, Faith and History, S. W. Sykes, ed. (London: Cambridge, 1972) pp. 131-144.

39. G. D. Nineham, "Epilogue" in The Myth of God Incarnate, J. Hick, ed., (Philadelphia: Westminster, 1977) p. 195.

40. N. Perrin, Rediscovering the Teaching of Jesus, p. 234.

41. Ibid., p. 235.

42. Ibid.

43. Ibid., p. 229.

44. Ibid., p. 234.

45. Ibid., pp. 240-241.

46. Ibid., p. 242.

47. Ibid., pp. 243-244.

48. Ibid., p. 244.

49. Ibid.

50. Ibid., p. 245.

51. Ibid., p. 237.

52. E. Käsemann, Essays, p. 25.

53. Ibid., p. 33.

54. Ibid., p. 18.

55. "...the community bore (and still bears) witness to history as being living and contemporary. It interprets out of its own experience what for it has already become mere history and employs for this purpose the medium of preaching. It is precisely by this method that the community rescues the facts of the past from being regarded only as prodigies and wonders. And in so doing, it demonstrates that in its eyes Jesus is no mere miracle-worker, but the *Kyrios*, from whom it knows itself to receive both grace and obligation. To state the paradox as sharply as possible: the community takes so much trouble to maintain historical continuity with him who once trod this earth that it allows the historical events of this earthly life to pass for the most part into oblivion and replaces them by its own message. It is not only at this point in history that the community does this. The same process is always being repeated in the course of Church history. Time and again, continuity with the past is preserved by shattering the tradition... The truth is that it is this variation which makes continuity possible at all. For mere history becomes significant history not through tradition as such but through interpretation, not through the simple establishment of facts but through the understanding of events of the past which have become objectified and frozen into facts... Mere history only takes on genuine historical significance insofar as it can address both a question and an answer to our contemporary situation; in other words, by finding interpreters who hear and utter this question and answer. For this purpose primitive Christianity allows mere history no vehicle of expression other than the kerygma." E. Käsemann, *Essays*, p. 20.

56. Ibid., p. 31.

CHAPTER 3

JESUS, HIS LIFE, MINISTRY AND MESSAGE

A. Introduction

We contend that New Testament Christology, while admittedly grounded in the early Church's subjective experiences of the risen Lord, is not totally unrelated to the historical person of Jesus and his message. While the Gospels do not intend to set out the life and character of Jesus, they are not totally unconcerned with the past. The Gospel's kerygmatic role did not lead to total disinterest in the life and character of Jesus. R. Bultmann accepts the fact that, in the primitive Church, Jesus the "proclaimer" became the "one proclaimed." It follows then that the very nature of this proclamation has important implications for any understanding of the early Church's use of Gospel traditions. The nature of Jesus' proclamation becomes relevant to the Gospel tradition's *sitz in leben*. Bultmann's insistence that the kerygma of the early Church was concerned with no more than the *dass* of Jesus' historical existence is no longer accepted without modification, even by scholars whom he has deeply influenced. /1/

Jesus' sayings and narrative traditions about his actions and his message permeate the Gospels. And while the traditions incorporated in the Gospels were shaped by the experiences, practices and needs of the early Church, the memory of Jesus was also a contributing factor. An empty tomb, the Resurrection, appearances, and religious enthusiasm could not possibly have called the Jerusalem Church into being unless the life and death of Jesus had already created the context within which the disciples interpreted their experiences.

The message of Jesus, his relationship to God, his manner of life and ministry is imbedded in multi-layered material. In order to define this message, various criteria can be applied to the sources. These criteria are well expressed in Norman Perrin's *Rediscovering the Teaching of Jesus*. /2/ First and most important is the criterion of "distinctiveness" or "dissimilarity." Material will be attributed to Jesus if it is distinct from emphases in the Judaism of Jesus' time and in early Christianity. Secondly is the criterion of "multi-attestation." Themes and concerns which occur in different forms can be attributed to Jesus' message. The third criterion is "coherence." Whatever is consistent with what has been established as authentic by the first two criteria can also be admitted.

These criteria must be used judiciously. This is especially true of the first criterion. It would be one thing to say that a statement attributed to Jesus is probably authentic if it is inconsistent with Judaism before him and with the Church after him. But to say that no statement attributed to Jesus can be authentic unless it is inconsistent with Judaism and with the Church after him is quite another matter. That is tantamount to saying that Jesus could never have agreed with Judaism and that the Church could never have agreed with him. We do not know enough about Judaism and early Christianity to make those statements.

Jesus had his roots in the culture and religion of Judaism; he is the product of the Old Testament. It is to be expected then that many aspects of his message can be found in the Old Testament. Yet there was something distinctive about his message and person; otherwise, it would not have had the impact it had.

While we know nothing about the personality of Jesus in the modern sense of his psychological make-up, this should not be interpreted to mean that the early Church was uninterested in Jesus of Nazareth. The Gospel traditions, descriptions of Jesus' actions, words and relationships, do indicate a great deal about who he was, enough to enable us to say that certain things would be inconsistent with his character. In fact the historicity of some aspects of the portrait of Jesus are essential to faith, for if historical research were ever able to prove conclusively that these aspects were really unlike those of the Jesus of history, it would certainly erode our faith.

The intent of this chapter is to show that New Testament scholarship has developed a consensus about the message of Jesus. This consensus centers on two major points: Jesus' radical proclamations, and his message of the breaking forth of the kingdom of God.

A KENOTIC CHRISTOLOGY

B. In the Form of Parables

In order to understand these major points, it is important to grasp the important and crucial role New Testament parables play in expressing Jesus' message. In fact, the recovery of their meaning has been one of the most important elements in the historical quest for Jesus. /3/

A major tendency in the study of the parables is to make them the object of linguistic and semantic analysis. A. Wilder's book on the rhetoric of early Christianity is a good example of such a study. /4/ Wilder sees the parables as stories that reveal how the fate of individuals is decided as they take positions in actual situations. D. Via considers the parables total entities with an autonomy and a cohesive unity which makes it impossible to divide them into form and content. Via underlines Wilder's position by insisting that the parables are language events that lead to a new possibility for the listeners in demanding that they take a personal stand. /5/ Jesus' parables were intended neither to convey timeless truths nor to simply illustrate his proclamations. They themselves were a "message," a language event.

That important dimension of the parables has been presented in a book by E. Linnemann. She defines a successful parable as an event that decisively alters a situation, creating possibilities that did not exist before in the situation of the one addressed by it. Moreover the parable not only creates this new possibility, it also compels the listener to make a decision with regard to it. "Jesus by compelling his listeners to a decision through telling a parable, gives them the possibility of making a change of existence, of understanding themselves anew from the depths, of achieving a new life." /6/

The parables of Jesus present this possibility because "something decisive happens here through what is said." /7/ Language, however, is subject to historical change and language which created a message event in one historical situation may not do so in another. "The parables of Jesus have been passed down to us, but the 'language event' they effected cannot be passed down." /8/ Although the language event of the parables cannot be transmitted, it can be made intelligible, and it is the task of interpretation to make the character the parables had for their original audience intelligible to later readers. The parables' language event character might then be repeated in Christian preaching. Linnemann applies this hermeneutical process to a number of parables. She speaks of Jesus using the story of the Good Samaritan to call men forth from "unauthentic existence" and to "authentic living." In the Lost Sheep and the Lost Coins, Jesus tells his contemporaries that repentance is "an event coming from God, the arrival of his Kingdom" and that here and how in these objectionable table companions this deed of God has happened. To agree with Jesus, his listeners had to alter their ideas radically.

D. Crossan finds the key to understanding Jesus' message about the Kingdom in the parables themselves. He expressed this dimension of the parables in three key words: the <u>advent</u> of new world and unforeseen possibilities; the <u>reversal</u> of man's entire past; <u>action</u> which expressed the new world and the new possibilities.

Crossan sees the parable of the Good Samaritan as a story challenging the hearer to put together two impossible and contradictory words for the same person, "Samaritan" and "neighbor." The story is a story of reversal, because when good (clerics) and bad (Samaritan) become respectively bad and good, a world is being challenged with polar reversal. /9/

In the case of the Good Samaritan the hearer is confronted with the necessity of saying the impossible and having his or her world turned upside down and radically questioned in its pre-suppositions. The metaphorical point of the parable is, in terms of the Kingdom, breaking abruptly into human consciousness and demanding the overturn of prior values, closed options, set judgments, and established conclusions. The result is that "the hearer struggling with the contradictory dualism of Good/Samaritan is actually experiencing the inbreaking of the Kingdom." "Not only does it happen like this," Crossan continues, "it happens in this. The original parable's point was the reversal caused by the advent of the Kingdom in and through the challenge to utter the unutterable and to admit thereby that other world was at that very moment placing their own under radical judgment." /10/

The parables convey to us now as they did to their original hearers the challenge of the historical Jesus. "They (the parables) challenge the hearer to explore the manifold possibilities of the experience of God as king, and they do so in ways which constantly remind the hearer that, on the one hand, God is to be experienced in the historicality of the world of every day, while on the other hand, they claim that God is to be experienced precisely in the shattering of that every day world." /11/

There is an inner connection between the language events of the parables and mode and motives of Jesus' work. In some way Jesus himself was a parable of the Kingdom of God. In Jesus' life, message, ministry, and person is a parable of God's offer of salvation. As Schillebeeckx writes: "The living parable that Jesus is in his own person and the impact of his parable stories confront us with the questions whether or not we also wish, venture, and are able to see in Jesus' activities a manifestation of God's regard for people." /12/ As a parable of God's offer of salvation, Jesus demands of his hearers an inward conversion, a _metanoia_.

C. The Kingdom of God

Jesus sees his cause as the approaching Kingdom of God, which, while at the center of his proclamation, is never exactly defined. In his parables, Jesus constantly described it in different ways to bring its meaning home to everyone. /13/ In the tradition of the Old Testament and of Judaism, the coming of the Kingdom of God meant the actual coming of God - the day on which God would be "all in all." The Kingdom of God did not primarily imply a realm, but God's lordship, the manifestation of his glory, God's Godhead. It implied a radical interpretation of the first commandment and a demonstration of it which would change the course of history. "I am the Lord, your God...you shall have no other gods before me." (Ex. 20:2,3).

In the Old Testament, the Kingdom of God was the power of God expressed in deeds, his activity as king. According to R. Schnackenburg, the Kingdom of God "...is characterized not by latent authority but by the exercise of power, not by an office but by a function. It is not a title but a deed." /14/ While

God's ruling was perceived by the Old Testament as ongoing, there was, especially in the prophets, an element of future to the ruling of God, "the idea of a future act of God which will be decisive for the salvation of the people in a way in which his past acts on their behalf were not." /15/ It would be a final act completely effective, an eschatological act. To this understanding of God's future, final, and all-encompassing act was added in the Apocalyptic literature other elements and imagery that the earth would be completely changed; that the dead would resurrect. What was essential here was that this final act of God would be decisive, all-transforming, redeeming for his people. This final act would bring about the "age to come," the time of salvation. Everywhere it was a question of a happening - in fact, the dynamic character of the Hebrew expression for the Kingdom of God radiates everywhere. It is an expression which cannot be rendered satisfactorily in translation; everywhere it is a question of how the reign of God makes itself known in what happens. Nowhere in the Old Testament was the Kingdom perceived as stereotype, an abstract idea.

Schillebeeckx writes: "What Jesus intends by it (Kingdom of God) is a process, a course of events, whereby God begins to govern or to act as king or Lord, an action, therefore, by which God manifests his being in the world of men." /16/ For Jesus' kingdom does not mean a territory or a sphere of domination. It means God's rule, the certainty of ruling which God will take over. "God's rulership," "God's Kingdom," thus becomes the designation for "God's cause." It cannot be earned by religious or moral effort imposed by political struggle. We cannot plan for it, organize it, make it, or break it. It is given; we can only inherit it. /17/ This is what comes out most clearly from the parables of Jesus: the coming of the Kingdom of God is notwithstanding all human expections, oppositions, calculations, and plans.

Jesus' proclamation of the Kingdom of God has a distinctly eschatological slant. He is certain that God will recognize him and give sanction to the ministry he has been called upon to perform on its behalf. The Kingdom of God which had such humble beginnings will ultimately be realized in power and glory. But this does not happen within this era. It lies beyond the limits of time and will come into being by God's direct intervention. At the same time it is of importance that that which is to come is seen as a fulfillment of that which has already begun. In this perspective, Jesus is an eschatological figure. This eschatological perspective is part and parcel of the message and cannot be eliminated without distortion. /18/ The Kingdom of God is seen as both of the future and of the present. The disciples experience the Kingdom of God in their present as they gather together in the table fellowship of the Kingdom; but they are also taught to pray "Thy Kingdom come." According to Jesus' teaching the experience of the present is a guarantee of the future. The present time of the disciple is filled with the reality of God. And what is expected is the consummation of the experience of this reality in the future. The reality experienced as fulfilling and meaningful is also known as ambiguous in terms of conflict or temptation. "A reality known in terms of Now, but also of Not Yet." /19/

According to Perrin those confronted by the ministry of Jesus are challenged to recognize that this is the beginning, not the end. One responding to the challenge of that ministry is assured that he or she does not know or have all that is to be known or had. "In the teaching of Jesus the emphasis is not upon a future for which men must prepare, even with the help of God; the emphasis is upon a present which carries with it the guarantee of a future. The present that has become God's present guarantees that all future will be God's future." /20/ Luke 11:20 emphasizes this when it sets Jesus' message about the Kingdom of God in the context of a ministry of exorcism, adding an important element to the nature of God's Kingdom as preached by Jesus. Exorcism can be seen as an intervention of God that restores the wholeness of one single individual and not of a whole nation. This dimension of the Kingdom is further elaborated in Luke 17:20 where Jesus tells the Pharisees that "the Kingdom of God is in the midst of you."

The presence of the Kingdom in our midst is not a threatening reality. It is an offer of salvation. Jesus' message is not one of fear but of joy. For that reason the synoptic Gospels often use the term "good news." /21/ This phrase points to an essential feature of Jesus' message. By his preaching of the Kingdom he promises the fulfillment of all human hopes, expectations and longings for a fundamental transformation of the order of things - a completely new start. When God's Kingdom comes, all suffering and oppression will be ended: the blind will see; the lame, walk; the lepers will be cleansed; the dead, hear; the dead will be raised up; and the poor will have the good news preached to them. /22/

D. Blessed Are the Poor

The "Good News" aspect of Jesus' message is emphasized by the formula "Blessed are you." All worldly blessing and values are to be considered of little value in comparison to the blessings of the Kingdom of God. But the nature of the blessings involves a total reversal of values, expressed in relation to their recipients. The blessings are not for virtuous people, but for the poor, the hungry, and the sorrowful, the outcasts, and the powerless.

In his inaugural sermon in Nazareth, Jesus can take up a saying of the prophet Isaiah (61:1) and say that he has been sent to preach the good news to the poor, to proclaim release to the captives and recovery of sight to the blind, to set at liberty the oppressed and to proclaim the acceptable year of the Lord (Luke 4: 18-19). The Goodness of God passing all understanding means joy and gladness for the poor. They have received redress before which all other values fade (Matt. 13: 44-46). They experience more than they have hoped for; God accepts them and, although they are empty-handed, Jesus himself rejoices with them.

Who are the poor to whom the Kingdom of God is promised? Poor is taken in a very broad sense; it includes the helpless, those without resources, those who suffer on account of their discipleship (Luke 6: 22-23). Jesus' poor are those who have nothing to expect from the world, but who expect everything from God. Those who have been driven up against the limits of the world and its possibilities. They are beggars before God - only from Him can they expect help.

The poor are the ones with whom Jesus associates - tax collectors, harlots, shepherds (Matt. 21:32) or sinners (Mark 21:17), that is, the Godless. The Godless included people who ignored the commandments of God and were held up to contempt. The whole lot were lumped together as ha-aretz, the poor, uneducated people who either did not know the complicated provisions of the Law or, if they did, could not keep them and were consequently despised by the pious. They were considered to be like Gentiles. While God's fatherhood extended to the Jewish people even when they were sinners, the same was not true for the Gentiles who were sinners almost by definition. Gentiles lived apart from the Law. A Jew who sinned could hope for mercy from his heavenly Father - but a Gentile could not count God as his Father.

Against this background we may appreciate the radical nature of Jesus' proclamation of the forgiveness of sins, as expressed in the parable of the Prodigal Son. By becoming a swineherd, the son had made himself like a Gentile. Any Jewish father listening to Jesus' parable would have considered this son as dead. Yet in the parable the father forgives in an extravagant way. Here was a situation of reversal; a situation in which God's love was being revealed in a new way. God is the compassionate one and salvation is available to the most abandoned. The Kingdom of God cannot be contained by existing structures and institutions. /23/ For God is no longer "clean" and "unclean," "Jew" and "Gentile" or "Jew who has made himself a Gentile."

According to N. Perrin:

> "The central feature of the message of Jesus is, then, the challenge of the forgiveness of sins and the offer of the possibility of a new kind of relationship with God and with one's fellow man. This was symbolized by a table-fellowship which celebrated the present joy and anticipated the future consummation: a table-fellowship of such joy and gladness that it survived the crucifixion and provided a focal point for the community life of the earliest Christians - and was the most direct link between the community-life and the pre-Easter fellowship of Jesus and his disciples...we are justified in seeing this table-fellowship as the central feature of the ministry of Jesus; an anticipatory sitting at the table in the Kingdom of God and a very real celebration of present joy

and challenge." /24/

Jesus' table-fellowship with sinners and the abandoned bears witness to the fact that Jesus, through his actions, carried his proclamation into effect.

To understand what Jesus was doing in eating with sinners, it is important to realize that in the East, even today, to invite a man to a meal is an honor. It is an offer of peace, trust, brotherhood, and forgiveness - in short, sharing a table means sharing a life. In Judaism in particular, table-fellowship means fellowship before God, for breaking bread shows that all who share the meal also have a share in the blessing which the master of the house has spoken over the bread. Thus Jesus' meals with the publicans and sinners were not only events on a social level, or an expression of his unusual humanity and social generosity, but they were an expression of his mission and message. The inclusion of sinners in the community of salvation, achieved in table-fellowship, is the most meaningful expression of the message of the redeeming love of God.

Jesus said again and again that salvation was for sinners, not for the righteous. God opens the Kingdom to children and to those who can say "Abba" like a child (Matt. 18:3): "I tell you this: unless you turn round and become like children, you will never enter the kingdom of Heaven." A person's response to God's activity must contain the ready trust and instinctive obedience of a child. Only in this way is one truly able to enter into the depth of the experience that has now become a real possibility for him or her. To experience God's activity as King requires a radically new attitude to life in the world - a radical reorientation. To accept it "like a child" means to accept it immediately, without any calculation. The prodigal son received a totally undeserved grace; his older brother's mistake was to count the whole time on a reward. This is where the message of Jesus about God's love and forgiveness, about the Kingdom, truly bursts the old wineskins. To accept Jesus' message demands a radical conversion from the old ways of seeing reality. God's Kingdom as forgiveness of sin is a challenge, for it constitutes a new relationship with God and with one's neighbor.

E. The Love of the Neighbor

There is an important correlative to the redeeming love of God. While experiencing God's love means experiencing that one has been unreservedly accepted, approved, and infinitely loved, it also demands that one do the same to one's neighbor. If God remits an enormous debt of ours, we, too, must be prepared to release our fellow men from their petty debts to us (Matt. 18:23-24). God's forgiveness gives us the capacity for limitless forgiveness (Luke 17:3-4).

The forgiveness of sins is a gift which God gives totally, unconditionally, and with absolute generosity. The father's reception of the prodigal son was unconditional. And the son's repentance was simply his willingness to set aside his pride and accept his father's graciousness. But because of the nature of the gift, we cannot keep it and simply enjoy it for ourselves; it will be wasted if we "do not forgive your (our) brother from the heart" (Matt. 18:35). To be forgiven means to forgive "seventy times seven"; that is, without limits. "As we also forgive" indicates that the experience of God's activity is linked to a proper response. In the context of God's forgiveness, men and women learn to forgive and to thus enter ever more deeply into an experience of the divine forgiveness. The all-surpassing love of God makes itself felt in the acceptance of human beings by each other.

Jesus' proclamation of the Kingdom of God demands a radical decision in favor of one's neighbor. His proclamation is related to the _shema_ with its dual command of God and the neighbor. The text of the _shema_ is from Deuteronomy 6:4-6: "Hear, O Israel, the Lord is our God, one Lord, and you must love the Lord your God with all your heart and soul and strength." For Jesus, the key word is "with all your soul" and it is encountered in the demand that one be prepared to sacrifice life itself: "If any man would come after me, let him deny himself and take up his cross and follow me." Everything that Jesus said concerning one's relationship to his neighbor is determined by the demand that one should be of help to him. Nothing may be allowed to stand in the way of care for the neighbor. Jesus' criticism of the Scribes and Pharisees belongs to this context: "They make up heavy packs and pile them on men's shoulders, but will not raise a finger to lift the load themselves." (Matt. 23:4-5). Religious obligations have no priority here, not even the rules concerning the Sabbath. For Jesus the Sabbath is for the sake of people and to serve God is to serve people in their need.

Although everything in Jesus' proclamation centers around the Kingdom of God, God is not to be loved simply in a ritualistic way but in care for the neighbor. The grace of God is compared to the gifts which are given by human beings. A man gets up in the middle of the night in order to give the help which has been requested (Luke 11:5-8). Jesus concludes: "...how much more will your heavenly Father give good things to those who ask him!" (Matthew 7:11).

The parable of the Good Samaritan underlines the same point about the reality of the Kingdom of God, for it is given in the context of a question about eternal life. It leads away from questions about personal salvation to questions about the other. In other words, eternal life is in our midst as compassion.

In Luke, the "neighbor" shifts from being the object of compassion (verse 24) to being the subject who shows compassion (verse 36). But the Samaritan's compassion in no way springs from faith in Jesus. He does not act religiously. In Jesus' teaching, love of neighbor is not simply a means to the love of God, for this would not really be love. In the parable of the Good Samaritan, the help given to the one who has fallen among the thieves is strictly given in response to the other's needs. According to G. Bornkamm, what the Samaritan does is aimed at the sufferer without side glances at God. This is referred to in the last judgment. The actions of those who are accepted were not meant for the judge but only for those in trouble. "I tell you this: anything you did for one of my brothers here, however humble, you did for me." (Matthew 25:39-41). Love of our neighbor can never be merely an indirect love, achieved by detour via a supposed love of God. /25/ The love of God and the love of neighbor are not the same thing.

What then is the meaning of this double commandment of love? The similarity is not in the object; the objects are infinitely different; the similarity lies in the nature of this love. According to Bornkamm:

> "It is in Jesus' own words the renunciation of self-love, the willingness for and the act of surrender there where you actually are, or which is the same, where your neighbor is, who is waiting for you. In this way and in no other God's call comes to us, and in this way the love of God and the love of neighbor become one. Surrender to God now no longer means a retreat of the soul into a paradise of spirituality and the dissolution of selfhood in adoration and meditation, but a waiting and preparedness for the call of God, who calls us in the persons of our neighbors. In this sense the care of our neighbors is the test of our love of God." /26/

In this context the one question which decides everything is the question "who is our neighbor?" In the story of the Good Samaritan, the scribe poses his question at a distance, as a theoretical problem, in the abstract. But such a question cannot be put at a distance since the neighbor cannot be put at a distance. As Kierkegaard wrote: "Indeed everyone has a distant knowledge of his neighbor, but only God knows how man really knows him from close at hand. And yet at a distance our neighbor is only a shadow which passes through our mind like a phantom. The fact, however, that the person we just passed at that same moment was in actual fact our neighbor we may unfortunately never discover." /27/

The neighbor then is not simply a friend. It is anyone, friend or enemy. The love of Jesus invites his listener to break through all boundaries established by religions or nationalities. God does not differentiate between friend and foe. "...only so can you be children of your heavenly Father, who makes his sun rise on good and bad alike, and sends the rain on the honest and dishonest." (Matt. 5:45-46).

The parable of the Good Samaritan teaches a radically new concept of neighborliness. It defines it in terms of need rather than mutual membership in a racial or religious group. The Kingdom of God is in our midst. It manifests itself when compassion and forgiveness are offered to the one in need. Through the coming of the Kingdom of God everyone can now know that love is the ultimate; that what is done out of love will endure forever.

The link between the Kingdom of God and the reception of this Kingdom on one's life is compassionate dedication to those in need. The *metanoia* demanded by the coming of the Kingdom of God takes concrete form in compassion. God's compassion and forgiveness precedes and forms the ground and source of our compassion to others. We are urged to be compassionate as God is compassionate, for God's mercy is expressed here on earth in our mercy just as God's compassion was demonstrated concretely in Jesus' compassion for the oppressed.

F. God as Father: The Sonship of Jesus

The major impact of Jesus' perception and proclamation of the Kingdom is in relation to an understanding of God. Jesus' message about the Kingdom of God is primarily a message about God, about who God is. Jesus' God is not purely transcendent contacted simply through the meditation of the Law. Jesus' God is near; his lordship consists in the sovereignty of his love. Jesus proclaims that, through his love, God has drawn near to man and woman so as to grant them the experience of his direct, immediate nearness. The experience of God's Kingdom is the experience of God's rulership not in power but in love. Experiencing the Kingdom of God means that one has been unreservedly accepted, approved, and infinitely loved. Jesus presents God as Father of the prodigal son, as Father of the abandoned.

Jesus' preferred way of speaking about God was as Father. Indeed, Jesus gave more importance to this title than did the tradition of the Old Testament. The Old Testament affirms in a variety of ways that God acts in history. For Jesus, the word "Father" symbolizes God's acts of compassion and mercy in history. In choosing the symbol "Father" to speak of God, Jesus was expressing his own experience of God. In the Gospels the term occurs 170 times on his lips. Jesus' use of the term "Father" to describe God crystallizes in a special way his view of God's Kingdom as God's loving rule. In his self-gift to man God goes to the root of things and knows no half means. Jesus' own response had to be equally radical.

A KENOTIC CHRISTOLOGY

The authentic term for God in the teaching of Jesus has been preserved in the original Aramaic - "Abba," indicating that the term was highly esteemed in primitive Christianity. To Jewish sensibility the term "Abba" is too familiar. For Jesus, it is the simplest and sincerest conceivable term to express God's attitude. The term does not imply a banal self-assurance which takes things for granted, but tells us that God is intimately close rather than a distant transcendent ruler.

According to Hammerton-Kelly, Jesus used the symbol Father on three levels of intimacy: "'My Father' when he prayed and when he revealed his identity as the son to his disciples; 'your Father' when he taught his disciples how to pray to a God who cared for them with compassion and forgiveness and assured them of a good time to come; 'the Father' when defending his message against doubters and attack." /28/

The real theological meaning of the use of "Abba" appears only when it is seen in connection with Jesus' message of the Kingdom of God. It then becomes clear that calling God "Father" is not a banal, almost automatic intimacy. The phrase "Father in heaven" (Matt. 5:9; 16:45; 6:1; 7:11) and the mention of the perfection of the Father (Matt. 8:48) indicate the difference between God and man. That is why Jesus forbids his disciples to let themselves be called Father, "for you have one Father who is in heaven." In the "Our Father," the invocation "Father" is connected with the prayer, "hallowed be thy name, Thy Kingdom come, Thy will be done." The dignity, sovereignty, and glory of God are in this way preserved, but they are imagined in a different way; God's lordship shows itself in his sovereign freedom to love and to forgive. Luke interprets the perfection of the Father in heaven as mercy (Luke 6:36). His perfection is not, as in the Greek system, a fullness of moral goodness but a "creature goodness" which makes others good, a contagious love. God's paternal love goes out to the lost and even restores to life what was dead (Luke 15:24). When God begins his rule as Father, it is the new creation - the old has passed away; all things are made new in his love. For Jesus, God's Fatherhood is not simply that of the chosen people. He is also Father of the unrighteous, the Gentiles, the oppressed. No one is excluded from God's fatherly care; there is equal dignity and worth for all. Reference to the Father always points first of all to God's active providence and care for all things. He is concerned about every sparrow and every hair on our heads, knows our needs before we ask him, makes our anxieties seem superfluous.

Jesus saw and understood God as a loving Father. He addressed him as Abba. But in what way did Jesus understand his own relationship to God? The exegetical evidence no longer enables us to affirm with any certainty the uniqueness of Jesus' sense of sonship. R. Brown writes: "The way in which Jesus speaks of God as Father certainly indicates that he claimed a special relationship to God. But it remains difficult to find in the Synoptic account of the public ministry an incontrovertible proof that he claims a unique sonship that other men could not share." /29/

Without speaking about the "complete novelty and uniqueness of Abba as an address to God," /30/ Jesus' use of "Abba" does seem to express an essential dimension of his relationship to God and, in some way, of his own self-understanding. Jesus spoke to God as a child to its father, with confidence and security and at the same time with reverence and obedience. To speak about Jesus' self-understanding is in no way to claim that he ascribed to himself a "Son of God" understanding.

Whatever self-understanding there is seems to be primarily in terms of Jesus' understanding of his mission. Fuller writes: "Sonship means to Jesus not a dignity to be claimed but a responsibility to be fulfilled." /31/ Sonship was a commission from God. According to Matthew 11:27, as son, Jesus was conscious of "being in a singular way the recipient and mediator of God." /32/ Fuller sees in this text from Matthew an affirmation of sonship based directly on Jesus' use of "Abba," and his admission of others through his eschatological message to the privilege of calling God "abba." So although we cannot accept the "thunderbolt" as directly from Jesus, it is an indirect witness to his self-understanding. /33/

F. Conclusion - The Compassion of Our God

From what we can gather about Jesus' message and self-understanding, the question of wider Christology poses itself to us: Was the uniqueness of his experience qualitative or quantitative - the experience of one other than man - more than man - or the experience of the "best" man, perfect man? Is this ultimately what Christian dogma is referring to when it speaks of the divinity of Jesus? The fact is that we cannot answer with any precision the question, "Who did Jesus think he was?" All we can say is that he lived out of a consciousness of sonship and power, of commissioning and authority which seems to have transcended the ordinary prophetic experience of inspiration. By how much it transcended the ordinary human experience we cannot say either qualitatively or metaphysically or existentially.

These questions can only be answered in light of the first Easter. Christological reflection cannot confine itself solely to Jesus' experience of God, or his claims or his ministry. It must include the Easter faith. What we can say and must say is that without this element of uniqueness in Jesus' experience of God the gap between the historical Jesus and the Christ of faith would be an unbridgeable abyss. Unless there is some correlation between Christian claims for Jesus and Jesus' own self-awareness these claims lose touch with reality.

The basic importance of Jesus' message concerning the Kingdom of God is reflected in the fact that this message provides a means for integrating and interpreting the whole of Jesus' proclamation. The importance of the Kingdom of God motif is found in the way it shapes and informs the message of Jesus, his ministry, and deeds. The Kingdom of God is about God. The Kingdom of God motif explains the basic character of God in his act of saving men and women. God's love is the supreme determinant of the divine action. And whoever accepts the Kingdom of God is united to love in a radical way. What the Gospel says about Jesus is that he loved in a radical way, and that therefore, in him, God the Father was manifest.

The Biblical history of salvation is one of changing strategems in God's search for men and women, a search characterized by a fatherly mercy exceeding all human comprehension. The prophet Jeremiah found in the following words the most moving expression for God's forgiveness: "Is Ephraim still my dear son, a child in whom I delight? As often as I turn my back on him I still remember him; and so my heart yearns for him, I am filled with tenderness towards him. This is the very word of the Lord." (Jeremiah 31:20). Here we have the "must" of God's incomprehensible love. The Gospel writers saw Jesus as the ultimate strategem of God's love for his people. As the writer to the Hebrews put it: "When in former times God spoke to our forefathers, he spoke in fragmentary and varied fashion through the prophets. But in this final age he has spoken to us in the Son whom he has made heir to the whole universe, and through whom he created all orders of existence..." (Hebrews 1:1-2).

God's ultimate strategem in expressing his love was the death of his Son for us. As Paul tells us: "And so, since we have now been justified by Christ's sacrificial death, we shall all the more certainly be saved through him from final retribution." (Romans 5:9). This is how primitive Christianity expressed what it saw in the person of Jesus, his message, and his ministry. It expressed it in light of the Resurrection. Yet, as we have seen, Jesus' message and ministry itself expressed a radical dimension of God's love.

A KENOTIC CHRISTOLOGY

NOTES

1. Cf. P. Gisel, *Vérite and Histoire. La Théologie dans la Modernite, Ernst Käsemann*, (Paris: Beau-chesne, 1977) pp. 90-189.

   N. Perrin, "The Kerygmatic Theology and the Question of the Historical Jesus," *Religion in Life*, XXIX, 1959-1960, pp. 86-97.

2. N. Perrin, *Rediscovering the Teaching of Jesus*, (New York: Harper & Row, 1976) pp. 236-238.

   R. Fuller, *Critical Introduction to the New Testament*, London, 1966) pp. 94-103.

3. Cf. C. H. Dodd, *The Parables of the Kingdom*, (New York: 1961).

   J. Jeremias, *The Parables of Jesus* (London: SCM, 1972).

   E. Linnemann, *Jesus of the Parables: Introduction and Exposition*, trans. J. Sturdy, (New York: Harper & Row, 1966).

   D. O. Via, *The Parables: Their Literary and Existential Dimensions* (Philadelphia: Fortress, 1967).

4. A. N. Wilder, *Early Christian Rhetoric: The Language of the Gospels*, (New York: Harper & Row, 1966).

5. D. O. Via, op. cit., pp. 2-109.

6. E. Linnemann, op, cit., p. 31.

7. Ibid., p. 32.

8. Ibid., p. 33.

9. J. D. Crossan, *In Parables: The Challenge of the Historical Jesus*, (New York: Harper & Row, 1973).

10. J. D. Crossan, op. cit., p. 56.

11. N. Perrin, *Jesus and the Language of the Kingdom*, (Philadelphia: Fortress Press, 1976) p. 199.

12. E. Schillebeeckx, *Jesus - An Experiment in Christology*, (New York: Seabury, 1979) p. 170.

13. Ibid., p. 141.

14. Cf. R. Schnackenburg, *God's Rule and Kingdom*, trans. J. Murphy, (New York: Herder & Herder, 1963) p. 13.

15. N. Perrin, *Rediscovering the Teaching of Jesus*, op. cit., p. 56.

16. E. Schillebeeckx, op. cit., p. 170.

17. Matt. 21:43, 25:34; Luke 12:32.

18. According to R. H. Fuller, "...Jesus understood his mission in terms of eschatological prophecy and was confident of its vindication by the Son of Man at the End." In *Foundations of New Testament Christology*, (London: Lutterworth Press, 1965) p. 130.

19. N. Perrin, *Rediscovering the Teaching of Jesus*, op. cit., pp. 90-91.

20. Ibid., p. 205.

21. Cf. Mark 1;14, 14:9; Matt. 4:23; 9:35; 24:14.

22. See Luke 7:22-23; Matt. 11:5-6.

23. Cf. N. Perrin, *Rediscovering the Teaching of Jesus*, op. cit., pp. 90-91.

24. Ibid., pp. 107-108.

25. G. Bornkamm, op. cit., p. 112.

26. Ibid.

27. Quoted by G. Bornkamm, op. cit., p. 112.

28. R. Hammerton-Kelly, *God the Father*, (Philadelphia: Fortress Press, 1979) p. 81.

29. R. E. Brown, "How Much Did Jesus Know?", CBQ, 29 (1967) p. 337.

30. J. Jeremias, New Testament Theology, op. cit., p. 67.

31. R. H. Fuller, The Mission and Achievement of Jesus, (London: SCM, 1954) p. 84.

32. J. Jeremias, The Prayers of Jesus, (London: SCM, 1967) p. 51.

33. R. H. Fuller, The Foundations of New Testament Christology, op. cit., p. 115.

CHAPTER 4

THE FORM OF A SERVANT

A. Introduction

The transition from Jesus, his message, and ministry to the beginning of Christianity, to the ecclesia, was operated through the salvific experience of Jesus' death and resurrection. The nexus of all the traditions about Jesus was the experience of salvation in him. And the early Christians named the one through whom this salvation occurred, Christ, Logos, Lord. These were common titles in the religious tradition of the early Christians. But they were changed as they were applied to Jesus, for they were used to claim that God was disclosed in Jesus.

These titles were attempts by the early Church to express its understanding of the person of Jesus. Yet they are certainly dependent on the socio-cultural context in which they were used. E. Schillebeeckx writes: "One must not lose sight of the historically contingent framework of Jesus' ministry when speaking of Jesus in the language of faith as the Messiah or Christ..." /1/ It is not possible to absolutize any of the titles and deal with them as abstractions from their historical situation. The structure of the New Testament seems to indicate that there was no one single starting point for Christology but a very complex interaction of different Christologies emerging from diverse cultural situations. The New Testament accepted a number of expressions of the salvific reality of Jesus. While these varying expressions were simultaneous, they were not harmonious. In fact, a historical/critical study of the New Testament demonstrates the impossibility of a unitary view of the New Testament Christologies. Form and redaction criticism have demonstrated that there is no single way to formulate the Christian message or to build Christian communities or indeed to live as a Christian. There are many different expressions of Christianity within the New Testament. No single form of Christianity can be singled out as normative in the first century. The same can be said about the various Christologies of the New Testament.

A critical question emerges from these affirmations: the issue of the authority and canonicity of the New Testament. /2/ If the New Testament is not a homogeneous collection of complementary writings, how does the New Testament function as a "canon," as a criterion for orthodoxy? According to Hans Küng:

> "The New Testament has continually proved its irreplaceable normative authority and significance and we are thrown back on this norm as long as we remain authentic Christians and do not want to be anything else. The New Testament as the original written Christian Testimony remains (fortunately) the unchangeable norm for all later proclamation and theology in the Church and provides against subjective whims and all kinds of fanaticism." /3/

Yet the New Testament has no independent authority from the living and worshipping ecclesial community. And in canonizing the Scriptures the Church did not absolutize the authority of the Scriptures.

In canonizing the Scriptures, the Church recognized and accepted the validity of diversity. As James D. G. Dunn writes:

> "If we take the canon of the New Testament seriously...we must take seriously the diversity of Christianity ...to recognize the canon of the New Testament is to affirm the diversity of Christianity. We cannot claim to accept the authority of the New Testament unless we are willing to accept as valid whatever form of Christianity can justifiably claim to be rooted in one of the strands that make up the New Testament." /4/

The New Testament as canon reveals how the reality of the Christ-event was expressed in diverse ways in the various situations of the first century; it does not dictate what the expression of Christian faith should be in each and every circumstance. As B. Child writes:

> "To distinguish between genuine and non-genuine oracles is to run in the face of the canon's intent. The canon seeks to preserve the authority of the whole witness and to resist all attempts to assign varying degrees of theological value to the

> different layers of Scripture on the basis of literary or historical documents." /5/

If the New Testament is pluriform, then one must question the relative importance of the various responses it engenders. Here New Testament scholarship has attempted to find some theological criteria or "canon within the canon" in order to evaluate the various traditions. These criteria have been formulated according to various frameworks, for they cannot simply be constructed in isolation from the Christian communities to which the New Testament text speaks today. The historical process of human response to the Christ-event was not terminated by the New Testament process of canonization. Human responses always exist within contexts. They are given by people and relate to their circumstances, cultures, and world views. That is why there must be an ongoing dialogue between the New Testament texts and our twentieth century. This dialogue would neither permit us to cling to formulations that are not meaningful to the contemporary situation nor to dictate the message and perspective of its faith. The Christ-event must interact with every generation, for the beginning of Christianity is a moving point that lies wherever the relationship between Jesus and the believer becomes visible and articulated.

Contemporary Christianity does not need to repeat or recite all the titles of the New Testament. There is no need to construct a single Christology out of the different titles and ideas connected with them. One does not need all of the New Testement for an authentic retranslation of faith. To do this would be to demand of every generation that which no one in the primitive Church succeeded in doing, for exegesis clearly indicates a variety of ruptures in New Testament Christology not unlike those now experienced as we retranslate the Christian heritage to a different cultural situation.

The starting point of contemporary Christology cannot be exclusively the Biblical dogmas about Jesus, nor the historical Jesus. What men and women of today experience and hope for must be one of the constitutive elements of the Christian response to Jesus' own question, "Who do you say that I am?" While a contemporary response is intrinsically conditioned by the history of Jesus and the New Testament sources, it is given in ever new historical situations. The contemporary situation has been described as one of the misuse of power and of manipulation, of the need for self-limitation. In this context the kenotic Christology of the New Testament seems most appropriate. I see this Christology as the most expressive of Jesus' own message and best reflected in Philippians 2:6-11 and in the Gospel of Mark.

Both Philippians 2:6-11 and the Gospel of Mark are very complicated texts and have a long history of interpretations. In relation to Philippians 2, M. Hooker quotes a comment made by A. B. Bruce in 1876: "The diversity of opinion prevailing among interpreters in regard to the meaning of Philippians 2:6-11 is enough to fill the student with despair and to affect him with intellectual paralysis." /6/ Hooker continues on her own, "Nearly 100 years later, the cause of the despair has increased out of all proportion - but the paralysis has apparently still not overtaken us." /7/ H. C. Kee begins his work on the Gospel of Mark by quoting W. C. Kümmel: "Ultimately a cloud remains over the question of Mark's aim--a clear explanation that takes into account all the facts concerning the Christological aim of the evangelist have not been elicited from the text." /8/ Yet as difficult as they may be, both texts are important sources for kenotic Christology.

B. Philippians 2

The first key in unlocking the meaning of Philippians 2:6-11 is to determine the literary style. It is important to decide whether the passage reflects the subtle distinctions of language that characterize formal theological language, or whether, like a liturgical hymn, it is essentially poetic in nature. It is clear that this passage is a hymn that probably grew out of the earliest Christian worship. It is pre-Pauline in origin. It was an established piece of tradition which Paul used as clinching evidence in his admonition to the Philippian Christians. It is a primitive liturgical form culminating in the confessional statement, "Jesus Christ is Lord." As such, it points back to the early unfolding of the mind of the Church about its Lord.

According to M. Hooker:

> "an unnecessary antithesis has been set

> up by interpreters between a rather superficial interpretation of Pauline ethics on the one hand - an interpretation implying that Christian behavior is simply a case of following Jesus - and on the other hand the conviction that the passage is to be understood only as a recital of saving acts, to which the Church responds in adoration." /9/

Following E. Käsemann, /10/ many exegetes interpret the passage as expressing the event of salvation as a drama. R. P. Martin sums up this position in the following way: "the hymn is loosely dependent upon the ethical dimension, yet...supplies the objective facts of redemption on which ethical appeal may be made. The Apostle's summons is not: Follow Jesus by doing as he did - an impossible feat - rather: Become in your conduct and church relationships the type of persons who, by that kenosis, death, and exaltation of the Lord of glory, have a place in his body, the Church." /11/ The hymn does enumerate the events of salvation. But it also invites the disciples to conformity, "for," according to Hooker, "what Paul urges the Philippians to do is to be conformed to what they ought to be - and what they did become in Christ - results from what Christ is and did; one cannot separate the Christian character of Christ himself." /12/ Whatever may have been the original intention and context of the hymn, Paul uses it as a basis for his ethical appeal to the Philippians and links the self-emptying of Christ to the life of the Christian community.

The everyday conduct of the authentic disciple should be characterized as the type of life Jesus Christ led himself. According to Hooker: "The appeal to act in a certain way is directly linked with the action of the Lord Jesus Christ." /13/ And what is the life of Jesus Christ? It is explained in terms of a contrast between Christ and Adam in the very first verses. Again according to Hooker: "An Adam created in the form and likeness of God misunderstood his position, and thought that the divine likeness was something which he needed to grasp; his tragedy was that in seizing it, he lost it. Christ, the true Adam, understood that Christlikeness was already his, by virtue of his relationship with God. Nevertheless, he empties himself." /14/

THE FORM OF A SERVANT

One of the most discussed questions in this hymn has to do with the meaning of _morphe theou_, the nature of Jesus' relationship with God. Classical exegesis has seen this word as the key term of the entire hymn. But this first-century liturgical hymn is far removed from the subtle distinction of thought found in the philosophy of Plato and Aristotle. So there are several clusters of interpretations. There is a philosophical one where _morphe theou_ is interpreted in a formal way. It would mean that Christ existed before his incarnation as essentially one with God. Another interpretation sees the roots of _morphe theou_ in the Septuagint. Here the word _morphe_ would have the meaning of the outward form or appearance of the thing so described. There is also a conviction that a doctrine of the primal man, the _Urmensch_, lies at the heart of the hymn. /15/ This position recognizes that the hymn uses the framework of a myth in order to set forth its Christological message. Within this framework, _morphe_ indicates not merely the outward form and shape in contrast to the being, but primarily the realm of existence. God quits his heavenly existence and takes instead a human existence, an existence of unredeemed man which is seen as that of slavery. Equality with God implies being of the realm of God without being the most high God. /16/ Equality with God is to be understood as Christ's present position - as something which did not need to be usurped.

The verb _kenoo_ which characterizes the all-important transition in verse seven from the divine to the earthly realm of existence has no particular philosophical use in Greek. It means simply "to empty" or it can mean "to make void, of no effect." "He emptied himself" is a graphic metaphor expressing the completeness of Christ's self-renunciation. The question has been asked "Of what did he empty himself?" Elsewhere in Paul the verb is used in a metaphoric way meaning "to make void" (Cf. 1 Cor. 9:15; Rom. 4:14). It could be translated "he made himself powerless." Making himself null and void, powerless, meant that he took the form of a slave. Now the slave is the one who has no rights or privileges, who does not even own his own body.

The verb "he emptied himself" has no second object, as if to define that of which he emptied himself. He empties himself as one pouring himself out. "For you know how generous our Lord Jesus Christ has been; he was rich, yet for your sake he became poor, so that through his poverty you might become rich" (II Cor. 8:9). According to Hooker, "the one who is truly what man is meant to be - in the form and likeness of God - became what other men are, because they are in Adam." /17/ Other men are in a position of enslavement, a position which leads ultimately to death.

One could, as C. D. Moule has done, translate the text in the following fashion: "Jesus did not reckon that equality with God meant snatching: on the contrary, he emptied himself." /18/ This would mean that, whereas ordinary human valuation reckons that God-likeness essentially means having your own way, getting what you can, Jesus saw God-likeness essentially as giving and spending oneself out. Precisely because Christ was in the form of God he recognized equality with God as a matter not of getting but of giving. Height is equalled with depth, humiliation is identified with exaltation. What is called emptying is really fulfilling, kenosis is actually plerosis which means that the human limitations of Jesus are seen as a positive expression of his divinity rather than as a curtailment of it.

According again to Hooker, the real paradox in the text

> "is precisely because he (Christ) is truly in the form of God (or God's image) that he is prepared to take on the form of a slave ... In becoming what we are, Christ becomes subject to human frustrations and enslavement to hostile powers; but his very action in becoming what we are is a demonstration of what he eternally is - ungrasping, un-self-centered, giving glory by all of his actions to God." /19/

God's glory is demonstrated in shame and weakness. Divinity in other words issued in generous self-giving, not in self-aggrandizement.

The last section of the hymn is opened by the conjunction dia meaning "in consequence of." It indicates a resultant or causal relation with what went on before. The exaltation resulted in a real change of status;

something was given and accepted which was not previously possessed. Christ became an object of worship. The relation of the exalted Christ to God is closer than that which he had in pre-existence. Traditional exegesis has tended to deny the real dynamic movement of God in Christ as pictured in this passage. The exaltation to a new and higher status was transformed simply into a return to the full glory of the Godhead. No new status could be given, since there is full equality with God from the beginning. Hence, exaltation was traditionally taken to mean the revelation of the true divine status which had been obscured during the earthly ministry because it was veiled in flesh.

But this is to overlook the evidence of the exaltation to new status. The new status given to Christ because of his obedience unto death is not simply a private possession to be enjoyed by himself alone. In Phil. 3:20-21, Paul affirms that the power given to him to transform will enable him to transform us into conformity with him; we shall become like him. "He will transfigure the body belonging to our humble state, and give it a form like that of his own resplendent body, by the very power which enables him to make all things subject to himself." (Phil. 3:21; 4:1). /20/

In recent times the concern of finding support for the kenotic Christologies in the exegesis of Philippians 2 has been displaced by a virtual consensus of opinion that the truth of the theory cannot be decided by the text. /21/ There are several accepted conclusions from contemporary exegesis of the text:

1. Understood in the context of the cultic life of the early Church, it is impossible to see the hymn as a pronouncement of dogmatic theology.

2. The hymn sets forth a soteriological drama and is not concerned with the relationships of the Father and the Son in the Godhead. /22/

3. Hellenistic Judaism is the source of the humiliation-exaltation motif. /23/

4. On strictly linguistic grounds, verses six and seven cannot mean that the pre-existent Christ

emptied himself of the _morphe_ _theou_ and instead took the _morphe_ _doulou_.

5. The kenosis of Christ is his Incarnation. The text does not affirm of what he emptied himself.

6. The Incarnation is truly an abasement and a mission. New Testament kenosis sees in Christ's full acceptance of the conditions of human existence the supreme manifestation of the limitless love of God for his unworthy creatures. When Paul wrote that "Christ died for us while we were yet sinners, and that is God's own proof of his love toward us," (Rom. 5:8), he summed up a truth inherent to the Gospels.

7. Although recent contributions to A. Feuillet and C. H. Talbert /24/ affirm that there is no question of pre-existence in the hymn, most exegetes regard the passage as referring both to Jesus' pre-existence and to his earthly life. This seems to be the consensus today as expressed by R. H. Fuller: "The attempts which have been made to eliminate pre-existence entirely from this passage...must be pronounced as a failure ..." /25/ The affirmation of pre-existence appears in the New Testament as a direct consequence of the community's confession of Jesus as Lord and as a reflection on the mystery of Jesus, his relation with God and his work. Pre-existence should not be seen as that of personal essence capable of choice. Nor can pre-existence in these texts be interpreted in the light of later developments of trinitarian doctrine not found in the New Testament itself. Historical study has shown it was only later trinitarian doctrine that made the pre-existent and exalted Christ of equal status. /26/

Jesus' message about God was a message of good news about forgiveness and compassion. God does not stand outside the range of human suffering and sorrow. Jesus proclaimed a new presence of God in Jesus the Christ. "God was in Christ reconciling the world to himself" (II Cor. 5:19). The Christological hymn of Phil. 2:6-11 presents the self-emptying of Jesus as the revelation that to be God is to be unselfishness itself. In his life, Jesus pursued a style of service even to the act of complete self-giving. He did so, not simply as a model of conduct, but as a revealer of divine reality. God's eternal happiness is not freedom from suffering but rather the victory of his suffering over evil. Divine suffering does not indicate any weakness or limitation in God, but rather a voluntary self-limitation and self-sacrifice and love for men and women. God knows no holding back, no selfishness, no fear of loss of power. The hymn presents the Incarnation as the expression of a divine pathos. The kenosis hymn must be read as a revelation of what it means to be God. As revealer of God's inner life, Jesus in the word of Mark came "not to be served but to serve" (Mark 10:45). The theology of Phil. 2:6-11 requires Calvary as the prelude to salvation.

C. The Gospel of Mark

Mark was the first to write a Gospel. In doing so he created a new literary form. /27/ It was also a major theological achievement. The result of the evangelist's literary creativity is a product of real symbolic dimension that served as much to shock the complacency of the Markan community as to support certain elements of its vision. In this perspective, Mark's Gospel functions as and approximates the intentionality of the parables. As we have seen earlier, the parables have as an objective the disruption of the world-view of the hearer for a radical change of heart. It is my contention that the Gospel of Mark is a parable about the kenotic love of God for us, in and through the person of Jesus Christ. /28/

According to Schillebeeckx, "For Mark the emphasis falls on the life of Jesus as *via crucis*..." /29/ The Gospel of Mark attempts to interpret the death of Jesus and especially God's rule in the death of Jesus, for the Gospel of Mark is truly "the Gospel of God" (Mark 1:14).

Mark begins his work by the words: "Here begins the Gospel of Jesus Christ, the Son of God" (Mark 1:1). Now the Gospel is the salvation of those who believe (Mark 16:15). The Gospel is the story of God's eschatological intervention in this world. It is the account of the unprecedented and incomprehensible love of God which in the person of Jesus seeks and finds man and woman despite many kinds of opposition.

Mark opens with the declaration that Jesus is God's

chosen agent to establish His sovereignty in the earth. The new situation that Jesus inaugurates (1:1) is announced as the fulfillment of the time of deliverance, the drawing near of God's rule (1:15). John, the herald of his coming, whose role is itself foretold in Scripture, points to Jesus as the mightier one - whose authority will be evident, through the divine spirit that he brings.

Mark's Gospel is an attempt to express the nature of Jesus' mission, and through this, the nature of the Kingdom of God. Christology is central in Mark. According to Perrin: "...A major aspect of the Markan purpose is Christological: He is concerned with correcting a false Christology and its consequences for Christian discipleship." /30/ While the interpretative key to Mark's Christology may not lie in understanding this Gospel as in some sense overcoming an erroneous theios aner ("divine man") Christology, /31/ Mark does present his own understanding of the titles "Son of God" and "Christos" primarily in the light of Jesus' passion and death. Throughout the Gospel the title "Son of God" is juxtaposed to that of "Son of Man." Mark's Christology is expressed in 8:31, "... the Son of Man had to undergo great sufferings, and to be rejected by the elders, chief priests, and doctors of the law; to be put to death, and to rise again three days afterwards."

Mark's Christology is expressed in two key sections of his Gospel: the incident at Caesarea Philippi (8:27-10:45) and the Passion Narrative (14-15). Norman Perrin has shown that in 8:27-10:45, there is a threefold repeated pattern: a passion prediction; the disciples' misunderstanding; and corrective teaching discipleship. According to Perrin, this section is intended to correct the disciples' misunderstanding of the authentic nature of Jesus' mission. The Christological climax of this section comes in 10:45; "For even the Son of Man did not come to be served, but to serve, and to give up his life as a ramson for many." This servant saying is preceded by an apothegm about the reception of children (10:13-16). Here Jesus identifies himself with a child emphasizing his powerlessness and total dependence upon God. God's power is to be manifested in Jesus' powerlessness. Jesus' authority, his exousia, is shown in the powerlessness of servanthood.

THE FORM OF A SERVANT

The disciples are invited to follow Jesus' "way" which for Mark is the way of the cross. They are invited to shed their "Christological blindness" to follow Jesus' way and to discover the authentic nature of Jesus' mission which is presented by Mark as being the same process. /32/ For Mark, discipleship is intimately bound up with Christology. The truth about Jesus Christ is to be found in the lives of the disciples together. Jesus chose his disciples "to be with him" (3:14). Mark intends to present Christ at work with his disciples. /33/ If the truth of Christ is compromised it is much more in terms of the disciples' life and fidelity than in terms of Christological polemics. For Mark there cannot be an abstract Christology; every Christology must be engaged (*engagée*). Christology in Mark is applied Christology. It is not possible without discipleship and authentic discipleship is an important factor in the process of understanding.

It is not possible to draw in the Gospel of Mark an absolute distinction between Jesus and his followers. The Gospel of Mark concentrates on the person of Jesus and the behavior of those who come face to face with him. In a sense we have in Mark an ecclesiological Gospel, if by ecclesiology we mean the doctrine of the gathering of men around Jesus.

The Christological titles, however they may have arisen, are employed in Markan tradition to highlight the continuity between Jesus' inaugural role in the redemptive purpose of God and the work in his name that the community has been commissioned to carry forward. Hence the corporate metaphors for the community; hence the designation "Son of Man" and "servant" which alternate in the Old Testament tradition between representing an individual and a community. Hence also the importance given to the reality of the Kingdom. In the fifteen opening verses, Mark affirms the triumph of God's Kingdom, points out who the agent of this triumph is and expresses what kind of suffering the real disciples must bear as God's Kingdom comes to fulfillment.

The motif of kingdom is announced in 1:15, is declared in 4:4 to be a mystery reserved for the elect, is promised as being disclosed within the lifetime of Jesus' contemporaries (9:1), is said to be accessible only to those willing to undergo self-denial (10:14 ff; 10:23 ff.), is described as being anticipated in the eucharistic meal (14:15), and is mentioned as the object of expectation (15:43). /34/

The Kingdom of God is understood as an eschatological reality. The followers of Jesus are told that some of them will live to see the Kingdom come with power (9:1). The futurity of the Kingdom is referred to explicitly elsewhere in Mark (14:25; 15:43). Christ's work continues in the world. It is deeply involved in the fidelity of the disciples to whom the Kingdom of God has been given.

The radicality of discipleship is made evident in Jesus' demand that all ordinary human obligations be set aside; to be a disciple requires a break with the family. The new family in which men and women find their true mother, brothers, and sisters is the community devoted to finding and doing the will of God (3:35).

The radicality of Mark's understanding of discipleship and of Christology is to be found in the second important section of the Gospel, the Passion Narrative. Jesus' passion begins in Mark by a description of Jesus, "as prostrated to the ground" (Mark 14:35). Jesus is in solitude. His disciples are sleeping. Even his Father to whom he addresses a cry of anguish seems distant. There is here a real solidarity of Jesus with humanity in its suffering and anguish.

The important concept of "being delivered up" appears at the end of the scene in Gethsemane. "Still sleeping? Still taking your ease? Enough! The hour has come. The Son of Man is betrayed to sinful men. Up, let us go forward! My betrayer is upon us." (Mark 14:14). The dimensions and depth of that being "delivered up" appears in Paul (Romans 8:32), "He did not spare his own Son but gave him up for us all..."

Jesus, the "Servant of God" (Acts 3:13, 26; 4:27), the "just" (Acts 3:14), was, like the Jews of the Old Testament, delivered by God, the "Abba," into the hands of sinners; and he who is delivered consents to be delivered up. He is the obedient one of Philippians 2:6-11. In the crucifixion scene (15:20-41), not only the Passion Narrative but the whole Markan drama reaches its climax. /35/ That the death scene is the climactic event toward which the entire Gospel points is an escapable conclusion thrust upon the reader.

It is clear according to Mark's description that Jesus' suffering exceeds that of physical pain. The cross marks his defeat by the forces of evil and his abandonment by God. Jesus suffers the absence of God. Jesus is "delivered up" (14:10, 11, 18, 21, 41, 44; 15:1, 10, 15) not merely into the hands of the Jewish-Roman power structure but beyond that into demonic darkness and God-forsakenness. God's non-interference at the cross, his abandoning Jesus in the hour of greatest need constitutes the ultimate depth of Jesus' suffering.

In the accounts of Mark and Matthew, Jesus dies with the words "My God, my God, why hast thou forsaken me?" (Mark 15:34; Matt. 27:46). This saying was considered a problem from the beginning. /36/ Luke already found it intolerable; he makes Jesus die with the words "Father, into thy hands I commit my spirit" (23:46). In John, Jesus dies with the cry of victory, "It is accomplished" (19:30). Even before the Biblical traditions had become fixed, therefore, it was felt to be scandalous that Jesus should die abandoned by God.

Exegetes can, of course, point to the fact that the cry "My God, my God, why has thou forsaken me" is a quotation from Psalm 22 which has influenced the whole Passion Narrative. According to the practice at the time, saying the opening verse of a psalm implies the whole psalm. And this psalm is a comment which turns into a song of thanksgiving. The religious man's suffering is experienced as abandonment by God - but in his suffering and in the agony of death the religious man finds that God has been Lord all along, and that he saves him and brings him into new life. Consequently, Jesus' words, "My God, my God, why hast thou forsaken me" are not a cry of despair but a prayer confident of an answer - and one which hopes for the coming of God's Kingdom.

Yet the text underlines that Jesus' faith did not give way, but he experienced the darkness and distress of death more deeply than any other man or woman. When he cried out to God in death, he called not just on the

God of the Old Testament but on the God he called Father in an exclusive sense, the God with whom he felt uniquely linked. In other words he experienced God as the one who withdraws in his very closeness, who is totally other. Jesus experienced the unfathomable mystery of God and his will, but he endured this darkness in faith. This extremity of emptiness enabled him to become the vessel of God's fullness. His death became the source of Life. It became the other side of the coming of the Kingdom of God - its becoming in love.

The Markan crucifixion drama contains various themes and motives. Among these, the motif of Christological identification (15:32) is not only central but it stands out as possessing crucial significance for the evangelist. The primal importance Christology has for this evangelist is manifested both by the fact that the centurion's Christological confession serves as the climactic point of the crucifixion scene and by the major role Christology plays in the crucifixion story and in the Gospels as a whole. /37/

It is in the context of the Passion that Mark shows Jesus to be the Son of God. Mark emphasizes the point that one can truly see Jesus as the Son of God only if one understands that Jesus shows himself to be such in the passion and death. For Mark to be God's son means to be dedicated unconditionally to God's purpose even to death. The Son of God title receives its definitive and correct meaning in the centurion's confession (15: 39). The centurion in contrast to others in the drama proclaims Jesus to be the Son of God - not because Jesus produced a miraculous feat, as Jesus' adversaries require for belief, but because he saw how Jesus died. The only person with real power in the eyes of the world paradoxically reinforces Jesus' Christological status not because Jesus awed him with his power but because Jesus died a suffering "powerless" death.

The confession of faith is not made by a pious disciple of Jesus, nor by a Jew, but by a Gentile Roman centurion. The centurion's confession means for the Jew the end of the significance of the temple and for the pagans the opening of the way to God through Jesus' death.

In the Gospel of Mark, an authentic Son of God Christology must always be perceived in light of a Son of Man Christology. The "Son of Man" title signifies the true nature of Jesus' Messiahship which includes suffering as well as glory. As the author of Hebrews wrote: "In the days of his earthly life he offered up prayers and petitions, with loud cries and tears, to God who was able to deliver him from the grave. Because of his humble submission his prayer was heard: son though he was, he learned obedience in the school of suffering,..." (Hebrews 5:7 ff.).

In Mark, the Resurrection is subordinated to the Crucifixion. The evangelist makes his Gospel culminate in a passion account and not in the narrative of Jesus' Resurrection appearance. Rooted in the Cross, the Resurrection does not carry in itself a soteriological significance. While Easter indicates the Cross, the Cross is the condition sine qua non of Easter. The Resurrection marks the beginning of Jesus' absence from the community. If the absence of Jesus from the community is a Markan experience, then the absence of God suffered by Jesus on the Cross appears in a new light. In his Godforsakenness Jesus suffers the plight of the Markan Christian. In his very Godforsakenness Jesus anticipates in exemplary fashion the traumatic experiences of the Gospel readers. The disciples' life is now conformed to the Cross. The actual way of the Christian community in this world has been traced out by the earthly, the crucified Christ, and not by the risen Christ in his glory. But it will one day be vindicated in the same way that Jesus' death on the Cross ended in Resurrection.

Mark's Gospel is at once radical and intensely personal. The message is "Follow me on the journey to the Cross" (Mark 10:32), "Follow me for my sake and the Gospel," "for the sake of my name" (Mark 10:29). To such a message the essential answer is action. The Gospel of Mark is salvation history and it places our response to it on the existential level of confrontation, decision, or deed. That decision and deed is to follow Jesus. Jesus' way is paradoxical: it is the way of the Cross; it is the way of powerlessness. "For you know how generous our Lord Jesus Christ has been: he was rich, yet for your sake he became poor, so that through his poverty you might become rich." (II Cor. 8:9). "For the divine nature was his from the first yet he did not think to snatch at equality with God, but made himself nothing, assuming the nature of a slave" (Phil. 2:6 ff.). "For even the Son of Man did not come to be served but to serve, and to give up his life as a ransom for many (Mark 10:45). Jesus' primary service is his self-sacrifice; in the ultimate renunciation of power the way of salvation is opened to all people.

D. Conclusion

Philippians 2 and the Gospel of Mark establish a paradox which must permeate all Christian life - salvation, well-being, are attained not by conquest, not by domination of the other, but by self-effacement and self-giving love which leads ultimately to self-realization. The coming of the Kingdom is realized through self-actualization of the other. Real authority and power lie in compassionate, persuasive love, in weakness.

The Passion Narrative in Mark effects a transvaluation of existing images of authority and power. While the prophetic destruction of the Temple was accompanied by a cry of triumph, the cry on the Cross is one of dereliction. Yet it is instrumental in causing the Roman centurion, the representative of the coercive power, to affirm the power of the powerless Christ on the Cross. The crucifixion story in Mark dramatizes the mysterious paradox of authentic Christian existence: "Power comes to its full strength in weakness" (II Cor. 12:9).

In I Corinthians 1:18, Paul says that the crucified Christ is a "stumbling block" for the Jews and "folly" for the Gentiles. A crucified Messiah, Son of God, must have seemed a contradiction in terms to anyone, Jew, Greek, Roman, or barbarian. In attempting to proclaim this paradox, the Gospel of Mark, as the hymn to the Philippians, shatters all analogies. In the person of Jesus the solidarity of the love of God with us is given historical and physical form. In Christ God himself took up the "existence of a slave and died the slaves' death for us." It is this radical kenosis, John's "Logos become sarx," that shatters all analogies and is the center of the Gospels. In this kenosis, God communicates himself and reveals who He is.

THE FORM OF A SERVANT

NOTES

1. E. Schillebeeckx, *Jesus - An Experiment in Christology*, (New York: Seabury, 1979) p. 50.

2. J. D. G. Dunn, *Unity and Diversity in the New Testament*, Philadelphia: Westminster, 1977) pp. 369-388.

3. H. Küng, *On Being a Christian* (New York: Doubleday, 1976) p. 466.

4. J. D. G. Dunn, op. cit., p. 377.

5. B. Childs, "The Canonical Shape of the Prophetic Literature," *Interpretation* XXXII, (January, 1978) p. 53.

6. A. R. Bruce, *The Humiliation of Christ*, (Edinburgh: 1976) p. 8.

7. M. D. Hooker, "Philippians 2:6-11) in *Jesus und Paulus*, Festschrift Für Werner Georg Kummel zum to Geburtstag. Heraugegeben von E. Earl Ellis und E. Grüsser, (Göttingen: Vanderhoeck and Ruprecht, 1975) p. 151.

8. H. C. Kee, *Community of the New Age: Studies in Mark's Gospel* (Philadelphia: The Westminster Press, 1977) p. 1

9. M. D. Hooker, op. cit., p. 156.

10. Cf. E. Käsemann, "A Critical Analysis of Philippians 2:5-11," *God and Christ: Existence and Promise, Journal for Theology and the Church*, (New York: 1968) pp. 45-88.

11. R. P. Martin, *Carmen Christi: Philippians 2:1-11 in Recent Interpretation and in the Setting of Early Christian Worship*, (Cambridge: Cambridge University Press, 1967) p. 153.

12. M. D. Hooker, op. cit., p. 156.

13. Ibid., p. 155.

14. Ibid., p. 162. Cf. also J. Murphy-O'Connor,

"Christological Anthropology in Phil. 2:6-11," in Revue Biblique 83 (No. 1, 1976) pp. 25-50.

15. On this topic confer M. Hengel's remarks in The Son of God, Philadelphia: Fortress Press, 1976) pp. 33-35.

16. E. Käsemann, op. cit.

17. M. D. Hooker, op. cit., p. 162.

18. C. D. Moule, "The Manhood of Jesus in the New Testament," in S. W. Sykes, Christ, Faith and History, (Cambridge: Cambridge University Press, 1972) pp. 95-111.

19. M. D. Hooker, op. cit., p. 164.

20. Cf. M. D. Hooker, "Interchange in Christ," in Journal of Theology No. 22 (1971) pp. 349-361.

What the early Easter profession of faith suggests is explicit in some early hymns to and confessions of faith in Christ. In these hymns and confessions we find a Christology of exchange. A great exchange has taken place in the divine-human history. "For you know how generous Our Lord Jesus Christ has been: he was rich, yet for your sake he became poor, so that through his poverty you might become rich" (II Cor. 8-9). The First Letter of Peter brings out this connection between the two-stage Christology and the Christology of exchange. "For Christ also died for our sins once and for all. He, the just, suffered for the unjust, to bring us to God" (3:18). In connection with the exchange Christology, the two-stage Christology carries a universal scope and dimension. This is underlined in I Tim. 3:16 when an older hymn is quoted: "He who was manifested in the body, vindicated in the spirit, seen by angels; who was proclaimed among the nations, believed in throughout the world, glorified in high heaven." Jesus Christ, heaven and earth, flesh and spirit are united.

21. H. W. Bartsch, "Die konkrete Wahrheit und die Lüge der Spekulation. Untersuchung uber den vorpaulinischen Christushymnus und seine gnotische Mythisie-

rung," Theologie und Wirklichkeit 1 (Bern: 1974).

J. F. Collange, L'Epitre de Saint Paul aux Philippiens (Neuchatel, 1973);
J. T. Sanders, The New Testament Hymns (1971).

22. E. Käsemann, "Kritische Analyse von Phil. 2:5-11," Exegetische Versuche und Besinnung: Easter Band (Göttingen, 1960).

23. P. Georgi, "Der Vorpaulinische Hymnus Phil. 2: 6-11," Zeit und Geschichte. Dankesgabe or R. Bultmann zum 80, (Geburtstag, 1964) pp. 263-293.

24. A. Feuillet, "L'Hymne Christologique," Revue Biblique 72 (1965) pp. 495 ff.

C. H. Talbert, "The Problem of Pre-existence in Philippians 2:6-11," J. B. L. 86 (1967) pp. 141-153.

P. Schoonenberg, "He Emptied Himself, Philippians 2:7," Concilium, Vol. II (1966) pp. 46-67.

25. R. Fuller, The Foundations of New Testament Christology, (London: 1963) p. 235.

26. R. G. Hammerton-Kelly, Pre-Existence, Wisdom and the Son of Man. A Study of the Idea of Pre-Existence in the New Testament, (Cambridge, 1973).

27. According to E. Auerbach, the Gospels as a literary genre portray "something which neither the poets nor the historians of antiquity ever set out to portray: the birth of a spiritual movement in the depths of the common people, from within the everyday occurrences of contemporary life, which thus assumes an importance it could never have assumed in antique literature," Mimesis, (Princeton: Princeton University Press, 1953) p. 426.

28. Cf. Lamarche, Revelation de Dieu Chez Marc, (Paris: Beauchesne, 1974).

P. H. Reardon, "Kenotic Ecclesiology in Mark," in Bible Today, No. 70 (1974) pp. 1476-82.

W. Harrington, "The Gospel of Mark: A Theologia Crucis," Doctrine & Life 26 (1976) pp. 211-33.

T. J. Weeden, "The Cross as Power in Weakness (Mark: 15:20f.-41)" in W. H. Kelber, ed., The Passion in Mark (Philadelphia: Fortress Press, 1976) pp. 115-135.

29. E. Schillebeeckx, Jesus - An Expirement in Christology, op. cit., p. 110.

30. N. Perrin, A Modern Pilgrimage in New Testament Christology, (Philadelphia: Fortress Press, 1974) p. 110.

31. See R. Fuller, The Foundations of New Testament Christology, (New York: Scribner's 1965) pp. 68-137.

32. See J. B. Tyson, "The Blindness of the Disciples in Mark," J. B. L. 80 (1961) pp. 261-268.

33. J. Donaldson, "'Called to Follow.' A Twofold Experience of Discipleship in Mark," Bibl. Theol. Bull. 5 (1975) pp. 67-72

34. W. H. Kelber, The Kingdom in Mark. A New Place and a New Time, (Philadelphia: Fortress, 1974).

35. Cf. W. H. Kelber, ed., The Passion in Mark, (Philadelphia: Fortress Press, 1976).

J. R. Donahue, "Are You the Christ? The Trial Narrative in the Gospel of Mark," SBL Dissertation Series 10 (Missoula: University of Montana Press, 1973).

E. Best, The Temptation and Passion: The Markan Soteriology, Society for New Testament Studies, Monograph Series, Vol. II (Cambridge: University Press, 1965).

36. See L. Mahieu, "L'abandon du Christ sur la Croix," MSR II (1945) pp. 209-242.

M. Rehm, "Eli, Eli Lema Sabachthani," BZ 2 (1958) pp. 275-78.

J. Gnilka, "Mein Gott, Mein Gott, Warum Hast Du Mich Verlassen?" (Mark 15:34) BZ 3, (1959) pp. 294-297.

G. Joussard, "L'abandon du Christen Croix dans la Tradition," RSR 25, (1924) pp. 310 ff.; 26 (1925) pp. 609 ff.

37. J. Moltmann, The Crucified God, (New York: Harper & Row, 1973) pp. 193-196.

CHAPTER 5

THE THEOLOGICAL IMPLICATION OF THE DEVELOPMENT OF CHRISTOLOGY

A. Introduction

"Here begins the Gospel of Jesus, the Son of God" (Mark 1:1). These are the very first words of Mark's Gospel and they express the major concern of contemporary as well as traditional Christology: What does it mean to confess that Jesus is the "Son of God"? Jesus' life, his ministry and message, his death and Resurrection confronted the disciples with fundamental questions about God, Jesus and themselves; about God who revealed himself in Jesus, and about their relationship to the God of Jesus. These questions were answered in light of the Resurrection. Yet in Phil. 2 and in the Gospel of Mark what is most revealing about God, Jesus, and themselves is to be found in Jesus' self-emptying. "And so, since we have now been justified by Christ's sacrificial death, we shall all the more certainly be saved through him from final retribution" (Romans 5:9). In Phil. 2, Jesus' saving action is expressed as self-negation and the disciples are invited to have the same self-negation in mind. "Whoever cares for his own safety is lost; but if a man will let himself be lost for my sake, he will find his true self" (Mt. 16:25-26).

Mark speaks of Jesus' earthly mission in terms of Sonship and is able to climax its presentation with its proclamation at Golgotha. For Mark, Jesus' Sonship comes to expression in his faithful fulfillment of the mission God had given him. His aim is to show that the Gospel of God was effectively proclaimed by Jesus. The Gospel is about God; Jesus' mission was to reveal who God is. Jesus' question "But who do you say that I am?" has no other aim than to provoke an answer to a question about God. Jesus is, in fact, asking "Who then is God if it is I who am the Christ, the Son of the living God?" Now the question about God is the existential question about the ultimate meaning of our own existence.

That Jesus is the Son of God or the Christ, does say something about Jesus; namely, that what is revealed to us in him is the answer to our question about God.

So the professions that were originally intended to express the event of Jesus in its meaning-for-us cannot be treated as though they were simply assertions about the person of Jesus in his being-in-himself. In Mark, the proclamation of the Gospel of God is embodied in the entire mission of Jesus ending in his death and Resurrection. He is the Servant of God who inaugurates the reign of God.

The earliest interpretations of the meaning of Jesus as the Christ were not "ontological" but functional. They were concerned not with who or what Jesus was but with what he was meant to do; namely, usher in God's definitive presence to man/woman. Hence all of the titles attributed to Jesus by his earliest followers did not explain Jesus' identity per se, but only his identification with God's saving action. These are, according to Schillebeeckx, first-order assertions about Jesus.

But as Christology developed it had to ask who Jesus himself was, the "ontological" question, as the one in whom man's salvation is achieved. This led, according to Schillebeeckx, to the relatively less important "second-order assertion" about the identity of Jesus as we find in St. Paul and, later, in St. John.

To affirm that God has saved us in Jesus Christ is already a confession of faith. To say something about Jesus in himself is a different kind of affirmation. Schillebeeckx sees the history of the Christological dogmas "...to lie in the plane of 'second order' affirmation, albeit with the purpose of, and real concern for bearing out the first order of affirmation." /1/ The relationship between first-order and second-order assertions raises the question about Jesus' divinity.

B. The Experience of Salvation and the Beginning of Christology

The experience of salvation in the early Church is the pre-supposition of Christology. The tradition has attempted to define the actual person of Jesus in terms of the salvation that Jesus brought about. In light of the Resurrection, the early Church concluded: God has acted decisively in the person of Jesus for the salvation of men and women. As Saint Paul wrote: "When anyone is united to Christ, there is a new world; the old order has gone, and a new order has already begun." (II Cor. 5:17). And "As in Adam all men die, so in Christ all will be brought to life" (I Cor. 15:22). The Christological titles are basically related to this. Jesus must be seen from within God's plan of salvation and his person as interpreted from God's standpoint. In the New Testament Jesus is from God, his activity is from God, and that defines him. If salvation has taken place in the person of Jesus then the question must be asked: Who is Jesus in himself and what is his "ousia," his "essential being"? How is it possible that when someone is in the presence of Jesus, he/she is faced with God's salvific action: What does this mean for the person of Jesus? The question is an attempt to interpret Jesus Christ as God's outreach towards humanity, God's self-disclosure and communication and giving of Himself to them. Christological titles expressed the conviction that Jesus encountered men and women from the side of God.

In the New Testament there is evident a momentum and directionality at work in the scope of its witness to Jesus as meeting men and women from God's side; from doxological affirmations taken from the language expressing the hope of Israel to the universal affirmation of Colossians. /2/ What took place in the life and death of Jesus of Nazareth, together with the occurrences after his death which brought the disciples to belief in the Resurrection, formed a complex historical event, the "Christ-event," which was placed by the early Church in the context of Israel's paradigmatic history. Inherent to Israel's history is the consciousness of being the chosen people. With Abraham, a new race (Gen. 12:1,2) is constituted and with the Exodus a new people is created (Dt. 4:35-40), "the people of Yahweh" Israel is a people different from other people, "for you are a people holy to the Lord your God; the Lord your God chose you out of all nations on earth to be his special possession" (Dt. 7:6). It is a people with a mission: "By my life I have sworn, I have given a promise of victory, a promise that will not be broken, that to me every knee shall bend and by me every tongue shall swear" (Is. 45:23). In fact, at the time of Jesus' appearance we find an unparalleled period of missionary activity for Israel. /3/ In Romans 2:17-23 Paul describes how the unshakeable certainty of the Jewish people that they possessed the revelation of God found expression in a sense of duty incumbent upon them to make this revelation known to the pagans.

Although the New Testament relates that Jesus forbade his disciples during his lifetime to preach to non-Jews -- "Do not take the road to gentile lands, and do not enter any Samaritan town; but go rather to the lost sheep of the house of Israel" (Matt. 10:5) -- we find the disciples involved in intensive missionary work very soon after the Resurrection. And the reason for this is that in light of the Resurrection, the early Church saw Jesus as the embodiment of all God's promises brought to fruition, and the Christ-event as the culmination of God's salvific action in the world. This gave the Christ-event both a universal and final import. The primitive community of faith understood itself as the new chosen people, the people of a new covenant, the "first fruits" of what was to be in the consummation of all things. What had happened to them in their little history was symbolic of the purposes of God in and for all creation.

The New Testament tells us that in Jesus Christ time is fulfilled (Mk. 1:15), the fullness of time has arrived (Gal. 4:4), and the Scriptures have been fulfilled (Lk. 4:21). The fourth Gospel begins with the affirmation that Jesus Christ is the Word of God through whom all things have been made. Jesus is the "last Adam" (I Cor. 15). In him is accomplished and fulfilled the promise made to Abraham for all the people of the world (Lk. 1:55, 73). Jesus Christ is presented as the one who sums up and fulfills in his own person the whole history of the people of Israel.

What Jesus represented for the early Christians was the right relationship to God. C. F. Moule writes: "It is in Jesus, as in no other figure in Jewish myth or history, that his followers found converging all the ideal qualities of a collective body of persons in a right relationship with God; and if Paul speaks of the Church as the Body of Christ (or as a body because incorporated in Christ), that is partly because he has found in Christ all that the People of God were designed to be." /4/

A KENOTIC CHRISTOLOGY

Paul affirms a universal Lordship to Christ. Christ dominates all the centuries and sums up all creatures in himself because he is risen from the dead and seated at the right hand of the Father, and also because he is the pre-existent Son of God. "He is the image of the invisible God; his is the primacy over all created things," (Col. 1:15). Jesus Christ is the one through whom God made everything there is (Heb. 1:2), the Son "sustaining the universe by his powerful command." The covenant established by God with creation, with Israel becomes focused in the one person of Jesus Christ. "There is no salvation in anyone else at all, for there is no other name under heaven granted to me, by which we may receive salvation" (Acts 4:12). Jesus' existence and words are understood as disclosive of God. Paul sees Jesus' significance as grounded in the fact that in him the final eschatological destiny of humanity to sonship has already appeared (Rom. 8:29). Everything is predestined toward Jesus and he is predestined to the summation of the whole cosmos.

The universalism of the New Testament has its source and foundation in one person, Jesus Christ. In every part of the New Testament, in every stage of the early tradition, we find that the coming of Jesus Christ has completely transformed the human situation. Man's/woman's eternal destiny depends on their decision concerning their relation to this one Jesus of Nazareth. It is because of him that the whole outlook for the future has so changed. As Schillebeeckx writes:

> "Although Jesus' historical message about the kingdom of God is of abiding value, there is no single instance, either pre-canonical or in the New Testament, of an attempt to implement the task of carrying forward this good news without linking it intrinsically with the person of Jesus. The heart of Christianity is not just the abiding message of Jesus and its definitive relevance, but the persisting eschatological relevance of his person itself." /5/

How seriously this definitive character of the person of Jesus is taken becomes especially clear in the fifth chapter of Romans. Here we find the synthesis of all the previous material. There is almost monotonous repetition that just as there has been a first Adam so there is a second Adam. His commission means a complete change in the situation of humankind - in that he brings new life and inaugurates a new and final era of history. Adam is the prototype who foreshadows Jesus Christ. Why? Because Adam is the father of the old humanity. With the coming of Jesus Christ a new age has been inaugurated, an age of Grace. Jesus Christ is seen as the fulfillment of all promises made in the past. /6/

As a fulfiller of the promise made in the Old Testament, Jesus is perceived by some of the authors of the New Testament as a supernatural agent; pre-existence is attributed to Him. It is this understanding that leads to the understanding of the Christ-event in incarnational terms. As a fulfiller of God's promises, Jesus has a mission that no one else has ever had or will ever have. "...here is the answer, for all of you and for all the people of Israel: it was by the name of Jesus Christ of Nazareth, whom you crucified, whom God raised from the dead; it is by his name that this man stands here before you fit and well" (Acts 4:10). Both understandings of Jesus, as fulfillment of God's promises and involved in a unique way in bringing about such a fulfillment, are expressed by the Christological title Son of God. The title is prominent in Paul, in the Epistle to the Hebrews, and in John, much more prominent, in fact, than the doctrine of the Logos which is explicit only in John.

C. Jesus, "Son of God"

R. Schnackenburg has listed the variety of opinions on the title, "Son of God," and has discerned four possible approaches. /7/ First, there is the conservative which affirms that Jesus himself used the title in a Messianic sense and understood himself as the unique Son of God. Second, there is the religio-historical explanation of the title in terms of the Hellenistic concept of the divine man, the Theios Aner. Third, some scholars have attempted to discern in the teaching of Jesus some starting point for the later development in the Church. J. Jeremias sees an original "servant" understanding behind the title Son of God, in the baptismal narrative which was later reinterpreted in terms of Sonship. /8/ Authors such as

O. Cullman and B. M. F. van Irsel see a link between the title with Jesus' own consciousness of a filial relation to God. /9/

According to R. Bultmann and F. Hahn, the traditio-historical approach accounts for all the uses of the title within the developing theology of the early Church. The self-consciousness of Jesus is not a legitimate concern, because we have no sources for such knowledge. According to Hahn and Fuller, the title Son of God was first applied to Jesus in the early Palestinian Church with reference to his future work as Messiah and only at a later stage (Hellenistic Jewish Christianity) was it applied to him with reference to his exalted position after the Resurrection. /10/ Hahn's basic evidence for his view is to be found in Luke 1:32f.; Mark 14:61f.; and I Thessalonians 1:9f. which testify to the Palestinian view, and in Romans 1:3f.; Acts 13:33; Hebrews 1:5; 5:5; Colossians 1:13, and I Corinthians 15:15-28 which testify to the Hellenistic-Jewish view.

Fuller bases his case on Romans 1:3f. This text has long been recognized as a pre-Palestinian formula established by Paul. Fuller affirms that the words "who was made of the seed of David...who was designated Son of God by resurrection from the dead" means that Jesus was fore-ordained to be the Son of God at the parousia. /11/ The Sonship referred to in this text expresses more fully a dignity and a function than a natural sonship. The function implied here is one of sanctifying (<u>pneuma agiosunes</u>). The dignity of Son of God with power designates a function which began at a certain moment in time and while it might presuppose the eternal divine nature in the one who exercises it, it does not designate it explicitly. The Resurrection is perceived as effective and declarative of Jesus' divine sonship.

According to Hahn it is from royal messianism that the use of the title "Son of God" in the primitive Christian tradition can be explained. /12/ As the concept Messiah went through a process of transformation, "Son of God" became a characteristic title of the exalted Jesus who has been adopted by God and installed at his right hand. /13/ Here the title "Son of God" pertains to a two-stage Christology already outlined in Romans 1:3ff. This is a passage already built up in two stages according to the flesh and according to the Spirit. The descent from the line of David qualifies the time of the earthly Jesus, denoting the Messiah in the condition of his humanity and lowliness. The second stage, the realm of the Spirit, is through appointment. Jesus is anointed Son of God. This Sonship of God cannot be taken in a physical sense but must be understood as the conferring of a dignity and office. The two stages simply indicate a contrast between the sphere of weakness and transience and the sphere of divine power, life and salvation. The designation as Son of God has taken place not under earthly conditions but under the exclusive operation and within the unlimited rule of the Spirit of divine holiness.

In his heavenly mode of existence the One born of the seed of David and risen from the dead has taken over the authoritative function of the Son of God and has assumed the office of Messiah. In a real sense Jesus was proclaimed Son of God by the Resurrection. The Resurrection authenticates and exercises a retroactive power. Some of the New Testament texts affirm a real effect of the Resurrection on the person of Jesus. It is clear that the Resurrection should not be reduced to a mere incident in the totality of the Christ-event. Jesus is not the same before and after the Resurrection.

According to Paul there is a uniqueness about the relationship of Jesus to the Holy Spirit. This uniqueness is underlined in texts like I Cor. 15:45 and in Paul's descriptions of the Holy Spirit as the Spirit of Christ, the Spirit of the Son, the Spirit of Jesus Christ (Rom. 8:9; Gal. 4:6; Phil. 1:19). Jesus, from being a man under the direction of the Spirit, Son of God, according to the Spirit, becomes by virtue of his Resurrection Son of God in full power of his Sonship, that is in full power of the Spirit. After the Resurrection and the exaltation, Jesus impressed his character and personality on the less well-defined personality of the Spirit. /14/

Within Hellenistic Jewish Christianity the dimension of the exaltation of Jesus is developed and affects the title "Son of God." Involved in the complicated process is the assumption of elements of the Theios Aner conception into the traditional "Son of God" concept.

But in Hellenistic Judaism, "the constitutive element of the Theios Aner conception, the divinity of man as the possibility of his participating in what is divine -- indeed of his deification -- is unthinkable in the Old Testament." /15/

In the Jewish context, the Theios Aner is conceived as a man under divine inspiration - as the equipment given by God to a man for a special mission. Because of his miracle-making powers Jesus had already been regarded as the new Moses, as a charismatic man of God. Jesus is equipped with the Spirit bestowed by God and therefore now has power over the unclean spirits. In the baptismal scene there is a connection made between the concept of Theios Aner as that of a man endowed with the divine Spirit and the concept Son of God. Here the Spirit of God descends in person and unites with the human person of Jesus. Jesus receives a permanent endowment and indwelling and obtains the messianic dignity of the Son of God, a dignity understood as a special supernatural power. Operative here is not a process of transformation but of bestowal of the Spirit of God.

The temptation narrative underlines the real value of the title "Son of God" -- "The Son of God may not misuse his power either in helping himself or in working a spectacular miracle - but must use it only in what he is commissioned to do." /16/ Divine Sonship implies obedience even unto death.

In the infancy narratives, the dimension of Divine Sonship is further determined by the theologumenon of the virgin birth. Here, through the begetting by the Holy Spirit, divine Sonship is predicated of Jesus not simply by indwelling "but by a special act which precedes the whole of his (Jesus') work on earth." /17/ Divine Sonship rests upon the creative act of election and separation in the mother's womb. /18/

In Luke, Jesus' sonship to God ("He will be great; he will bear the title 'Son of the Most High'"(Lk. 1:32) is traced back to a special creative act by God at his begetting although nothing is said yet of a physical Sonship to God. But when Matthew simply formulates: "This is the story of the birth of the Messiah. Mary his mother was betrothed to Joseph; before their marriage she found that we was with child by the Holy

Spirit" (Matt. 1:18), this formulation "approaches" the conception of physical Sonship to God.

In Hellenistic Gentile Christianity, the title "Son of God" passes through a twofold process: first, "the divine Sonship established through the bestowal of the Spirit is understood in the sense of a pervasion of being, and this then leads on to the idea of an original giftedness in nature." /19/ Here the endowment by the Spirit is not understood in the sense of an equipment, but as an apotheiosis. /20/ "Therefore the step was taken from a concept of the divine Sonship that was messianically and therefore functionally determined to one that was understood in reference to being, even if to begin with an act of appointment was still adhered to." /21/ Hellenistic Christianity interpreted the divine Sonship in the sense of giftedness in nature. Here two approaches were available - "The one provided from the event of a virgin begetting; the other, from the idea of pre-existence..." /22/

For Paul, the title "Son of God" contains both the dignity of the Son and his subordination to the Father. The Father is the One to whom final honor belongs and his power and honor are the goals of all history. In Rom. 5:10; 8:32; Gal. 2:10, Paul finds the divine Sonship particularly in his suffering. "Son" describes the close bond of love between God and Jesus and emphasizes the greatness and the sacrifice. Although Paul presupposes the pre-existence of the Son of God, he does not stress this traditional dimension. The title, Son of God, has for him the function of describing the greatness of the saving act of God who offered up the One closest to him. The deepening of Paul's understanding of the divine Sonship as compared with the tradition lies in the fact that he no longer grounds this sonship in the heavenly glory of the Exalted or general institution as King of the end time but in his suffering and rejection.

There are only several places in the epistles that are surely of Paul where he uses the word Son in a context which seems to refer to a pre-existent relationship with God: Rom. 8:3, 32, and Gal. 2:20; 4:4. In these texts, what seems to be meant by Paul is that in the sending of the Son it is really God giving himself;

it is the self-giving character of God that is expressed in the pre-existent Sonship of Jesus.

In John, the title "Son of God" does not appear very frequently, but it is used very emphatically. Yet the few passages do not allow a very exact definition of the meaning. A more precise meaning can only be discerned when we hold in view the statements about the Son which are actually characteristic of John. E. Schweizer writes about John:

> "When one considers what was already the formalized use of 'Son of God,' especially in demarcation from false faith, one can hardly deny that the title has already become a cipher which presupposes a unity of essence between Father and Son without defining it more precisely. But when one examines the basic passages, it is also evident that this unity of essence is grounded in the love between Father and Son and is thus an ever new unity of willing and giving on the part of the Father and of seeing, hearing, and responsive obeying on the part of the Son. It is not an ephemeral unity which has to be attained and which might be broken off at any time, but is grounded in the depth of God's being... The heart of Johannine theology is to be found in the emphasis on the unity of love which lives on in Jesus' dealing with his people." /23/

The whole event of salvation is anchored in the most intimate union between Father and Son. The Son lives only on the basis of the Father (6:57), that he is one with Him (10:30) and that he has unlimited participation in Him (16:13; 17:10). The main accent falls on the basic statement: "The Father loves the Son" (3:35). This is not meant emotionally or mystically. It is closely bound up with the commissioned work of the Son (8:16, 29). Love, then, is the deepest expression of the relation between the One who reveals himself and His agent (15:9, 17:23f).

In the title "Son of God" are revealed both attributes given to Jesus; that of being the fulfillment of God's promise and his special agent.

THE THEOLOGICAL IMPLICATION OF
THE DEVELOPMENT OF CHRISTOLOGY

The various stages evident in the attribution of the title "Son of God" to Jesus indicate clearly that there was a real development in New Testament Christology. The designation of Jesus as God's Son happened within the Church. This designation was connected with various aspects of Jesus' life and ministry and always contingent on the Resurrection. What is being said with this title is that Jesus in his life, ministry, death and Resurrection is the genuine revelation of the one God and Father.

Whether the filial relation of Jesus to the Father leads to affirming a distinction within the Godhead is a question that is not dealt with in the New Testament.

According to B. Vawter:

> "it would be a mistake to regard the functional sonship...as a provisional level of Christology from which the Church graduated into a higher conception of Christ's relation to God. On the contrary the theology of adoptive or functional sonship continued throughout New Testament times to protect the truth it had first asserted, namely that the work of salvation was one of grace and not of value, that Jesus Christ was Savior not in virtue of the 'flesh' but of the 'Spirit.'" /24/

D. Jesus - Logos as Revelation of God

While one of the Christological climaxes in the Fourth Gospel is to be found in the affirmation, "I and the Father are one," yet it is impossible to blur the distinctions between Jesus and the Father. What is essential for John is that Jesus is the true revelation of God: "Anyone whose teaching is merely his own, aims at honour for himself. But if a man aims at the honour of him who sent him he is sincere, and there is nothing false in him" (John 7:18). As God's agent and fulfillment of his promises, Jesus is from God and stands for God.

In the writings of Paul and John, Jesus is presented as the definitive Word of God to men and women as the unique and absolute Revealer. The office of revealer is so closely bound up with the person of Jesus that He himself becomes the embodiment of revelation.

The climax in the New Testament development of Christological thought is reached in John. The affirmation that the "Word became flesh" (o logos sarx egeneto) becomes the most influential New Testament text in the history of dogma. "The Word dwelt with God, and what God was, the Word was" (John 1:1). John identifies Jesus with this Logos - and in so doing makes it personal. In an Hellenistic context no greater opposition could be conceived than that of Logos and Sarx. Sarx points to what is most ordinary in man and woman, to their frailty and weakness. John's affirmation underlines the sharpness of the antitheses and the depth of the synthesis of Logos and Sarx. When predicated of the Logos, sarx underlines the fact that God's Word has entered completely into our human existence, even down to its ordinary and limited dimension. From John's Logos Egeneto Sarx, "the Word become flesh," no triumphalistic Incarnational theology can be deduced. /25/

The subject of becoming is the Logos. It is first said of the Logos that from eternity the Logos is with God and that the Logos becomes flesh. The Logos is the subject of the event. Divine and human attributes are asserted of one and the same subject. It would be historically mistaken to seek the fully developed two-nature doctrines in the Johannine writing. The emphasis here is not on two natures in one subject but with a succession of events in history.

In the Logos become sarx, in Jesus Christ, God is revealed as a personal God in the concreteness of his free activity. The answer to the question, "Who is God?" can only come to the question, "How has humanity experienced God in its history?" God's omnipotence is primarily revealed through his free operation in salvation history. God's attributes are not to be deduced in an a priori way from a metaphysical understanding of God, but from the nature, from the reality of his Word made flesh. His attributes are to be understood in relation to the free revelation of Himself in Jesus Christ. As K. Rahner writes: "A person does not, strictly speaking, have attributes with respect to another person: he has freely and personally adopted attributes." /26/ The question about God's attributes is a question about how God behaves in relation to his creature and not simply what can be deduced from the essential structure of his nature. /27/

In the New Testament, God's attributes of love and forgiveness, His "I must have mercy," and His compassion are not deduced through a philosophical process, are not simply metaphysical attributes, but have been made objective and have been revealed, have appeared in Jesus Christ. "It was there from the beginning; we have heard it; we have seen it with our own eyes; we looked upon it, and felt it with our own hands; and it is of this we tell. Our theme is the word of life" (I John 1:1). And the letter continues: "We have come to know and to believe in the love God has for us." St. Paul has a profound conviction of being loved by God: nothing "...will be able to separate us from the love of God that comes to us in Christ Jesus our Lord." It is in the Christ that God's love is concretely objectified and made present and finally realized once and for all since nothing in the future can ever make this presence void (Rom. 8:38). In the person of Jesus, God is revealed as absolutely free. God's love is not a calculable principle but an unfathomable mystery of his freedom. This unfathomable mystery of God's free love is most fully expressed in the kenotic statements. The self-emptying of Jesus is the revelation that to be God is to be unselfishness itself. Being God means being the giver. To say that in Jesus Christ God is revealed, is to affirm that in God there is no un-Christlikeness at all, there is nothing in God that is in contradiction with what has been revealed in his human face, Jesus the Christ. God can know no holding back, no selfishness, no fear or loss of power. When we think of the Passion, we are meditating on the mystery of God. This revelation of God in the Passion is a shattering revelation because it contradicts all our conventional ideas of God, everything that has been commonly believed about God.

The divinity revealed in Jesus is the divinity whose whole and total activity is the activity of self-emptying. Jesus' kenosis is a manifestation, a revelation of the kenosis of God. Jesus' self-emptying, his kenotic love in the poverty and humility of his historical existence points to the eternal kenosis of God; instead of impairing the fullness of God's revelation it contains, in fact, the very heart and substance of that disclosure. In the vulnerability and precariousness of Jesus' love we have a disclosure of the nature and activity of God.

God does not reveal himself in the wisdom and power of the world but in the foolishness and weakness of the cross (I Cor. 1:18-25) and he communicates himself to the weak, to the foolish of the world (I Cor. 1:26-9:2; I Cor. 12:9; 13:4; Mt. 11:25). That which is equal to God, the morphe theou, issues in poverty, lowliness, the death on the cross. He who is Wisdom, Logos become sarx, is temporal, frail, delivered up to the power of sin and death (John 1:14).

In the kenosis of Jesus, God is revealed as a loving and compassionate God. The Christ-event is revealed as a loving and compassionate God. The Christ-event as kenotic is fully and thoroughly a free act on the part of God in which God's love, his innermost life, is communicated and revealed.

E. Jesus as "Very God of Very God"

It is clear that in understanding Jesus as the fulfillment of God's promise to Israel and as God's special agent in bringing about salvation, the early Church attempted to define more fully the person of Jesus. It was inevitable that questions would be asked which would lead directly into classical doctrines; such questions as: what must have been the case about Jesus, for Jesus to have been what he was and to be what he continues to be in the structuring and restoration of human existence? The basic question that is being asked about the person of Jesus is the question of his relationship to God. This question will ultimately lead to the Christian dogma of consubstantiality of Jesus with the Father, to the "very God of very God." In the New Testament we find a variety of formulations relative to the question of the human and the divine in Jesus: the Son of God becomes man (Gal. 4:4; Rom. 1:3; Phil. 2:7); he gives up in some fashion his divinity to take on our humanity (Phil. 2:7). The fullness of the divinity dwells in him corporally (Col. 1:19; 2:9); he appears or is manifested in the flesh (I Tim. 3:16). He is the Word become sarx (Jn. 1:1). In the New Testament we find a variety of groundings for the doctrinre about the relationship of Jesus to God: there are passages of adoption, of identity, of distinction and derivation. It is the passages of derivation that ultimately control the development of Christology. These passages refer to Jesus as being of the Father, not only in time but also eternally. The two basic titles expressing that dimension of derivation are the titles "Son of God" and "Logos." These titles simply reinforce the conviction that Jesus, his person, life, message, death and Resurrection is from the side of God. They also underline the theocentric dimension of salvation history.

The passages of derivation became eventually the key to the orthodox understanding both of the passages of identity and the passages of distinction. While the title "Son of God" is more prominent than that of "Logos" in the New Testament, it is the "Logos" title that is most prominent in the development of Christology in the Patristic period. The Christological formula of John 1:14 became the most influential text in the history of the Christological dogmas. In the Old Testament the term "Logos" gradually underwent a transformation as it developed from its basic meaning of an eternal word spoken by Yahweh, through the notion of an inner word or thought of Yahweh, to signifying God's personal appearance to men. There is a clear tendency to hypostasize the Logos. This is evident in those Biblical passages where the Word is understood as subject of personal actions. This is apparent primarily in Wisdom literature. In Proverbs 8:22, we read about the pre-existence of Law, the identity of Law with God's plan for his creation and also the understanding of Law as the instrument of creation. It is this tradition that lies behind the prologue to the Gospel of John.

The dimensions of pre-existence attributed to Law and Wisdom are transferred to the Logos of the prologue. In Paul the only really explicit references to pre-existence come where Paul identifies Jesus with pre-existence Wisdom (I Cor. 8:6: Col. 1:15ff.; I Cor. 1:24). What is radically new in John's and Paul's use of Wisdom language is the application of such titles as Logos and Wisdom to an historical person, to Jesus of Nazareth.

F. The Impassibility of God and the Development of Logos Christology

In the transition of New Testament Christology to its development in the Patristic period, the foremost influence was the use of the term "Logos" by the Apologists. The Apologists made something special out of the Logos doctrine and gave it a key position in Christology. The term "Logos" is probably the most characteristic word in the Greek language. It relates to philosophy, science and religion and offered a comprehensive term for an overall understanding of reality. /28/ In this understanding, the Logos was regarded as the reasonable principle of the cosmos, of the knowledge of truth and morality. The Logos is understood as the interpretation, revelation and expression of the Father. It is most suitable for the interpretation of the words of God outside, in the creation of the world and the Incarnation. It provided the Apologists with a fruitful way of dealing with the relationship of Jesus and his Father within the Godhead.

Central to the use and development of the Logos concept in the Apologists is the influence of the Jewish philosopher Philo. Philo's thought concerning the Logos involves the blending of the Old Testament, Middle-Platonic and Stoic ideas. Philo believed that the Logos had three stages of existence: two before the creation of the world and one after creation. First, the Logos existed from eternity as the thought of God. Then, before the creation of the world, the Logos was created by God as an instrument and as a plan in the creation of the world. After the creation of the world, the Logos was inserted in the world to be an instrument of God's providence.

The Apologists adopted and changed Philo's concept of the Logos. But they did not change the basic understanding lying behind Philo's development and use of the Logos: the absolute transcendence of God. God the Father is thought to have such an absolute transcendence that he could not possibly deal actively with his creation.

With the concept of the transcendence of God, the idea of the impassible God was imported into theology. This idea is so foreign to Hebraic-Christian thought that it seems to make nonsense of the Revelation of

God in the Old Testament, it makes the Incarnation no real Incarnation, the kenosis, an impossible contradiction and it reduces the suffering and death of Christ to a purely human work. The idea seems simply to be assumed rather than argued for and is placed in paradoxical justaposition with the New Testament affirmation that God was in Christ in his suffering and death reconciling the world to himself.

This paradoxical juxtaposition is evident in one of the earliest of the Fathers, St. Ignatius. In his "Letter to the Romans," he writes: "Let me imitate the Passion of my God," but in the letter to Polycarp (3.2) he writes: "Be on the alert for him who is above time, the Timeless, the Unseen, the One who became visible for our sakes, who was beyond touch and passion, yet who for our sakes became subject to suffering, and endured everything for us." /29/ Again, in the "Letter to the Ephesians" (7:2) Ignatius writes: "There is only one physician - of flesh yet spiritual, born yet unbegotten, God incarnate, genuine life in the midst of death and suffering, from Mary as well as God, first subject to suffering, then beyond it - Jesus Christ, our Lord." /30/ The paradox is explicit: God is impassible - yet in Christ he suffers.

A good example of the influence of such thought in the concept of God and therefore in Christology is to be found in Irenaeus. Irenaeus held that God is impassible (Adv. Haer. 2.17,6) and that the Logos who is also from God is impassible (2.17,17). Irenaeus stressed the eternal co-existence of the Logos with the Father. Because the Logos is divine, the Logos is thereby immutable. The Logos could descend to take up his dwelling in a human life. But the work of the Logos was limited to those activities that were compatible with divinity.

> For just as he was man in order that he might be tempted, so, too, he was Logos in order that he might be glorified. When he was being tempted and crucified and dying, the Logos remained quiescent: when he was overcoming and enduring and performing deeds of kindness and rising again and being taken up, the Logos aided the human nature. /31/

The same problematic is found in the writings of Clement of Alexandria: If God is immutable how can He experience genuine incarnation?

> God is impassible, free of anger, destitute of desire. And He is not free of fear, in the sense of avoiding what is terrible; or temperate, in the sense of having command or desires. For neither can the nature of God fall in with anything terrible, nor does God flee fear; just as He will not feel desire, so as to rule over desires (Str. iv., XXIII). 151.1ff). Man, on the other hand, possesses "flesh with its capacity for suffering...by nature subject to passion"(Str. vii, II, 6,7). /33/

Clement's Christology is conditioned by his concept of impassibility. And yet Clement does not deny the reality of the Incarnation. He does write about "the God who suffered." /33/ Yet the incarnational suffering of Jesus is not essential to his role: Jesus' suffering is accidental to the divine condescension and Salvation. /34/ What Jesus brings about is a noetic redemption. Jesus' role in the redemption is that of being a teacher. Clement sees Jesus as being the "impassible man." /35/ While the Logos has taken to himself our flesh, so that the Incarnation is real <u>sarko phoros</u> /36/ he trains this flesh towards impassibility. The incarnate Logos leads humanity to an imitation of the immutable God. According to Clement, "the way to the Immutable is by immutability." /37/

While Origen knows better than Clement that Jesus' passion and death are at the heart of divine love and salvation, yet the divinity of the Logos means absolute impassibility, so that his entry into humanity does not allow him genuine participation in the suffering of the human soul and body he assumed. Origen feels compelled to grant that God experiences suffering; yet he cannot fit this affirmation into his philosophical-theological framework. /38/

G. The Arian Controversy

The implications of the doctrine of the impassibility of God for Christology became evident in the Arian controversies. The fundamental premise of Arius' system is the affirmation of the absolute uniqueness and transcendence of God, the unoriginate source of all reality. If the Logos is truly flesh, then according to Arius, the Logos cannot be equal to God, since the transcendent God cannot become flesh.

In his opposition to Arius, Athanasius affirmed the consubstantiality of the Logos with the eternal Father. At the same time he also insisted on the unchanging nature of the Logos.

> For the Father is unalterable and unchangeable, and is always in the same state and the same; but if, as they (the Arians) hold, the Son is alterable, and since not always the same but an ever-changing nature, how can such a one be the Father's Image, not having the likeness of his unalterableness... /39/

The Son, since he is of the same substance as the Father, is also unchangeable. This same Logos is the sole principle and unique subject of all statements about Christ. The human element in Christ is governed by the Logos. The relation between the Logos and flesh is not accidental. Yet no change is possible in the Logos who becomes flesh. The suffering and weakness of Jesus cannot be attributed to the Logos for that would be attributing them to God and, as Athanasius wrote, "... the faith of Christians acknowledges the blessed Triad as unalterable and perfect and even what It was, neither adding to It what is more, nor imputing It any loss..." /40/

The unchanging character of the Logos has direct consequences in relation to the nature of Redemption. Redemption is the restoration of human nature into the incorruptible image of God. "For he was made man that we might be made God; and he manifested himself by a body that we might receive the idea of the unseen Father; and he endured the insolence of men that we might inherit immortality." /41/

While Athanasius is so concerned in affirming the unity of the Logos with the flesh that he is sometimes moved to affirm that the Logos suffered, yet he never fully follows that inclination, as he writes: "It becomes the Lord, in putting on human flesh, to put it on whole with the affection proper to it; that, as we say that the body was his own, so also we may say that the affections of the body were proper to Him alone, though they did not touch Him according to his Godhead." /42/ All weakness and suffering are attributed to the flesh. Yet Athanasius writes that the Logos is the sole physical subject of Christ's life and actions.

At Nicea, Jesus Christ was confessed to be the Second Person of the Trinity, co-equal, consubstantial with the Father. Consubstantial with the Father, his being is eternal and unchangeable. At Nicea, the unchangeableness of the divine nature in Jesus Christ was emphasized. At the same time any suggestion of subordinate in Christ is eliminated. In reaction to Arianism, the true divinity of Jesus Christ was so emphasized that the true humanity was lost sight of. This is evident in the words of Apollinarius. His problematic is the relation of God, who is immutable, to a finite human life. That relation is only possible if the humanity of Jesus is not complete, if the Logos takes the place of the human soul. The Logos uses the human sarx simply as an instrument.

H. Chalcedon and the Doctrine of the Hypostatic Union

Later Christologies such as that of Cyril of Alexandria affirm the full humanity of Jesus while maintaining the impassibility and immutability of the divine Logos. The subject of suffering is the human Jesus. There is a risk here of loosening the intimate link between the divine Logos and human nature of Jesus. In expressing the nature of the Incarnation, Cyril used the phrase "hypostatic union." Cyril writes: "We believe therefore, not in one like us honoured with Godhead by grace...but rather in the Lord who appeared in servant's form and Who was truly like us and in human nature, yet remained God, for God the Word, when he took flesh, laid not down what he was, but is conceived of the Same God alike and man." /43/ The two natures, divine and human, are so united in Jesus that we may speak of one Person. Because of this unity we may speak in such terms as God suffered, God died. Yet the Logos remains in his own nature impassible; he remains "...external to suffering as far as pertains to His own Nature, for God is Impassible." /44/ Cyril must simultaneously affirm the impassibility of the Logos and the suffering of the Logos since the suffering and death of a mere man could not have effected redemption. The Logos suffered in the human flesh and since this flesh is the Logos' very own the Logos suffered, but impassibly. Cyril's difficulties with this question of Jesus' suffering and divinity can be seen in the following quotation:

> And though Jesus be said also to suffer, the suffering will belong to the economy; but is said to be His, and with all reason, because His too is that which suffered, and he was in the suffering Body, He unknowing to suffer (for He is impassible as God); yet as far as pertained to the daring of those who raged against Him, He would have suffered, if he could have suffered. /45/

In Cyril's doctrine on the Incarnation, we have a clear expression of the difficulties inherent in accepting an understanding of God as changeless, eternal and impassible, of identifying the Logos to such a God and of attempting to attribute real suffering to the incarnated Logos. The Logos is sympathetic to the suffering of the flesh, but does not suffer himself. The divine in Christ is untouched by the suffering of his human nature. Instead of being affected by becoming flesh, the divine Logos imparts its attributes to the human nature. There is a deification of the human, but no humanization of the divine.

Hilary presses the idea of impassibility to a point where the exemplary nature of Christ's experience in His human nature almost completely disappears. Writing about the Logos' human nature, Hilary affirms "When, in this humanity, He was struck with blows, or smitten with wounds, or bound with ropes, or lifted on high, He felt the force of suffering, but without its pain... He had a body to suffer, and he suffered: but He had not a nature which could feel pain. For His body possessed a unique nature of its own." /46/ In fact Hilary believes that Jesus Christ never needed to satisfy bodily longings. He writes, "...it is never said that the Lord ate or drank or wept when he was hungry or sorrowful. He conformed to the habits of the body to prove the reality of his own body, to satisfy the custom of human bodies, by doing as our nature does. When he ate and drank, it was a concession, not to his own necessity but to our habits." /47/ This approach seems to evacuate the Passion narratives of their force: suffering undertaken for the sake of men and women yet without pain is not suffering. Later for the Monophysites it is an act of pure grace on the part of the Logos that allows the body of Jesus to experience suffering since apart from such grace, suffering could not touch it.

At Chalcedon the Orthodox faith was expressed in terms of the doctrine of two natures and one person. This solution to the Christological controversies was a logical consequence of the earlier Trinitarian doctrine. It resulted from the affirmation at Nicea that the Son is consubstantial with the Father. It resulted from the rejection by Nicea of those who claimed there was a time when the Son did not exist or that he did not exist before he was begotten. Its framework is still that of an impassible God and Logos. Being of one substance with the Father, the Second Person of the Trinity shares the immutability of the Father. This immutability must necessarily affect the nature of the Logos' consubstantiality with us. Consubstantiality cannot mean any real sharing in the experiences of suffering, want or change. The doctrine of the two natures involves the fundamental distinction of the two natures. It also involves a specific soteriological motif: human nature finding salvation and immortality by participating in the divine nature. God becomes man that men and women might participate in God. It seems evident that the Patristic idea of God colored the whole development of classical Christology and has posed a problem for theology ever since. It set the stage for real difficulties in the understanding of the Incarnation because it operated with an understanding of God that was inadequate to carry the full meaning of the New Testament texts. The Fathers insisted at all costs on the impassibility of God and his Word. For the Greek mind, one of the predominant ideals of life is stability and permanence, and the idea of perfection is inseparable from the idea of changelessness. Becoming is the opposite of being and being is reality. The very idea of change is to be excluded from the essence of the divine and the life of God is a life of eternally changeless contemplation of the eternally changeless. The stoic ideal of *apatheia* was transferred in an idealized form to the inner life of God. In this framework it was difficult for the Fathers to find a proper place for the humanity of the Logos and for the reality of suffering. For the Fathers, God has to be understood as eternal, without change and impassible. The Fathers' struggles with the issue of Jesus' suffering provide a clear example of the way in which the theology of God influenced their understanding of the Incarnation. If the Son is consubstantial with the Father and, therefore, inherently perfect and incapable of change, progress or suffering, how is he truly one with us, consubstantial with us, authentically a mediator? The Christological controversies that took place in the early Church were concerned with the seemingly insoluble problem of how the eternal Logos, incapable of change or suffering, could be incarnate at all. The two major opponents in the controversy that finally led to the formula of Chalcedon, were both unable to solve the problem. Since the Logos, like God, could not really be involved in the world, the Antioch

and had real difficulties in accounting for the unity between them. Although the Alexandrians stressed the oneness of the nature of the Logos enfleshed, nevertheless the Logos could not suffer on the cross.

P. Van Buren states the problem clearly:

> On the one hand, the Fathers said that God was in Christ in an indissoluble union with Christ's human "nature." On the other hand, they said that Jesus Christ had actually suffered and died on the cross. If they had been more consistent in saying that God is unknown apart from his self-revelation and that we must begin with Jesus Christ in order to know anything about God at all, they might have been able to begin with the cross as the event of self-revelation of a God who is quite able to take suffering to himself and whose glory is so great that he can also humble himself. Had this been done, the course of the development of classical Christology would have been quite different. /48/

Because this was not done, the kenosis motif lost its constitutive role in Christological thinking. It was increasingly interpreted within the narrow limits of the divine immutability and the doctrine of the two natures. On the basis of these doctrines, the only meaning the Church could give to the kenosis was that of a condescension of the divine to the human realm in which and by which it was to be veiled. As a result of this, traditional Christology came very near to docetism according to which Jesus only appeared to suffer and only appeared to die abandoned by God; that the kenosis really did not occur.

According to Chalcedon, it is given that we have in Christ someone who is God and someone who is man. There is only one and when the exigencies of thought forced the Fathers to answer the question, "one what?" they settled on hypostasis, person, as the best word to express their own notion. This someone is God, the eternal Logos, the eternal Son; there is no human person. Yet it is as person and not as flesh that man is passible, both in the sense of being capable of emotions and capable of suffering. To affirm as some of the Fathers did that Christ suffered in his human nature, is to lead us to a two-person view of Christ which goes against Chalcedon. This understanding introduces an intolerable dualism in the person of Christ and robs the Incarnation of most of its religious and moral value. In light of the Chalcedonian formula, this conclusion about the reality of the Incarnation seems unavoidable. Leontius of Byzantium and John of Damascus developed the doctrine of the enhypostasis; the human nature of Jesus has its hypostasis in the Second Person of the Trinity. John, as the other Greek Fathers, insists on the impassibility of God and therefore of the eternal Son.

I. The Personal Humanity of Jesus - Christ

The whole development of the Christology from Chalcedon up to our own time has been dominated by the "God-man" formula: Jesus Christ is "truly God" and "truly man." All the formulas that have emerged in the course of the history have been intended as logical explanations of this union. The core and crucial question of the whole Christological tradition is the question of the living unity of God and man in Jesus Christ, with the continuing differentiation of the two:

the personal unity of God and man in Jesus Christ. The unity of God and man in Jesus Christ has been classically expressed in the doctrine of the hypostatic unity. The hypostatic unity means that God is so radically present to Jesus' own subjectivity that Jesus' own identity is God-given and yet his own. The hypostatic union is the affirmation that while God and man are radically different yet they are one in Christ.

During the Christological controversies, there occurred a shift from the radical monotheism of the Bible to trinitarian monotheism. This transformation involved the development of the concept of person and its application to the Godhead. The development did not occur in the same way for the Latin and Greek Fathers. According to T. DeRegnon, the Greek Fathers began with the three divine persons and then arrived at the one divine nature. The Latin Fathers started from the one divine nature and then proceeded to the three persons. /49/ R. Cantalamessa has pointed out that while there is some truth in DeRegnon's observation, it is more precise to say that while both the Latins and Greeks start from God's unity "...this unity is conceived by the Latins as impersonal or prepersonal - it is God's essence which then becomes specified as Father, Son and Holy Spirit (although of course this essence is not thought of as preexisting the persons). The Greeks on the other hand conceive of an already personalized unity." /50/ This is a personalized unity because it is that of the Father from whom proceeds the other two persons. "For the Latins, God is the divine essence, for the Greeks, the person of the Father." /51/ The Latin view has been criticized because it gives too much importance to the impersonal God of the philosophers; the Greek, for leading to subordinationism.

While in the Christological controversies both *persona* and *hypostasis* were used to mean an objective individuality, *persona* stressed the individuality, and *hypostasis*, the objectivity. But the word *persona* did not involve the idea of a subject implying self-consciousness. The word *persona* meant substance and not self-reflecting consciousness. Augustine writes: "When we speak of the person of the Father, we mean simply the substance of the Father." /52/ According to the formula of Chalcedon, the person of Christ does not first come into being from the concurrence of the Godhead and manhood, but is already pre-existing. The Logos was already in the full sense a person. At the Incarnation he did not become an individual, he became human without ceasing to be divine. The Incarnation is the mystery of the Logos uniting himself hypostatically with Jesus' human substance. Thus the formula of two natures and one person.

Trinitarian theology in its classical affirmation states that there are three "persons" in God. The Logos is one of these persons and is such from all eternity and independently of the Incarnation of the Son. This divine person assumes a complete human reality through a union which is affirmed to be hypostatic because the union is not a mingling of natures but has to do with the Son's hypostasis. The human nature of Jesus is joined in such a fashion to the Logos' hypostasis that this hypostasis becomes this nature's subject and is united to it substantially. So the human nature is truly predicated of the Eternal Logos. The divine and human natures exist "unseparated." The union is not a merging into a third nature; the subject does not emerge from the union but pre-exists prior to the union. The uniqueness of the subject is the ground for the doctrine of the <u>communicatio idiomatum</u> - the interchange of predicates.

This formula led to a theological explanation of the unity of the two natures in the one person termed "enhypostasis." According to this doctrine, the man Jesus in his concrete reality has the ground of his existence, his hypostasis, not in himself as man but "in" the eternal Logos, "in" the second person. The human nature of Christ is enhypostatic; it exists in the divine hypostasis of the Logos. According to Pannenberg:

> "The unity of the man Jesus with the Son of God is expressed in post-Chalcedonian Christology with the formula of the enhypostasis of Jesus in the Logos. According to the Chalcedonian decision, an independent reality (hypostasis) of its own form of manifestation (person) could no longer be attributed to Jesus' human nature. By itself Jesus' humanity would not only be personal in the modern sense of lacking self-

> conscious personality, but taken by itself Jesus' human being would be non-existent. Hence it can be conceived by itself only by abstracting from the actual reality of Jesus' existence. In his concrete reality the man Jesus has the ground of his existence (his hypostasis) not in himself as man but 'in' the Logos." /53/

During the medieval period, the enhypostasis led to various forms of explaining the action of the eternal Logos relative to the human nature of Jesus. W. Pannenberg sees three categories: the *assumptus* theory, the *habitus* theory, and the subsistence theory. According to the *assumptus* theory, the Logos assumed a complete man at the Incarnation, yet that man is not a person. The *habitus* theory sees the Incarnation as a form of vesting, of putting on clothes. The eternal Logos simply dons a human nature taken on by the Logos and united by him having its subsistence in the Logos. According to this theory the human nature of Jesus loses nothing by receiving its subsistence from the eternal Logos: it receives a higher dignity than if it had possessed a human personality and existence of its own.

All of these theories demanded the establishing of a distinction between nature and person or hypostasis. /55/ The theories developed to explain what the person is in itself were basically metaphysical in nature. In a contemporary context when it is assumed that a person is a psychological subject of interpersonal relations, the traditional enhypostasis theory has been challenged. What is being affirmed today is that a person is a psychological subject of interpersonal relations, and the traditional enhypostasis theory has been challenged. What is being affirmed today is that one cannot be truly a human being without being a human person. If we are to think of Jesus as truly a man, we have to think of him as a historical person. Contemporary Catholic theology has attempted to take into consideration this new development in the concept of the person, and attributes to Jesus a human subjectivity, a human "I." /56/ These contemporary discussions have pointed out quite clearly the difficulties of the enhypostatic way of understanding the hypostatic unity. According to this doctrine, the man Jesus in his concrete reality has the ground of his existence, his hypostasis not in himself as man but "in" the Logos. The absence of individual concreteness in Jesus' human nature as such, apart from its unification with the Logos, makes the completeness of Jesus' humanity problematic. According to this doctrine the divine person substitutes for this human person in Christ. The subject of Jesus' thoughts, feelings, and actions is the divine Logos. Foremost as problematic is the fact that personal subsistence is an important element in a human being. Can one be truly a man without being a human person? According to G. H. W. Lampe, reflecting the thought of many contemporary theologians, "The great defect of this idea is that in the last resort it almost invariably suggests that Christ's manhood is no more than an outward form, like a suit of clothes in which God the Son was dressed up as a man - the king disguised as a begger." /57/ The theory of the enhypostasis makes the personal agency of Jesus' humanity problematic. According to P. C. Hodgson, "The Logos is conceived as an active, personal suprahuman agent who incarnates himself in generic human flesh or nature and who constitutes the personal individual subjectivity of that flesh in lieu of a human subjectivity, while the flesh itself is merely instrumental to the action of the Logos." /58/

While the whole theological tradition sees the unity of Jesus as hypostatic in and with the eternal Logos, the Second Person of the Trinity, the New Testament sees the unity of Jesus primarily as that of Jesus to the Father. According to the New Testament, Jesus' human consciousness is turned not to the Logos but to the Father. Jesus knows himself to be one with the Father, not with a divine hypostasis differentiated from him. Jesus' unity with the Father is expressed in his behavior towards the Father, one of obedience and total dedication to the point of self-sacrifice. Jesus relates to the Father as a free subject to a free subject. According to Karl Rahner:

> "...the human nature of Christ as the person of the Logos must be understood in such a way that Christ in reality and in all truth is a man with all that involves: a human consciousness which is aware in adoration of its own infinite distance in relation to God: a spontaneous human interior life and freedom with a history which because it is

> that of God himself, possesses not less but more independence, for the latter is not diminished but increased by union with God." /59/

Jesus stands before God in free human obedience. He is Mediator, according to K. Rahner, "not only in virtue of the ontological union of two natures, but also through his (Jesus') activity, which is directed to God (as obedience to the will of the Father) and cannot be conceived of simply as God's activity in and through a human nature thought of as purely instrumental, a nature which in relation to the Logos would be ontologically and morally, purely passive." /60/ The unity of Jesus with God can be found only in the historical existence of Jesus in his message and actions. The starting point for the question of the hypostatic unity is the history and destiny of Jesus of Nazareth, his relation to the Father in dedication and obedience.

J. Conclusion

From what can be discerned about Jesus' own message, it is apparent that he was all about God and God's Kingdom. Jesus was a pointer to the Father and to the Kingdom of the Father. As Jesus is confessed to be the Christ by the early Church and becomes the focus of its preaching, the centrality of the Father is not forgotten. God the Father still remains the focus of the New Testament. /61/ The basic question in Christology is the question about God; more specifically, it is the question about God and man; it is the question about the transcendence and immanence of God: God being fully God and man being fully man.

When we deal with the hypostatic union, we are basically concerned with the basic question of the relationship between God and the world. Therefore, the question of the hypostatic unity must be located within the sphere of the more fundamental question of God's relationship to the world. The hypostatic unity should be seen within the single mystery of God's self-gift to his creation. This relation of God to his creation is the one and absolute and essential mystery of Christian faith. The hypostatic union, while specifically the property of Jesus Christ, expresses something decisive about God's self-communication to His total creation.

A KENOTIC CHRISTOLOGY

The hypostatic unity must be set in the broader context of the ontological relationship between God and creation. Christology cannot be isolated from the major symbols and doctrines of the Christian faith. While it is true that the question of the hypostatic unity is not specifically the question about the unity of God and man in general but the unity of God and man in Jesus Christ, basically the hypostatic unity poses the formidable question of how God can exist as origin, ground, and goal of man and his world and yet not be ontologically identified with them.

God's relationship to Jesus' humanity has been expressed in the symbol of the Incarnation. This symbol can already be discerned at work in the New Testament even if the language is not specifically its own. /62/ At Chalcedon, the symbol of Incarnation attained classical formulations in the notion of hypostatic union. While there has been a marked tendency in recent Christologies to abandon this symbol, /63/ the question about Jesus the Christ still remains a question about God and man. As a theological symbol, Incarnation speaks in a very specific way of God's presence and initiative, of God's graciousness and self-communication in Jesus Christ. The specificity of the symbol has been described as a "from above" approach to the mystery of the self-communication of God in Jesus Christ. /64/ While this approach may prove to be problematic, the primary question in any Christology remains that of the relationship of God to the human, the unity of God and the human, the transcendence and immanence of God. In its theological meaning the symbol of Incarnation says that God belongs to the world of his creatures; the Incarnation is a characteristic of God's being with us. God's transcendence is not from another world. It is a transcendence for men and women. The Incarnation as a symbol expresses something decisive about the relationship of the human to God, and this specifically in Jesus Christ. /65/

Theologizing about Jesus becomes a real discussion about God, about God who has joined Himself at a particular point in time with the earthly corporality of the man Jesus. /66/ The primary function of Christology is that of illuminating our experience and understanding God. God remains the one, absolute mystery which defines all other mysteries including that of Jesus Christ. While the person of Jesus Christ leads us into the mystery of God, he is himself defined by God. The underlying and critical question in Christology is the queston of God, of God's agency and causal relation to His creation, to the human reality of Jesus. Is a human history capable of mediating the action and presence of God? Can the history of the man Jesus be at the same time the history of God? W. Kasper sees the primacy of God in Christology in terms of the fundamental problem of freedom. Human freedom that is not grounded in the freedom of God is destined to self-destruction. The question of a unity of God and man in Christ has to be rethought in such a way as to show that this unity is not the antithesis of human emancipation, but the condition of its possibility. /67/

A KENOTIC CHRISTOLOGY

NOTES

1. E. Schillebeeckx, Jesus - An Experiment in Christology, (New York: The Seabury Press, 1979) p. 549.

2. I Col. 15:22.

3. Cf. F. Hahn, Mission in the New Testament, (Studies in Biblical Theology 47, London, 1965).

   J. Jeremias, Jesus' Promise to the Nations, (London: SCM Press, 1967).

4. C. F. Moule, The Origin of Christology, (New York: Cambridge University Press, 1977) p. 131.

5. E. Schillebeeckx, op. cit., p. 438.

6. W. Kasper writes about the New Adam:

   > "In fact by entering into the world in person as the Son of God, he changes the situation of everyone. Every man's living space acquires a new dimension and the man himself has become new. Every man is now defined by the fact that Jesus is his brother, neighbor, comrade, fellow-citizen, fellow man. Jesus Christ is now part of man's ontological definition. With Christ's coming a new kairos, a new opportunity of salvation is opened to the whole world and to all men. With him the situation of all has become new, because in the one humanity the existence of each and everyone is determined by the existence of all."

7. R. Schnackenburg, in Lexicon Fur Theologie Und Kirch, (1964) IX, Cols. 851-854.

8. J. Jeremias, New Testament Theology I, (London: SCM, 1971) pp. 53-55.

9. B. M. F. van Irsel, "'Der Sohn' in Der Synoptischen Jesusworten," Nov Test Suppl III (1964).

10. F. Hahn, The Titles of Jesus in Christology, Their History in Early Christianity, trans. H. Knight, (London: Lutterworth Press, 1969) pp. 284-288.

THE THEOLOGICAL IMPLICATION OF
THE DEVELOPMENT OF CHRISTOLOGY

R. H. Fuller, The Foundations of New Testament Christology, (London: Collins, 1965) 164-167.

11. R. H. Fuller, op. cit., pp. 165 f.

12. F. Hahn, op. cit., p. 281.

13. Ibid., p. 288.

14. W. Pannenberg, Jesus - God and Man, (Philadelphia: Westminster, 1978).

15. F. Hahn, op. cit., p. 289.

16. Ibid., p. 295. Cf. J. B. Metz, Poverty of Spirit, (New York: Newman Press, 1968).

17. F. Hann, op. cit., p. 297.

18. Cf. R. E. Brown, The Birth of the Messiah, (New York: Doubleday, 1977) pp. 160-162; 298-310; 517-534.

19. F. Hahn, op. cit., p. 299.

20. Cf. R. H. Fuller, op. cit., p. 166.

21. F. Hahn, op. cit., p. 300.

22. Ibid., p. 203. Cf. Rom. 4:4; Phil. 2:6; Jn. 1:14.

23. E. Schweizer, art. "UIOS" in TDNT Vol. VIII, pp. 387-388.

24. B. Vawter, This Man Jesus: An Essay in N. T. Christology, (New York: 1973) p. 132.

25. W. Kasper, op. cit., p. 198.

26. K. Rahner, "Theios in the New Testament," Theological Investigations, Vol. I, (New York: Seabury Press, 1974) p. 112.

27. Ibid.

28. W. Pannenberg, op. cit., pp. 158-168.

29. St. Ignatius, Letter to Polycarp, 3.2.

30. St. Ignatius, Letter to the Ephesians, 7:2.

31. St. Irenaeus, Against the Heretics, III, 19.3.

32. Clement of Alexandria, Stromata, VII, II, 6.77.

33. Clement, Protrepticos, 106.4.

34. Stromata, IV, XXIV, 153.6.

35. Stromata, V, XIV, 94.57.

36. Stromata, V, VI, 34.1.

37. Stromata, II, XI, 51.6.

38. Cf. R. M. Grant, The Early Christian Doctrine of God, (Charlottesville: University of Virginia Press, 1966) p. 291.

39. St. Athanasius, Discourse Against the Arians, III.4.

40. Discourse Against the Arians, I.18.

41. On the Incarnation. Page numbers refer to Christology of the Later Fathers, eds. J. Baillie, J. T. McNeill, (Philadelphia: The Westminster Press, 1954) pp. 107-108.

42. Discourse Against the Arians, III.32.

43. Cyril of Alexandria, "Scholia on the Incarnation," in Five Tomes Against Nestorius, ed. E. B. Posey, (Oxford: James Parrer and Co., 1881) 12, p. 197.

44. Ibid., 13, p. 202.

45. Ibid.

46. St. Hilary, On the Trinity X, 23.

47. Ibid., X, 24.

48. P. Van Buren, The Secular Meaning of the Gospel, (New York: Macmillan, 1963) p. 42.

49. Cf. T. DeRegnon, Etudes de Theologie Positive sur la Sainte Trinite, Vol. I (Paris, 1892) p. 433.

50. R. Cantalamessa, "The Development of a Personal God," Concilium, Vol. 103, (New York: Seabury Press, 1977) p. 61.

51. Ibid.

52. St. Augustine, On the Trinity, VII, 6.11.

53. W. Pannenberg, op. cit., pp. 337-338.

54. Ibid., p. 295.

55. W. Kasper, op. cit., pp. 240 ff.

56. K. Rahner writes:

> "The Jesus of the Chalcedonian dogma, which was directed against Monophysitism and Monothelitism, likewise has a subjective centre of action which is human and creaturely in kind, such that in his human freedom he is in confrontation with God the inconceivable, such that in it Jesus has undergone all those experiences which we make of God not in a less radical, but on the contrary, in a more radical - almost, we might say, in a more terrible - form than in our own case. And this properly speaking not in spite of, but rather because of the so-called hypostatic union."

"The Position of Christology in the Church Between Exegesis and Dogmatics," Theological Investigations, Vol. XI, (London: 1974) p. 198.

P. Schoonenberg takes a similar direction in his Christology, and affirms that one must speak of a human person when one speaks about Jesus Christ. Cf. The Christ, (New York: Herder & Herder, 1969).

57. G. W. H. Lampe, "The Holy Spirit and the Person of Christ" in S. W. Sykes, ed., Christ, Faith and History, (Cambridge: Cambridge University Press, 1972) p. 111.

58. P. C. Hodgson, Jesus - Word and Presence. An Essay in Christology, (Philadelphia: Fortress Press, 1971) p. 65.

59. K. Rahner, "Incarnation," in Encyclopedia of Theology. The Concise Sacramentum Mundi, (New York: The Seabury Press, 1975) p. 695.

60. K. Rahner, "Current Problems in Christology," in Theological Investigations, Vol. I, (Baltimore: Helican, 1965) p. 161.

61. On this point E. Martinez writes:

> "Jesus did not proclaim himself - his whole life was a proclamation of the Father and the coming of the Kingdom of God his Father. Faith in God the Father who saves is what Jesus proclaimed and this shines through all the expression of his teaching. After Jesus' Resurrection the early Church did not change this emphasis: the disciples proclaimed the God who has raised up Jesus."

"The Identity of Jesus in Mark," Communio 4, (Winter, 1974) p. 342.

62. Cf. J. Knox, The Humanity and Divinity of Christ, (New York: Cambridge University Press, 1967).

63. Cf. J. Hick, ed., The Myth of God Incarnate, (Philadelphia: Westminster Press, 1977).

64. W. Pannenberg, Jesus - God and Man, (Philadelphia: Westminster Press, 1968) pp. 33-37.

65. K. Rahner make the point in the following way:

> "This Savior, who represents the climax of this self-communication, must therefore be at the same time God's absolute pledge by self-communication to the spiritual creature as a whole *and* the acceptance of this self-

communication by this Savior; only then is there an utterly irrevocable self-communication on both sides, and only thus is it present in the world in a historically communicative manner."

Theological Investigations, Vol. V, (Baltimore: Helicon Press, 1961) p. 176.

66. To concentrate too exclusively on the Christ-event and not on what the Christ-event reveals about God is to run the risk of reductionism. Such a concentration gives rise to the death-of-God theology.

67. Cf. W. Kasper, Jesus the Christ, (New York: Paulist Press, 1976).

CHAPTER 6

KENOTIC CHRISTOLOGY: ITS HISTORY, PROBLEMATICS AND POSSIBILITIES

A. Kenotic Christology in the 19th Century

It is our contention that a very fruitful approach to the mystery of the Incarnation can be found in what has been termed a kenotic Christology. Kenotic Christology, in its technical expressions, has been particularly associated with a group of theologians of the latter part of the 19th century in Germany, such as Gottfried Thomasius, /1/ and of the early part of this century in England, such as P. T. Forsyth and H. R. Mackintosh. /2/ The stimulus for the earlier kenotic Christologies arose out of a real desire to deal seriously with the newly emerging conception of personality and the critical restudying of the New Testament that emphasized the reality of Jesus' humanity. The Chalcedonian doctrine of person had been expressed in ontological terms and did not in any way consider the psychological dimension of the person, with its insistence on consciousness and growth.

The exponents of kenotic Christology see in "kenosis" the means of integrating the new doctrine on person to the traditional understanding that the personalizing center of Jesus' person was the second person of the Trinity. For these theologians, God in some way had to limit himself so that the presence of the divine in Jesus did not destroy the human dimension of his personhood. Kenotic Christology asserted some real modification of the divine attributes as a necessary condition of the true and personal entrance of the Son of God into human history and human experience. Kenosis was interpreted as the emptying of certain aspects of the divine being, and, as such, became a principle of intelligibility, an interpretive framework, for the resolution of the questions pertaining to the unity of the human and divine in Christ.

Kenotic Christology had its roots in Germany where it received its most comprehensive expression in the works of Gottfried Thomasius. /3/ He was the most important defender and articulator of the kenotic position and made clear the theory's presuppositions and possibilities. Thomasius's definitive statement is found in his book Christ's Person and Work. /4/ Here Thomasius argues that if the Incarnation is to take place, this can only happen through a voluntary self-limitation of the eternal Logos. According to Thomasius this self-limitation happens without any limitation of the divinity of the Logos, because, in Thomasius's words, it is of the very essence of love "to accept every limitation...what seems to be alienation or finitization of deity itself, the concentration of its energies on one point which, in its significance, far outweighs the most inclusive manifestation of omnipotence." /5/

According to Thomasius, the eternal Logos in his kenosis laid aside the relational attributes of omnipotence, omniscience, and omnipresence that are not essential to God himself, but are expressive of a relationship God has entered into freely and from which he can withdraw. But the incarnated Logos retains the immanent attributes, those of power, truth, and love, since these attributes characterize God as God and are essential. While the relational attributes would vitiate the reality of Christ's humanity since no humanity could be omnipotent, omniscient, or omnipresent, the immanent attributes are capable of expression in and through a human personality.

In expressing his kenotic Christology, Thomasius redefined the concept of divine absoluteness in such a way that real change would be possible in God. Self-emptying implied in Thomasius's mind a real change in divine life. For Thomasius, the absoluteness of God does not lie in immutability but in his ability to change. God is most totally and completely God in his power to change himself, even to limit himself in his will of love for mankind. Thomasius also saw that although there is a distinction between the self-emptying of the Logos in the Incarnation and the suffering undergone in the Logos' earthly life, yet there is an intimate relationship between the two, the earthly suffering and humiliation being continuous with God's own act of humility and suffering. /6/ In conjunction with this, Thomasius affirmed that there is within ourselves the capacity to receive and be penetrated by God, and that such a capacity is an essential presupposition of incarnation. Thomasius's insistence on the reality of the divine self-emptying challenged the traditional teaching on the immutability and impassibility of God.

Thomasius's views were opposed from the very beginning. The opposition came in terms of kenotic Christology's inability to safeguard the traditional Trinitarian doctrine - where the divine absoluteness is rooted in the very co-inherence of the others. As long as the absoluteness of the Godhead is defined in terms of its co-inherence, the lessening of one person of the Trinity destroys the unity and absoluteness of the divine. The only theologians who could get around this objection were those who accepted the Hegelian doctrine of God which accepted the changes and limitations demanded by kenosis as a necessary stage in the development of the Absolute. The previous objection, expressed in different ways, /7/ became the predominant source of opposition to the kenotic Christology: it seemed to place the whole doctrine of the Trinity in jeopardy. According to W. Pannenberg, "An incarnation thus understood as incapacitation of the Son necessarily draws the doctrine of the Trinity into difficulties as well. Is not the Son, who had given up His relative divine attributes in the flesh, excluded from the Trinity for this period since during His humiliation he was apparently not equally God with the Father and the Spirit?" /8/

The criticism directed at Thomasius underlined a basic difficulty - the impossibility of developing a workable kenotic Christology without changing the traditional conceptual framework. These criticisms made clear the inherent impossibility of fitting the kenotic theme into the traditional Trinitarian doctrine. They also indicated the need for a more radical reconstruction of the doctrine of God. The inadequacies of the traditional doctrine about God created insoluble problems for any kenotic Christology.

While the kenotic Christologies failed in their promise of making intelligible the traditional Christology, they understood the humanity of Jesus with a new depth and reality that marks a clear advance in Christology. Kenotic Christology got away entirely from docetism and affirmed the full humanity of Christ including the necessary limitations of his knowledge and the need for growth and development. Even in their failure, they focused the attention of theologians on the need to reformulate the doctrine of the divine absoluteness.

KENOTIC CHRISTOLOGY: ITS HISTORY, PROBLEMATICS AND POSSIBILITIES

B. Contemporary Protestant Approaches to Kenotic Christology

While the solemn warnings of many theologians /9/ of the unavoidable and insolvable problems of kenosis should have sounded the end of the Christological model, it would now seem that such a conclusion was premature. While J. A. T. Robinson accuses the kenotic Christologies of being "fruitless expenditures of theological ingenuity" since they were founded in supranaturalist categories, where Christ is "presented as stripping Himself of those qualities of transcendence which make Him the Revelation of God," /10/ yet "the development of kenotic Christologies in the latter half of the nineteenth century, first in Germany and later in England and Russia was a response to the felt inadequacies of the static doctrine of the two natures with its presupposition of divine immutability and impassibility. Under the impact of historical studies and evolutionary theories, kenoticism performed a valuable function as a bridge from the past to the present." /11/

According to John Macquarrie, the mediating nature of kenotic Christology is perhaps what we now need "...since we may well be again today in need of a mediating Christology, it is possible that we still have something to learn from the kenoticists." /12/ According to Macquarrie, the only way to understand the real contribution of kenotic Christology is to place it in its historical setting and to appreciate the radical context in which it had to operate. /13/ In their attempt to go along with the humanistic thrust of Schleiermacher's Christology, the kenoticists were "genuinely concerned to retrieve a deeper and more genuine understanding of the humanity of Christ," yet they were determined to do so while retaining the full divinity of Christ and the complex dialectic of Christological language.

The greatest weakness of the kenoticists was that they did not go far enough. "The new humanistic thrust in theology demanded nothing less than that Christology be stood on its head, so to speak, and that it should find its starting point in the humanity of Christ." /14/ In their fear of the extreme positions of men like Strauss and Feuerbach, they held on to the traditional framework as alone making possible a real Incarnational theology. /15/ The key problem for Thomasius was metaphysical; it was the question of the being of God in the historical person, Jesus Christ, the question of the union of God and man in Christ. In the new humanistic thrust the humanity of Jesus Christ had become the pivot of reconstruction. A new question is asked: Given the integrity of human existence, how is it possible to speak of the presence of the divine?

Most contributions to kenotic Christology have come out of the Protestant tradition. With Kierkegaard, kenosis is no longer accepted as a principle of intelligibility, a solution to the Christological question but as a paradox of grace. /16/ Kenosis is the absolute paradox over which all attempts to rationalize Christianity must come to failure. The final measure of God's love is that God loves man for what he is. Kenosis is the link relating the finitude and sinfulness of man to the love of God. The acceptance by God of the servant form is the final measure of the offense of Christianity. For, in becoming man, the Eternal God has become a particular historical fact. God has done what seems to be totally contrary to his nature, he became unlike himself and yet remained God. Kierkegaard writes about the God-man: "He is God, but chooses to become the individual man. This, as we have seen, is the profoundest incognito, or the most impenetrable unrecognizableness that is possible; for the contradiction between being God and being an individual man is the greatest possible, the infinitely qualitative contradiction." /17/

While accepting Kierkegaard's concept of paradox, Karl Barth accepted kenosis as a theological framework and contributed to its contemporary expression. /18/ In his commentary on Philippians, Barth described kenosis not as a loss in divinity but as the affirmation that God is Lord even in his humiliation. In becoming man, God did not become unlike himself. The kenosis is the highest affirmation of God's transcendence.

> The way of the Son of God into the far country, i.e., into the lowliness of creaturely being, of being as man, into unity and solidarity with sinful and therefore perishing humanity, the way of His incarnation is as such the activation, the demonstration, the revelation of His deity, His divine Sonship. /19/

The basic questions about God's nature and man's nature have to be asked in the light of God's lordship even in his humiliation. This will lead to a major reconstruction of the doctrine of God and the rejection of natural theology with its concept of God as changeless Being.

For Barth, God is the one who loves in freedom, and the free acceptance of limitation is of the very nature of God. We have here the clue for the understanding of how God can combine in himself constancy and change. /20/ God is free to enter fully into realities different from himself, while remaining himself. The divine self-emptying is the expression of God's will to love. His absoluteness and immutability are expressed in terms of his constant will to love. In relation to us, there is a holy immutability about God.

> "In the work of the reconciliation of the world with God, the inward divine relationship between the One who rules and commands in majesty and the One who obeys in humility is identical with the very different relationship between God and one of His creatures, a man. God goes into the far country for this to happen. He becomes what He had not previously been. He takes into unity with his divine being a quite different, a creaturely and indeed a sinful being. To do this He empties Himself, He humbles Himself. But, as in His action as Creator, He does not do it apart from its basis in His own being, in His own inner life. He does not do it without any correspondence to, but as the strangely logical final contribution of, the history in which He is God. He does not need to deny, let alone abandon and leave behind or even diminish His Godhead to do this. He does not need to leave the work of the Reconciler in the doubtful hands of a creature. He can enter in Himself, seeing He is in Himself not only the one who rules and commands in majesty, but also in His own divine person, although in a different mode of being, the One who is obedient in humility." /21/

A KENOTIC CHRISTOLOGY

W. Pannenberg has criticized Barth's kenotic doctrine on the grounds that no answer has been given to the question of the unity of God and man in Christ in their continued differentiation. We have in Barth a functional unity and not a personal unity. According to Pannenberg this is due to Barth's reluctance to take seriously the kenosis of God as a real giving of himself. /22/ Although Pannenberg criticizes quite strongly the kenotic Christologies of both the 19th and 20th centuries, he sees in these Christologies elements that are necessary for the structuring of a contemporary Christology. The discussions on God's self-emptying have contributed to a better understanding of how God, who is one himself, can become something and precisely in so doing remain true to himself and the same. /23/ "To the extent that it shows how God can be one with himself in the other, the dialectic of self-differentiation forms an important aid to the understanding of the Incarnation." /24/ Pannenberg also understands Jesus' unity to the Father in kenotic terms. On the part of Jesus, his unity to the Father had to be expressed in terms of dedication to the point of self-sacrifice. "He reserved nothing for himself in his human existence, he lived entirely from God and for the men who must be called into his kingdom. Thus Jesus is one with God through his dedication to the Father that is confirmed as a true dedication by the Father's acknowledgement of him through Jesus' resurrection." /25/ Pannenberg quotes Hegel in terms of understanding the person as essentially self-dedication. /26/ "Jesus' unity with God is mediated through his human dedication to the Father." /27/ "This dedication... penetrates, surpasses, and envelops all expressions and elements of his existence..." /28/ In a sense all human existence is designed to be personalized by its dependence upon God, to be integrated into a person through its relation to God the Father.

Within the Protestant tradition, a radical interpretation of kenosis was given in the "Death of God Movement." This radical interpretation was preceded by a less radical but more pervasive use of the kenosis motif. In Bonhoeffer we have a new style of kenoticism, a type of Christology which sees the ultimate meaning of Jesus in his human self-emptying. /29/ While Bonhoeffer does not negate or minimize the divinity of Christ, we find in him an emphasis on the humanity of Jesus, on his weakness and humiliation. The "enfleshed"

God is the only God we know; whatever is to be said of God's transcendence is what we can say of the Biblical Christ. Bonhoeffer wrote from prison shortly before his death:

> "God lets himself be pushed out of the world and on to the Cross. He is weak and powerless in the world, and this is precisely the way, the only way, in which he is with us and helps us. Matt. 8:17 makes it quite clear that Christ helps us, not by virtue of his omnipotence but by virtue of his weakness and suffering... Only the suffering God can help ... That is a reversal of what the religious man expects from God. Man is summoned to share in God's suffering at the hands of a godless world." /30/

Through his self-emptying, God is weak and powerless. In Bonhoeffer's words:

> "Faith is participation in this being of Jesus (Incarnation, Cross, and Resurrection). Our relation to God is not a 'religious' relationship to the highest, most powerful, and best Being imaginable --that is not authentic transcendence-- but our relation to God is a new life in 'existence for others,' through participation in the being of Jesus. The transcendental is not infinite, unattainable tasks but the neighbor who is within reach in any given situation. God in human form-- not, as in oriental religions, in animal form, monstrous, chaotic, remote, and terrifying, not in the conceptual forms of the absolute, metaphysical, infinite, etc., nor yet in the Greek divine-human form of 'man in himself,' but 'the man for others,' and therefore the Crucified, the man who lives out of the transcendent." /31/

Christ's divinity adds nothing to his humanity. Christ is fully God in his humiliation. For Bonhoeffer, God does not sit in another world of unchanging lordship, but he becomes flesh and world so that we can speak of him in worldly terms. For Bonhoeffer, when God is no longer needed as a problem solver, he does not disappear but he truly appears in his authentic transcendence at the very center of human potential and progress.

With the "Death of God" theologians and specifically with T. Altizer we have a radical interpretation of kenosis: the self-emptying of God in Jesus Christ is really his death. The Incarnation has to be understood as actually effecting the death of God. According to Altizer, "Theology is now called to a radically kenotic Christology." /32/

> "An authentically kenotic movement of 'Incarnation' must be a continued process of Spirit becoming flesh, of eternity becoming time, or of the sacred becoming profane." /33/

> "'God is dead' are words that may only truly be spoken by the...radical Christian who speaks in response to an Incarnate Word that empties itself of Spirit so as to appear and exist as flesh (in such a way that) flesh negates itself as flesh so as to become Spirit." /34/

> "God has negated and transcended himself in the Incarnation and thereby he has fully and finally ceased to exist in his original form. To know that God is Jesus is to know that God himself has become flesh; no longer does God exist as transcendent spirit or sovereign Lord, now God is love." /35/

Attributing his thought to Hegel, Altizer affirms the necessity of a Christian atheism, "Hegel and Nietzsche were Christian thinkers who grasped the necessity of a theological atheism." /36/ This form of kenosis is a radical solution to the Christological question of how God can become one with man through the act of self-emptying, since it sacrifices the person of God. In so doing it eliminates one essential aspect of Jesus of Nazareth - his openness towards God, his community with the Father. Without this openness, the unique quality attributed to Jesus as revealer of the truly human seems to be without foundation.

C. Duquoc has pointed out the lack of a doctrine

of the Trinity in the radical kenotic Christologies. /37/ Altizer cannot conceive of a God who gives himself to the Son through the Holy Spirit. The Logos is identified to God and the Incarnation of the Logos is the Incarnation of God. Although Altizer accepts the initial distinction of the Father and the Son, this is an opposition that must be reduced since it corresponds to the separation of God and the world. The Father as distinct from the Son is really God in his initial form of transcendence. Through kenosis, this transcendent God-Father must disappear so that only the Incarnated Word subsists. /38/ We have here the suppression of the dialectic, the negation of the transcendent pole and the exclusive affirmation of the immanent pole. The polarity and the dialectical tension of the Gospel's Father and Son is suppressed. The Trinitarian doctrine is an attempt to affirm both the transcendence and the immanence of God.

J. Moltmann agrees that the "Death of God" theology has lacked a Trinitarian dimension. With Moltmann the conceptual framework for kenotic Christology is the doctrine of the Trinity. There must be "a Trinitarian understanding of kenosis. In contrast to the traditional doctrine of the two natures of the person of Christ, it (the kenosis) must begin from the totality of the person of Christ and understand the relationships of the death of the Son and the Father and the Spirit." /39/ He quotes approvingly Losky's affirmation, "The kenosis...and the work of the Incarnate Son is the work of the entire most Holy Trinity, from which Christ cannot be separated." /40/ What happens on the Cross manifests the relationship of Jesus the Son to the Father, and makes possible the movement of the Spirit from the Father. Jesus' death is not the death of God, but death in God. Moltmann writes the following:

> "In the forsakenness of the Son, the Father also forsakes himself... To understand what happened between Jesus and his God and Father on the Cross, it is necessary to talk in Trinitarian terms. The Son suffers dying, the Father suffers the death of the Son. The grief of the Father here is just as important as the death of the Son. The Fatherlessness of the Son is matched by the Sonlessness of the Father, and if God has

> constituted himself as the Father of Jesus Christ, then he also suffers the death of his Fatherhood in the death of the Son." /41/

Moltmann accepts fully Martin Kahler's affirmation that the Cross is the basis and standard of Christology: the crucified Christ "becomes the general criterion of theology." /42/ The converging trend in contemporary theological thought is to understand God from the death of Jesus. "What does the cross of Jesus mean for God himself?" /43/ There can be no theology of the Incarnation which does not become a theology of the Cross. /44/ The suffering of Christ must be thought of "as the power of God and the death of Christ as God's potentiality." /45/

With the doctrine of two natures the event of the Cross, the primordial self-emptying must be understood statically "as reciprocal relationship between two qualitatively different natures, the divine nature which is incapable of suffering and the human nature which is capable of suffering." /46/ Within the Trinitarian context the relationship is dynamic, between persons who constitute themselves in their relationship with each other. "What is in question in the relationship of Christ to his Father is not his divinity and humanity in their relationship to each other but the total, personal aspect of the Lordship of Jesus." /47/ In Moltmann's mind this perception overcomes the dichotomy between immanent and economic Trinity. God both transcends the world and is immanent in history. "He is transcendent as Father, immanent as Son, and opens up the future as the Spirit." /48/

The acceptation of the kenotic Christology within a Trinitarian framework leads to a serious questioning of the doctrine of immutability and impassibility of God. "For the doctrine of the Trinity speaks of God in respect to the Incarnation and the death of Jesus and in so doing breaks the spell of the old philosophical concept of God." /49/ The Christian God is one who is able to love. "If love is the acceptance of the other without regard to one's own well-being, then it contains within itself the possibility of sharing in suffering and freedom to suffer as a result of the otherness of the other." /50/ Since God is love by nature, humiliation even unto death corresponds to God's nature. "God is not more powerful than he is in this helplessness; God is not more divine than he is in this humanity." /51/

In insisting on a Trinitarian framework for this kenotic Christology, Moltmann has avoided collapsing the divine transcendence into immanence. He has also inserted the kenosis within the Godhead. The suffering of Christ involves process within God's own life. The self-limitation of Christ on the Cross is an expression of the self-limitation within God himself. "Here God has not just acted externally, in his unattainable glory and eternity. Here he has acted in himself and has gone on to suffer in himself... So the new Christology which tries to think of the 'death of Jesus' as the 'death of God' must take up the elements of truth which are to be found in kenoticism." /52/ Moltmann sees kenotic Christology as the necessary basis of a theology of liberation. The cross reveals that "God's being is in suffering, and suffering is in God's being itself." /53/ A "revolution in the concept of God" is needed to establish the proper foundation for any solidarity with the oppressed world.

C. Contemporary Catholic Positions

The contemporary forms of kenotic Christology that we have examined up to now have been influenced quite directly by Hegel's thought. Less influenced by Hegelian thought for whom God and the world are engaged in dialectical interaction, Roman Catholic theology has consistently refused to accept any form of limitation or mutability within the Godhead. Kenosis has been understood as a process within the humanity of Jesus, as the veiling of the fully divine nature in human flesh. /54/ The rigidity of modern Roman Catholic tradition on the question of kenotic Christology must be attributed to rigidity in God doctrine.

This situation has changed quite radically. Hans Küng has suggested in his book Mensh-Werdung Gottes /55/ that a new look at classical Christology could be helped by Hegel's own thought patterns. /56/ Küng is attracted to Hegel because Hegel dealt creatively with the concept of the unchangeableness of God. Hegel's God is close to humanity, one who suffers and dies. /57/ Küng regards Hegel's theological thought as "prolegomena to a future Christology." He suggests that Hegel's insight can be used to build a theology which would appeal to contemporary thought, and help bridge the God of the philosophers and the God of our fathers and of Jesus Christ. Hegel works out his Christology in the pattern of humiliation and exaltation. The human, the finite, the negative becomes a divine element in God himself. Kenosis is the pattern of the inner life of the Trinity. Finitude is a necessary aspect of the divine life. Here the notion of kenosis is not extraneous to a conception of God, but is in reality an eternal aspect of God. Kenosis is not only an explanation of Jesus' real humanity, but it is also the pattern of all reality. The threefold movement or pattern of all reality in Hegel's ontology is really the pattern of kenosis described in the New Testament:

> "Actual reality (nature)...and implicit being (logical structure) are two moments, and by the reciprocity of their kenosis, each relinquishing or 'emptying' itself of itself and becoming the other, spirit (the highest level of reality) comes in existence as their unity." /58/

Hegel understands the nature of person in kenotic terms. It is of the very nature of the person to exist in dedication. "In friendship and love I give up my abstract personality and win thereby concrete personality. The truth of personality is just this, to win it through this submerging, being submerged in the other." /59/

While Küng is critical of Hegel's concept of necessity in God, /60/ he fully approves his contribution towards a better understanding of God's absoluteness. /61/ Kenotic Christology needed a totally different framework than traditional theology has transmitted. Küng sees Hegel's doctrine of God, where self-limitation becomes integral to divine life itself, as establishing that framework. Küng feels that classical Christology demands to be surpassed, to be taken seriously, more so that it could take itself since it has been handicapped by its own static understanding of God. Christology for Hans Küng means a reflection on the history of the suffering and death of Christ. It is only on the cross that one can perceive the supreme depth and the supreme seriousness of what happens in the man Jesus - the meaning of that event for God - _Passio Christi_, _Passio Dei_; _Mors Christi_, _Mors Dei_.

God suffers, contrary to Greek thought, not out of imperfection, but out of the plenitude of his love. The essence of the living God has the power within himself of self-exteriorization. /62/ The living God is one who includes within himself his contrary, a life which includes death, a domination which includes servitude, an eternity which includes time. "The being of God is in the becoming." /63/

> "If we wish to think Christologically within the framework of Greek metaphysics, we would rather have to say: it is precisely because God is Pure Act, a superabundant fullness, immutable perfection, because he is the exalted God and not a creature, that he can undergo in his Word and Son such a self-emptying, without losing himself, that he can enter worldly mutability without giving up his immutable, divine perfection, that he can afford this seemingly godless descent into the depths without miserably perishing in this transition into otherness. God can do all this, he does not have to do it. And, although he does not have to do it, he wills it, once more out of the superabundance of his gracious love, which wishes to identify itself with man and his fate in this world." /64/

Küng considers the Incarnation in the light of God's personal Incarnation. The history of Christ's humanity in the Incarnation became the history of the Word. For Küng the reality of the Incarnation hinges on the possibility of real becoming or change in God. Küng regards Karl Rahner's position as being about as far as theology has been able to go. /65/ While Küng does not accept the earlier expression of kenotic Christology, he does see in kenosis a viable way of dealing with the affirmation that Jesus is God and man.

For Karl Rahner, the basic way of understanding the Incarnation is not the concept of an assumption, but that of a self-emptying, of a kenosis, through which God poses the other as his own reality.

> "God, in and by the fact that he empties <u>himself</u>, gives away <u>himself</u>, <u>poses</u> the other as his own reality. The basic element to begin with is not the concept of an assumption, which presupposes what is to be assumed as something obvious, and has nothing more to do than to assign it to the taker--a term, however, which it never really reaches, since it is rejected by his immutability and may never affect him, since he is unchangeable, when his immutability is considered undialectically and in isolation--in static concepts. On the contrary, the basic element, according to our faith, is the self-emptying, the coming to be, the kenosis and genesis of God himself--because, being love, that is, the will to fill the void, he has that wherewith to fill all--the ensuing other in his own proper reality. He brings about that which is distinct from himself, in the act of retaining it as his own and vice versa, because he truly wills to retain the other as his own, he constitutes it in its genuine reality. God himself goes out of himself, God in his quality of the fullness which gives away itself. /66/

When the Logos became man, his humanity is not prior but it comes to be, insofar and inasmuch as the Logos empties himself. Jesus as such is the self-utterance of God "because God expresses himself when he empties himself." /67/ Jesus of Nazareth is the one who, from the very depths of his being, a being grounded in God, has surrendered himself to God and has been accepted by God. In the case of the Incarnation we have the verification of the axiom which governs all relationship between God and creature:

> "namely, that the closeness and the distance, the submissiveness and the independence of the creature do not grow in inverse but in like proportion. Thus Christ is most radically man, and his humanity is the freest and most independent, not in spite of, but because of its being taken up, by being constituted as the self-utterance of God. /68/

The degree in which true selfhood is realized is the co-efficient of the constitutive transcendental relation to God. Dependence and freedom are not in inverse proportion but in direct proportion. Human freedom perfects itself through dedication to God. Jesus is the man whose life is one of absolutely unique self-surrender to God. For Rahner, the kenosis of God, the self-emptying, is not simply a metaphor. In the context of a traditional affirmation of God's immutability and unchangeability, Rahner has a startling theology of God. The Incarnation implies a real change for God. God in his unrelatedness has the possibility of becoming something else. While remaining immutable "in himself" the Incarnate Word really changes in his divine nature and in his human nature. /69/ Rahner is able to affirm that God in his relatedness has the possibility of becoming something else. Through auto-limitation God constitutes the finite other, in whom the Word can express himself through personal union. God is really involved in world history. "The Logos became man, the changing history of this human reality is his own history; our time became the time of the eternal, our death, the death of the immortal God himself." /70/ When the Word expresses himself in human nature, He really becomes. God himself undergoes change in the Incarnation.

On the basis of a dialectical understanding, Rahner affirms that God really suffers in the crucifixion. We can speak of the death of Jesus as the death of God. Jesus' death belongs to God's utterance, it is a statement of God about himself.

> "If it is said that the Incarnate Logos died only in his human reality, and if this is tacitly understood to mean that this death therefore did not affect God, only half the truth has been stated. The really Christian truth has been omitted. The immutable God in himself of course has no destiny and therefore no death. But he himself (and not just what is other than he) has a destiny, through the Incarnation in what is other than himself... In that case, however, this death of God in his being and becoming in what is other than himself, in the world, must clearly belong to the law of the history of the new and eternal covenant in which we have to live." /71/

A KENOTIC CHRISTOLOGY

For Rahner the possibility of change in God can only be perceived from within the trinitarian dimension of God. /72/ The real possibility is the becoming of the Son within the immanent Trinity and this constitutes the transcendental presupposition of change. /73/ Both Creation and Incarnation have their possibility within the immanent Trinity. For Rahner there is an intrinsic metaphysical connection between the processions "ad intra" and the processions "ad extra." /74/ Creation and Incarnation are understandable only in terms of their relation to the procession of the Word within the Godhead. /75/

With Urs von Balthasar, we have another form of kenotic Christology. /76/ Von Balthasar traces the self-surrender and the death of Christ back to the inner mystery of God himself and finds in the death of Jesus the fullness of the trinitarian relationship. Von Balthasar outlines his kenotic Christology in the context of an exegesis of Phil. 2. In the exegesis of Philippians 2, Von Balthasar accepts as proven that the subject who empties himself in taking the condition of a slave is not the Incarnated Christ but the eternal Logos. What the eternal Logos abandons is nothing else but the glory of the Father, which is his by right. In accepting kenosis seriously, we must admit an event happening within the immutable Godhead, a letting-go of an equality with God concerning the precious possession of glory. The theological problem in admitting this event lies in the reconciliation of this event within the Godhead and the doctrine of the Immutability of God. According to the Old Testament, God holds on to his glory and does not share it with anyone else. In this context the self-emptying is impossible to understand. This was the constant problem facing the older kenotic Christologies: they considered God's divine attributes in the framework of the Old Testament and located the Incarnation there. The event of self-emptying must be understood within the trinitarian context where the Divine Persons are considered in their processions, relations, and missions. The Old Testament God's unwillingness to let go of his glory is not characteristic of the Second Person who is so divinely free he can let go of his glory. This "letting go" on the part of the Second Person reflects on the Father - who does not hold on to his Son but gives him up "<u>tradere</u>." /77/

In the same way the Spirit is described as the "gift" of the two persons. What is essential here is our understanding of God. God is not primarily absolute power but absolute love, and his power manifests itself not in holding on to what is his, but in the letting go. The exteriorization of God in the Incarnation has its ontic possibility in the eternal exteriorization of God, in his tri-personal gift. The ultimate presupposition for the kenosis is the selflessness of the divine Persons as pure relations. This divine way of acting and being becomes for us also the accepted rule. We subsist and become not in ourselves but in the going out of ourselves. The concepts of poverty and richness are dialectical. The divine power is such that it can let go of itself. Christology must take seriously the fact that God, in his Son, has really suffered and died, while remaining fully God. Christology must begin with the Cross and must recognize as a divine law that "power comes to its full strength in weakness." (2 Cor. 12:9).

D. Problematics and New Directions in Kenotic Christology

It is not possible to deny that the 19th and early 20th century forms of kenotic Christology were inadequate. Therefore, it is understandable that for many theologians the kenotic Christologies received such devastating criticism that in their minds they could never be reinstated as viable models. Shocked by earlier and vulnerable forms of kenotic Christology, the theory was abandoned. Yet, recent contributions in Christologies have clearly indicated a renewed interest in kenotic Christology. It is my contention that many objections directed to earlier forms of kenotic Christology do not apply to contemporary expressions, and that, in fact, these contemporary expressions contain new developments in theology which make it possible to establish a new kenotic Christology that is faithful to the past tradition and meaningful for contemporary Christianity. One of the problems with the earlier kenotic Christologies and, for that matter, with most other Christologies was the fact that it was established on too narrow a basis. The only way in which a kenotic Christology can become intelligible is if it is perceived within the whole divine life and economy. A kenotic Christology must be rooted in the Trinitarian mystery; it must become evident in the creation and redemption of the world. Kenotic Christology not only must be rooted in this broad framework of God's mystery as he is in himself and as he is for us, but it must shed light on what the nature of God must be. A kenotic Christology must have real implications for a Christian view of life; as a theological model it should function as a transformation model. /78/ The self-emptying of God in the person of Jesus Christ is the model for human generosity and compassion.

One basic objection raised against the kenotic Christologies is its mythological appearance. In the New Testament, the kenotic motif is expressed through mythological thought forms. The conception of God is intensely personalistic and dynamic. God is understood as freely taking upon himself human suffering; he feels sorrow and joy, is moved to compassion and to anger. It would seem that to be able to express the truth about the Incarnation as a kenosis one is bound to tell a myth. In fact, according to G. MacGregor:

> "...every significant religious idea in human history has to be mythologically expressed. Why haggle at a mythological element in kenoticism? Consider only, for example, the eternal begetting of the Son, the coming down from heaven, the sitting at the right hand of the Father, the Spirit descending in tongues of fire and settling upon each of the apostles. Surely we were never meant to suppose that this Son of God came down from the sky or has gone thither to sit upon a throne adjacent to his Father's." /79/

A. Dulles writes: "In some sense the Incarnation is a myth. Like other myths, it is a tale that holds us in its grip because in some way its symbolism casts light upon the riddles of our life and enables us to deal creatively with forces that threaten to destroy us." /80/ Yet while expressed in metaphors and in mythological categories, kenosis has a meaning or a series of meanings that can be expressed in conceptual language forms and organized in a systematic way.

At Chalcedon the Incarnation was given a conceptual framework whose meaning is not obscure. Nevertheless, there is present in the minds of many theologians today that historically it has been impossible to unpack the concept of Incarnation. Every attempt to determine more specifically the idea that Jesus was both God and man has been broken down. It would seem more appropriate in this context to express a kenotic Christology in the framework of a model. /81/ This would imply the need to correlate doctrine and the existential involvement of the believer. It would also engender "humility and tentativeness in the claims made on behalf of any model." /82/ As David Tracy writes:

> "...theological models do not purport to provide exact pictures of the realities they disclose. Rather, theological models seem to disclose or represent the realities which they interpret... Theologies do not--or should not--claim to provide pictures of the realities they describe--God, humanity, and world; they can be shown to disclose such realities with varying degrees of adequacy." /83/

One of the reasons for the failure of the 19th century kenotic Christology was its determination to retain the traditional incarnational framework of Christology. This framework has recently been described as a Christology "from above." It is a Christology that orients itself first of all to the divinity of Jesus. Pannenberg writes: "For Christology that begins 'from above,' from the divinity of Jesus, the concept of the Incarnation stands in the center." /84/ In a Christology "from above" the doctrine of the Trinity is presupposed and the question posed is: how has the Second Person of the Trinity (the Logos) assumed a human nature./85/ Rahner described the Christology "from above" as "the metaphysical type." /86/ In this Christology "the pre-existence of the Logos," his divinity, his distinction from the Father, the predicate "Son of God" ascribed to the divine Logos as he who pre-exists in this Christology, are regarded as manifestly belonging to him from the first, and assumed more or less to be statements based upon the verbal assertions and convictions of Jesus himself. /87/

Macquarrie suggests what would seem to be a very important step for any contemporary focus of kenotic

Christology: the Incarnational framework "must emerge only at the end and must not be presupposed." /88/ Pannenberg had already made the point.

> "Methodological reasons (he affirms) do not permit us to work with the Incarnation as a theological presupposition. To do so would be to make the humanity of Jesus' life problematic from the very beginning. To be sure, all Christological considerations tend toward the idea of the Incarnation; it can, however, only constitute the end of Christology. If it is put instead at the beginning, all Christological concepts are given a mythological tone." /89/

What is being asked by Macquarrie and Pannenberg is a methodological shift, a Christology whose starting point is "from below." A Christology "from below" directs itself to the historical man, Jesus. According to Rahner, the starting point for a Christology "from below" "...is the simple experience of the man Jesus, and of the Resurrection in which his fate was brought to its conclusion." /90/ "...Jesus in his human lot is the (not a!) address of God to man, and as such, eschatologically unsurpassable." /91/ A Christology "from below" views the life, ministry, passion, death and resurrection of Jesus as an act of God's self-giving. The life of Jesus is the revelation of God's self-giving love. A Christology "from below" simply states that all Christological language must take its beginning in the historical Jesus; that this historical man, Jesus, is the criterion of Christology. The historical Jesus is the locus where one can learn to speak about God. Starting "from below" is not an attempt to prove the divinity of Jesus from his own history. In Jesus, there is a movement from above; from God to Jesus where Jesus is the receiver. The Resurrection is the expression of this movement.

One cannot begin Christology with a fully developed concept of God in himself and in his trinitarian life and then by some process, kenotic or other, "say how much the divine being can be brought within the limits of human existence." /92/ But we cannot avoid affirming the full divinity of the one whom we confess to be Lord. This should follow the full acceptance of Christ's humanity. The Jesus of history cannot be separated from the Christ of faith. The risen one is the one who died on the cross. According to Küng, "The resurrection adds no new revelation: it is the revelation of Jesus himself: He now acquires final credibility." /93/

In a kenotic Christology, starting "from below" means that it is the crucified, the suffering humanity of Jesus that is the locus of God's revelation and God's being. God is known to us in the complete human obedience of Christ, an obedience perfected in suffering. Our guiding idea must be that the historic life of Jesus is the revelation and the characteristic action of God, of God's love. God's love is not simply revealed through the words of Jesus but through action and deeds through a kenosis, a self-emptying which led to the Cross, a kenosis through which God put himself at man's side to suffer with him and for him--authentically as "fellow-sufferer." As St. Thomas wrote: "The love of God to men is shown not merely in the assumption of human nature for other men." /94/ And as Karl Barth once wrote: "In Jesus Christ...God activates and proves his Godhead by the fact that he gives himself to the suffering and limitation of the human creature." /95/

Macquarrie suggests that within this methodological shift, the eternal self-emptying of the Logos should be spoken of in the light of human self-emptying. "The theological value of this idea lies in the fact that it points to what is deepest both in man and in God and so in the God-man, Jesus Christ." /96/ We first experience and understand self-emptying in our own experience and we then encounter it as a unique depth in Christ and confess it as the manifestation and presence of God. /97/

> This is the paradox of personal existence, that emptying and fulfilling, <u>kenosis</u> and <u>plerosis</u>, are the same; and he who utterly emptied himself, Jesus Christ, is precisely the one who permits us to glimpse that utter fullness that we call divine. /98/

The kenosis of Christ is not a dimming down of the divine nature, a curtailment of it, but a positive expression of it, "the very expression of that nature at its deepest and most significant level." /99/ J. A. T. Robinson accepts kenosis in that form.

> "But if it is used, as I think the New Testament uses it, to show how a man, and an utterly humilited man, could nevertheless be the self-expression of the wisdom and the power, the freedom and the triumph, of the love that 'moves the sun and other stars,' then it provides a marvellously rich vein for theological exploration. For it declares that profound truth that 'the form of a servant' is not a derogation from or even a modification of the glory of God, but precisely the fullest expression of that glory as love. For of no other omnipotence than that of love could a man riveted in impotence be the supreme exemplification and chief declaration. Equally, 'the chief end of man,' his true glory, is by utterly generous obedience to be the transparency of that love, so that there is no 'inference,' and nothing of self gets in the way." /100/

One of the objections directed to kenotic Christology was that it tended to dominish the divinity of Christ in order that there be a true human life. The earlier forms of kenotic Christology affirm that Christ forgoes the divine being in some of its attributes, in order to become human. Chalcedon spoke of a fully divine and fully human nature in the one person of Jesus. Kenosis as understood here is not a negation of God's nature in Jesus Christ; it is the opposite; it is the revelation and affirmation of God's nature as Love. When we see in Christ God as a God for us, we really see him as he is. Kenosis is not a self-emptying in the form of a renunciation of the nature of God himself, but a self-emptying that is the very nature of God himself. Kenotic Christology affirms that there is a self-limitation at the heart of God and exalts humiliation as a primary dimension of God.

In a kenotic Christology there can be no a priori understanding of God - nor is there an a priori understanding of man. A Christology "from below" does not necessarily mean that Christological reflection necessarily begins with a priori anthropology. But it does mean that its point of departure is a humanity to which God is already present. The presupposition for thinking "from below" is the opennness of that "below" of historical existence in general to the divine "above." According to Pannenberg,

> "...the essence of man, like his salvation, the fulfillment of his destiny consists in openness for God. Openness for God is the real meaning of the fundamental structure of being human, which is designated as openness to the world in contemporary anthropology although this designation means an openness beyond the momentary horizon of the world. Man's question about his destiny expresses itself in this openness. Only when man lives in the openness of this question, when he is completely open towards God, does he find himself on the way leading towards his destiny." /101/

We have previously seen that the background for the original kenotic Christologies was the humanistic approach to Christology initiated by Schleiermacher. This direction led, according to many, to the abandonment of one of the poles of the mystery of the Incarnation, the transcendence of Christ. With Karl Rahner, we have a theologian who is willing to begin with Jesus Christ as a genuine historical fact which can be understood through human experience approached transcendentally.

> "We merely observe that anthropology and Christology mutually determine each other within Christian dogmatics if they are both correctly understood. Christian anthropology is only able to fulfill its whole purpose if it understands man as the *potentia obedientialis* for the "Hypostatic Union." And Christology can only be undertaken from the point of view of this kind of transcendental anthropology: for in order to say what the "Hypostatic Union" is without being suspected of merely reproducing no longer feasible "mythologies," the idea of the God-man needs proof of a transcendental orientation in man's being and history under grace. A purely *a posteriori* Christology, unable to integrate Christology into an evolutionary total view of the world, would not find it easy to dismiss the suspicion of propounding mythology." /102/

A KENOTIC CHRISTOLOGY

We cannot recognize who Christ is without knowing what it means to be human, nor can any knowledge of what it means to be human fail to be an incipient Christology. To approach a human experience "transcendentally" means in the realm of Christology to inquire into those conditions already given within man himself, which rendered the Christ-event possible at all.

> "Therefore, if one wishes to pursue dogmatics as transcendental anthropology, it means that whenever one is confronted with an object of dogma, one inquires as to the conditions necessary for it to be known by the theological subject, ascertaining that the *a priori* conditions for knowledge of the object are satisfied, and showing that they imply and express something about the object, the mode, method and limits of knowing it." /103/

Our kenotic Christology will begin "from below," from the transcendental nature of human personhood and suffering. It will then proceed to examine both phenomenologically and transcendentally Jesus' life and suffering. Our next step will be a theology of God as Personal Agent. It is in light of these different processes that our kenotic Christology will be developed.

KENOTIC CHRISTOLOGY: ITS HISTORY, PROBLEMATICS AND POSSIBILITIES

NOTES

1. C. Welch, ed., God and Incarnation in Mid-Nineteenth Century German Theology, (New York, 1965).

2. H. R. Mackintosh, The Doctrine of the Person of Jesus Christ, (London, 1912).

3. G. Thomasius, Christi Person und Werk, (Erlangen, 1853).

4. The translation of Thomasius's work is to be found in C. Welsh, op. cit., pp. 31-101.

5. Ibid., p. 61.

6. Ibid., p. 67; p. 71.

7. D. M. Baillie, God Was in Christ, (New York, 1948) pp. 94-98.

8. W. Pannenberg, Jesus - God and Man, (Philadelphia: Westminster Press, 1977) p. 310.

9. Cf. J. A. T. Robinson, The Human Face of God, (Philadelphia, 1973) pp. 206-209.

   P. Schoonenberg criticizes the kenotic Christology in the following way:

   > "To think along such lines sacrifices Christ's human person to the divine person - but the kenoticists refuse to do the reverse. The Logos as the Son remains the divine person who rids himself in freedom from his relative attributes, so that there is during the emptying still a divine person... For them, Jesus does not become a human person."

   The Christ, (New York: Herder & Herder, 1971) p. 77.

10. J. A. T. Robinson, op. cit., p. 206.

11. Ibid., p. 207.

12. J. Macquarrie, "Kenoticism Reconsidered," Theology 77 (1974) p. 116.

13. Ibid., p. 120.

14. Ibid., p. 121.

15. Cf. W. Pannenberg, Jesus - God and Man, (Philadelphia, 1968) pp. 310-313.

16. S. Kierkegaard, Training in Christianity, trans. W. Lowrie (Princeton, 1941) p. 131.

17. Ibid.

18. Cf. D. Dawe, The Form of a Servant, (Philadelphia, 1964) pp. 160-176.

19. Karl Barth, Church Dogmatics, tr. by G. W. Bromiley, (Edinburgh, 1956) Vol. IV, Part I, p. 211.

20. Cf. D. Dawe, op. cit., p. 166.

21. K. Barth, op. cit., pp. 203-204.

22. W. Pannenberg, op. cit., pp. 313-315.

23. W. Pannenberg, op. cit., p. 320.

24. Ibid., p. 319.

25. Ibid., p. 336.

26. Ibid.

27. Ibid., p. 339.

28. Ibid., p. 342.

29. D. Bonhoeffer, The Cost of Discipleship, (London, 1958); Ethics, (New York, 1965); Letters and Papers from Prison, (London, 1967).

30. D. Bonhoeffer, Letters, op. cit., p. 360.

31. Ibid., p. 210.

32. T. Altizer, W. Hamilton, Radical Theology and the Death of God, (Indianapolis, 1966) p. 135.

33. Ibid., p. 152.

34. Ibid., p. 154.

35. T. Altizer, The Gospel of Christian Atheism, (New York, 1966) p. 67.

36. T. Altizer, Radical Theology, op. cit., p. 134.

37. C. Duquoc, Christologie, L'Homme Jesus, (Paris, 1968), Vol. 1, pp. 329-336.

    Cf. also J. Richard, "La Kenose de Dieu dans Le Christ d'apres T. Altizer," Eglise et Theologie 2 (1971) pp. 207-228.

38. T. Altizer, The Gospel of Atheism, op. cit., p. 68.

39. J. Moltmann, The Crucified God, (New York, 1974) p. 206.

40. A. Losky, Theologie Mystique de L'Eglise d'Orient, (Paris, 1940) p. 140.

    For S. H. Bulgakov (1871-1948) kenosis is rooted in the inner life of the Trinity and is revealed in the creation and redemption of the world. He sees the inner life of the Trinity as an ongoing process of mutual self-giving and self-emptying between the divine Persons, the Trinity as a whole.

41. J. Moltmann, op. cit., p. 243.

42. Ibid., p. 4.

43. Ibid., p. 204.

44. Ibid., p. 205.

45. Ibid., p. 215.

46. Ibid., p. 245.

47. Ibid.

48. Ibid., p. 256.

49. Ibid.

50. Ibid., p. 230.

51. Ibid., p. 205.

52. Ibid.

53. Ibid., p. 227.

54. Cf. C. Duquoc, op. cit., pp. 177-186.

Traditional exegesis constantly affirms that kenosis involves no change in the divine nature of the Word. It is well summed up by Thomas Aquinas:

> "Because he was full of divinity, did he therefore empty himself of divinity? No, because what he was he remained, and what he was not he took... For as he came down from heaven, not because he ceased to be in heaven, but because he began to be in a new manner on earth, so also he emptied himself, not by laying down the divine nature, but by taking up human nature. Super Epistolas S. Pauli Lectura, Ad Phil., cap. 2, lec. 2 (Turin: Marietti, 1953, ii, 101).

55. H. Küng, Menschwerdung Gottes, (Freiburg, 1970). Cf. the following review: J. Fitzer, "Hegel and Incarnation, A Response to Hans Küng," Journal of Religion, 52 (1972) pp. 240-267.

56. Cf. E. L. Fackenheim, The Religious Dimension in Hegel's Thought, (Indiana, 1960); A. Leonard, La Foi Chez Hegel, (Paris, 1971); W. L. Shepherd, "Hegel as a Theologian," Harvard Theological Review XLI (1968) pp. 583-602; W. D. Marsch, "Logik des Kreuzes, Uber Sinn und Grenzen Einer Theologischen Berufung Auf Hegel," Evangelische Theologie XXVIII (1968) pp. 57-82.

57. H. Küng, op. cit., p. 524.

58. G. W. F. Hegel, The Phenomenology of Mind, tr. by J. Baillie, (London, 1955) p. 756.

59. G. W. F. Hegel, Lectures on the Philosophy of Religion, tr. E. B. Speirs, (London, 1895) p. 24.

60. H. Küng, op. cit., p. 353.

61. Ibid., Excursus 2, pp. 622-631; Excursus 4, pp. 637-646.

62. Ibid., p. 548.

63. Ibid., p. 552.

64. Ibid., p. 551.

65. H. Küng, op. cit., 648 ff.

66. K. Rahner, "On the Theology of the Incarnation," Theological Investigations Vol. IV, (Baltimore, 1966) pp. 114-115.

67. Ibid., p. 116.

68. Ibid., p. 117.

69. K. Rahner, "On the Theology of the Incarnation, op. cit., p. 114.

70. Ibid., p. 113.

71. Karl Rahner, Sacramentum Mundi II (London, 1969) p. 207.

72. Cf. Karl Rahner, "Trinity," in Encyclopedia of Theology, (New York, 1975) pp. 1758-1762.

73. Karl Rahner and Herbert Vorgrimler, Dictionary of Theology, (New York, 1965) p. 115.

74. Ibid.

75. W. Pannenberg has criticized Rahner's kenotic Christology as not being radical enough. For Rahner "the idea of self-emptying loses the radicality of self-relinquishment... If God remains the same, he is still God even in the deepest humiliation, and the question remains unsolved as to how he can at the same time and

in unity with his divinity be a man as we are... It will hardly suffice to speak only of a becoming 'in the other' as if an inner being of God were to be distinguished that remains completely untouched by such becoming." Jesus - God and Man, op. cit., p. 320.

76. Urs von Balthasar, Le Mystere Pascal, Coll. Mysterium Salutis, (Paris, 1972) pp. 13-275.

77. Cf. Jn. 19:11; Rm. 11:25.

78. For an extensive analysis of pertinent transformation-models cf. D. Browning, Generative Man, (Philadelphia: Westminster, 1961) pp. 105-126.

79. G. MacGregor, He Who Lets Us Be. A Theology of Love, (New York: Seabury Press, 1975) pp. 81-82.

80. A. Dulles, "Incarnation 1973," Commonweal Vol. XCIX, No. 13, (Dec. 28, 1973) p. 329.

81. J. McIntyre, The Shape of Christology, (Philadelphia, 1966); I. Barbour, Myths, Models and Paradigms, (New York, 1974); E. Cousins, "Models and the Future of Theology," Continuum 7 (1969) pp. 78-91.

82. I. Barbour, op. cit., p. 8.

83. D. Tracy, Blessed Rage for Order, (New York: Seabury Press, 1975) p. 22.

84. W. Pannenberg, op. cit., p. 33.

85. Ibid., pp. 33-34.

86. K. Rahner, "The Two Basic Types of Christology," Theological Investigations XIII (New York: Seabury Press, 1975) p. 216.

87. Ibid., p. 217.

88. J. Macquarrie, op. cit., p. 121.

89. W. Pannenberg, op. cit., p. 279. For a criticism of this position cf. J. Moltmann, op. cit., pp. 87-92.

90. K. Rahner, "The Two Basic Types of Christianity," op. cit., p. 215.

91. Ibid., p. 216.

92. J. Macquarrie, op. cit., p. 122.

93. H. Küng, _On Being a Christian_, (New York: Doubleday, 1966) p. 302.

94. Thomas Aquinas, _S. T._ III, Qu. 4, art. 5, ad. 2.

95. K. Barth, _Church Dogmatics_, Vol. IV, The Doctrine of Reconciliation, Part I, (London: T. & T. Clark, 1958) p. 134.

96. J. Macquarrie, op. cit., p. 121.

97. Cf. K. Kitamore, _Theology of the Pain of God_, (Richmond, 1965); J. Moltmann, op. cit., pp. 267-291.

98. J. Macquarrie, op. cit., p. 123.

99. Ibid.

100. J. A. T. Robinson, op. cit., p. 208.

101. W. Pannenberg, op. cit., p. 195.

102. K. Rahner, "Theology and Anthropology," _Theological Investigations_, Vol. XI, (New York, 1972) pp. 28-29.

103. Ibid.

CHAPTER 7

PERSON AND SUFFERING: KENOTIC ANTHROPOLOGY

A. Introduction

The renewal of kenotic Christology has been made possible by a radical shift in methodology. There is a commitment to begin Christology with concrete human experience approached transcendentally. To approach a human experience transcendentally means, in the realm of Christology, to inquire into those conditions already given within the human reality, which render the Christ-event possible at all. The inner logic of a kenotic Christology is dependent upon the possibility of locating transcendence in the act of human self-emptying and suffering. The eternal self-emptying of God can only be spoken of meaningfully in light of human self-emptying. The disclosive and revealing dimension of Jesus' life and death can only be perceived in light of the transcendent dimension of human self-emptying and suffering. There is a conviction here that we can understand the Christ-event kenotically only if we attentively re-evaluate the fundamental kenotic nature of human reality itself. Kenotic Christology needs to stand on the solid and concrete grounds of a kenotic anthropology, which examines both transcendentally and phenomenologically the realities of personhood and suffering.

B. Person as Agent

A contemporary author has attempted to show how the kenotic theme is found in the personality theories of such men as R. D. Laing and H. Fingarette. /1/ What some of these contemporaries are telling us is that human unfolding and becoming is a painful act. They are affirming the paradox that self-realization and self-divestment are mutually reinforcing. A more elaborate development of a kenotic concept of person is to be found in the works of John Macmurray. /2/

It is J. Macmurray's fundamental contention that a dialogical and act-centered understanding is the best way to interpret reality. To accept subjectivity as a starting point for dealing with reality is to implicitly destroy the bridge between subject and object, knower and known. Within the tradition inherited from Descartes, the self is pure subject considered in its moment of reflection while directing its activity to acquire knowledge. Descartes established a dichotomy between the self, constituted by thought, and the body, constituted by extension and understood in purely mechanical terms with the rest of the material universe. The self in reflection can withdraw into itself and into contemplation; it does not act nor does it involve itself with the life of the world which it perceives as object. For this reason, the traditional point of view is not only theoretical but also egocentric. The self in reflection knows the world but isolates itself from it. It thus insures that it will relate to the world only with its imagination and only as a spectator. The traditional theoretical view protects the self in reflection from the challenge, growth and change by providing it a habitation other than the real world. It provides for it the ideal world of the mind in which it need only to think, certain that the exercise of reason will automatically lead to truth. While the self remains the self in reflection, it also remains in a static and impersonal framework and as long as this framework is maintained, a dynamic relationship between the self and the other in the real world of real action will not only be unnecessary and undesirable but even impossible.

According to Macmurray, the adoption of the "I think" as the starting point of philosophy leads to atheism, /2/ to the impossibility of doing justice to religious experience. "For thought is inherently private; and any philosophy which takes its stand on the primacy of thought, which defines the Self as the Thinker, is committed formally to an extreme logical individualism. It is necessarily egocentric." /3/ But religious experience demands that God be seen as a "Thou," as an other who can be related to in a personal way. Otherwise, God becomes simply an object of thought, of understanding.

It is J. Macmurray's aim to leave aside Descartes's starting point and begin with the fact of existence and affirm that "to exist is to have a being which is independent of thought." /4/ To exist is not simply to be independent of thought but it is "to be part of the world in systematic causal relation with other parts of the world." /5/ In place of Descartes's <u>cogito</u>, J. Macmurray begins with the experience, concept, and phrase, "I do." The self is primarily conceived as agent, as doer. And, since primarily conceived as agent, as "doer," the subject is not isolated but in relation with others; not "I" alone, but "you" and "I." The idea of an isolated agent is self-contradictory. Any agent as agent is necessarily in relation to the other. Apart from this essential relation he does not exist. Further, the other in this constitutive relation must itself be personal. Persons, therefore, are constituted by their mutual relations to one another. /6/

If action is primary, thought is secondary, serving the ends of action. Thought is a derivative of experience. When the self is considered as person with action as the primary mode of being and thought included within it as the secondary and subordinate, the correlative of the person cannot be the material world, nor the organic world. For neither provides the necessary poles for an action which is constitutive of the person. In other words, the self as agent cannot exist in a personal sense in insolation. The personal is constituted by personal relatedness, but its relation to the other self. As a person, I begin to exist as one pole in the complex "you and I." According to Macmurray "...the unit of personal existence is not the individual but two persons in personal relations:...we are persons not by individual right, but in virtue of our relation to one another. The personal is constituted by personal relatedness. This unit of the personal is not the 'I,' but the 'you and I.'" /7/ The process of becoming a person is heterocentric and not egocentric. The center of interest and attention is the other and not oneself.

While the person's primary mode of being is that of agent, the person is also a subject. But as "subject" the person is separated from the other and withdraws into itself. In subjective withdrawal it is possible to see the other objectively. The person is doer and thinker, agent and subject, but the thinker's subjectivity arises as a consequence of an initial encounter and exists for the sake of action. There is a positive and negative dimension to the person. According to J. Macmurray, the form of the personal is conceived as a positive that contains and is constituted by its own negative. (Positive and negative can be understood here as formal and structural.)

The same self is at the same time both agent and subject. But its unity is neither substantial nor organic nor dialectic; it is personal. "The unity of the Self is neither a material nor an organic, but a personal unity. The logical form of such unity is one which represents a necessary unity of positive and negative modes. The Self is constituted in its capacity for self-negation. It must be represented as a positive which necessarily contains its own negative." /8/ The unity of the person is contrapletal. /9/

The action of the agent also involves two aspects: "I move" and "I know." Without knowing there is no action but mere happening or activity which are impersonal in character. Moving and knowing are contrapletal. It is not enough to say that the self is agent; one must say that the self is an intentional agent and, therefore, a thinking agent. The self that reflects and the self that acts is the same self; action and thought are contrasted modes of activity. But it does not follow that they have equal status in the being of the self. In thinking, the mind alone is active. In acting, the body indeed is active, but also the mind; action is not blind. When we turn from reflection to action we do not turn from consciousness to unconsciousness. Action is always intentional; the action of a person is the realization of an intention. /10/

Every action involves a transcending of the person's individuality to the other agent. As an agent, I transcend myself, my individuality in my action. At the same time, transcendence to the other is not my withdrawal from him/her into the inaccessible realm of individuality, but an action with him/her by which he/she knows me as a person in relation. Rationality and intentionality are the capacities for self-transcendence; i.e., the center of interest resides in another person.

By intention, however, I can isolate myself, and reduce the other to the impersonal. Within the relation with the other person which is constitutive of one's existence "...I can isolate myself from you in intention so that my relation to you becomes impersonal. In this event, I treat you as an object, refusing the personal relationship. This is always possible because the form of the personal involves its own negation. Impersonality is the negative aspect of the personal; since only a person can behave impersonally, just as only a subject can think objectively." /11/ Personal knowledge always involves a transcendence of self to the other.

"I can know another person only by entering into personal relation with him." /12/ To treat the other as an object is to treat oneself also objectively, impersonally. As Macmurray writes: "Since Self and Other are primary correlates, our determination of one of them must formally characterize the other also... How then is it possible for the Other to be known as non-personal? Only by a reduction of the concept of the Other which excludes part of its definition; only, that is to say, by a partial negation; only by downgrading the 'You' and the 'you and I' to the status of 'It.' If we do this, however, we necessarily reduce its correlate the 'I' in the same fashion." /13/

Since rationality is the capacity for self-transcendence and the action that is constitutive of the self is intentional, self-revelation is essential. "All knowledge of persons is by revelation - my knowledge of you depends not merely on what I do, but upon what you do; and if you refuse to reveal yourself to me, I cannot know you, however much I may wish to do so." /14/ Since the "I" and "You" are constituted by their relation, self-knowledge is only possible when I reveal myself to you. Self-revelation is primarily practical; it is a "giving of oneself away" in contrast with the "keeping of oneself to oneself." While self-revelation is primarily practical, action centered, it also demands communication. The basic condition for communication is language. Human language reveals that human subjectivity exists only in intersubjectivity in existence with another and for another. The form of the personal emerges as dialogical. /15/

The self as person is an intentional agent; his/her actions are the realization of intentions. Action can only be understood by reference to the intention of its author, of its agent. A distinction must be made between "what is done" and "what simply happens" between an action and event. /16/ "Actions are the realization of intentions; event, the effects of causes." /17/ For an event there is a cause and for an act there is a reason - "If we believe a change to be an event, and wish to understand it, we must ask, 'What caused it?'; if we think it an act, we have to ask, 'Who did it, and why did he do it?'" /18/ Since action is intended, the intender, the agent, while immanent in his action, necessarily transcends it. What has been done, the existent, is what has been determined, and the agent is the determinant. What the agent has determined is the past, but the agent transcends the past. "His reality as agent lies in his self-transcendence." /19/ The terms "transcendent" and "immanent" refer to the nature of persons as agents, and they are strictly correlative. Pure immanence, without transcendence is meaningless. "Whatever is transcendent is necessarily immanent; and immanence, in turn, implies transcendence." /20/

Because the person is an agent who acts intentionally, the person is characterized by freedom. To act is to determine intentionally. In action, the agent generates a past by actualizing intentionally a possibility. In a real way, to act is to determine the future. To be characterized by freedom is to be able to determine the future. To be free is the correlate of "I do." /21/ The other does not simply represent a limitation of freedom but its very condition. Freedom is really possible only in solidarity, in being free for others. The freedom of the subject is simply a potentiality; it depends for fulfillment on the encounter with free persons. The social dimension is essential to freedom.

C. Person as Person-With

While the person as agent is characterized by freedom, its development is dialogical. Development is interpersonal just as communication is interpersonal. Persons in relation are correlative and mutually evocative of each other. It is not the self which stands as the foundation of our life and thought, but self and other. Personal life and dignity emerge not in reflection of the self upon itself, not in isolation from the other, but in a collaborative movement acting and responding to the other. The uniqueness and identity of a person is not constituted by an abstract self-consciousness, but only the character and unity of his/her life history. The structure of our experience as human beings is such that it is dependent on the experience of what is other then ourselves. We really live in the other. Our dependence on what is not ourselves, is the core of our reality. Individual independence is not appropriate for persons. Macmurray, speaking about the dependence of the child or the mother writes: "If the 'terminus a quo' of the personal life is a helpless, total dependence on the Other, the 'terminus ad quem' is not independence, but the mutual interdependence of equals." /22/

We need one another to be ourselves. "This complete and unlimited dependence of each of us upon the other is the central and crucial fact of personal existence." /23/ Absolute autonomy, individual independence is but an illusion; the totally autonomous self is a nonentity. "It is only in relation to others that we exist as persons; we are invested with significance by others who have need of us; and borrow our reality from those who care for us. We live and move and have our being not in ourselves but in one another; and what rights or powers or freedom we possess are ours by the grace and favors of our fellows." /24/

The basic fact of our human condition is that we are servant to one another, which implies that each of us values all the others for themselves. No one outgrows dependence on others or being-for-others. This is why the capacity to love is fundamental to our becoming persons. The capacity to love is the capacity to place the other within the reality of self-existence in such a way that real modification occurs for each. In light of this one can say that the essence of the person is love. Hegel had already affirmed this: "It is in the nature or character of what we mean by personality or subject to abolish its isolation or separateness. In friendship and love, I give up my abstract personality and in this way win it back as concrete personality." /25/ Hegel considers the person as becoming concrete by entering into community with the other or by surrendering to the other. One becomes a person by loving oneself in the other. In the process of self-emptying the self is enriched and embodied in a genuine presence to others. The person is the bringing together of universality and particularity; and that is the realization of the essence of love. Love implies the possibility of eliminating distinction while keeping it.

There is a for-otherness that is constitutive of the person as person. The essence of human personhood is a being-there-for-others. It is the self turned toward others which finds fulfillment. The question of authentic self-hood turns on the question of love for neighbor. We are authentic selves only in direct proportion to our ability to be affected by and related to other selves. The substance-self of the classical tradition is at best an abstraction. I am the person I am precisely because of my relationship to this history, this family, these friends. I am a profoundly relative, not substantial, being. Whether I know it or not, I am the person I am because this friend, person, idea, have literally entered my life.

While for-otherness is constitutive of personhood so is from-otherness. The fact that we derive from others, that we live from others is fundamental. It is through being loved that we learn to love; we have to be given to in order to be able to give. /26/ The fact of derivation from others is fundamental to personhood and a breakdown in this basic from-otherness may lead to a radical breakdown of self. Since we are not autonomous or self-sufficient, we have to be given to in order simply to be. So interdependence is the basic structure and dynamic of personal existence. The interdependent life is made up of mutuality, exchange, and reciprocity. Interdependence is founded on kenosis.

D. Suffering

It is because personal existence is interdependent that suffering occurs. Suffering is the potential result of the malfunctioning of interdependence. Interdependence includes within itself the twofold possibilities of fulfillment or suffering.

Suffering in its widest sense means being acted upon. It means to bear, to undergo. There is a basic connotation of passivity as distinct from activity in suffering: "Receptivity" is essential to suffering./27/ Yet, while there is an essential dimension of passivity in suffering, there is also a great deal of activity. /28/ The contrast in suffering is not simply between activity and passivity. Suffering is not to be equated with evil. Although there is within us a tendency to equate suffering with evil, the two are different realities. It is easy to identify the two since suffering is directly or indirectly linked to all forms of evil. Suffering is the price we have to pay for our limitations, our finitude, while evil resides in the world. As L. Lavelle writes: "There is perhaps no evil in the world that does not bear some relationship to suffering; but evil is not to be identified with suffering; it is the will's attitude toward it that matters.

Sometimes the will lets itself be overcome by the suffering in question; sometimes it imposes it on others; and sometimes it accepts it in order to alleviate, enter and transcend it." /29/ While suffering should not be equated with evil, neither should it be equated with pain. /30/ Pain has a physical dimension to it that is not essential to suffering; while pain is endured passively, suffering involves an active role. One usually says, "I am in pain," while relative to suffering, one will say, "I suffer." In a sense pain concerns only a part of ourselves, but suffering involves the whole self, and can penetrate to its essence.

By suffering we mean an anguish which we experience not only as pressure to change, but as a threat to our composure, our integrity, and the fulfillment of our intentions. Suffering has the character of a threat to our self-direction and therefore implicitly to our being. It challenges our capacity to maintain ourselves and retain the poise of self-direction. In Heidegger's understanding, suffering has the aspect of a threat of non-being. Suffering is disclosive of our own radical contingency, of the fact that ultimately our situation is neither one of our own making nor under our control.

The major difference between pain and suffering is the basic existential dimension of suffering. As existential, suffering is always an interpersonal phenomenon. Even though we experience it as if it were totally within ourselves, both its locus and source are in relationship. However we construe it, suffering is always an interpersonal phenomenon. While pain is primarily related to the body and can be inflicted by things, suffering is personal, it is related to our personhood. We primarily suffer in our relation to others. Lavelle writes:

> "The possibility of suffering measures the intimacy and the intensity of the bonds which unite us to another being. We do not suffer in our relations with those who are indifferent. In fact, indifference in some sense protects us against suffering. When indifference ceases, our capacity for suffering returns, and it is proportionate to our interest in and our affection for one another. It emerges as soon as the bonds which unite us

to the other are threatened; it is then that the bonds of friendship testify to their existence and their depth."/31/

Suffering is the result of the breakdown of interdependence. Because suffering is essentially interpersonal, it therefore has a social dimension. That dimension of suffering has been called affliction. Affliction involves isolation, abandonment. The infant's most despairing cry is not the one he/she utters when he/she feels pain, but rather when he/she feels himself/herself abandoned, when he/she no longer sees familiar faces around, and when all contacts with the universe seem to be suddenly broken off. Affliction involves abandonment and degradation or the fear of it in some form or another. The degradation shows itself in the isolation that accompanies affliction. The lack of solidarity with the afflicted is a common phenomenon. The dimension of affliction is more fully understood when one realizes the significance of the ongoing quest for the esteem of others.

Because suffering is essentially interpersonal, it must be looked at from within the dimension of human freedom, from within the realm of the will. Seen independently of freedom it is an absurdity. Within the context of freedom, suffering can be given a meaning. As human beings, we are aware of the limitations of our existence, of the uniqueness and unrepeatability of our existence. This implies that the success or failure of one's existence is as unrecallable as existence itself. As great a threat to man and woman as death is the threat of a lived futility, of meaninglessness. Meaning transforms the whole person and gives a definite directedness to existence. Suffering as an interpersonal reality must be given meaning. Two basic questions must be asked about suffering: what causes suffering and how can it be eliminated? Both questions need to be asked simultaneously in order to avoid any form of masochism. Suffering always remains an attack on human life. It can never be glorified nor sought masochistically. Taken by itself suffering is meaningless. There is also a sharp distinction between suffering before which we stand powerless and meaningful suffering. Suffering can be so acute and so long lasting that the sufferer feels powerless to break away from it.

Here one experiences a total loss of freedom.

One's consciousness loses its resources and is thus greatly restricted. The prospect for the hopeless sufferer is nothingness; the future does not exist for such a suffering person. Certain forms of suffering are so radical that they lead to the abandonment of all hope, to the most extreme forms of apathy. As D. Soelle writes: "Feelings for others die: suffering isolates the person and he no longer cares about anyone but himself." /32/ In this condition, everything else becomes unessential; nothing really matters anymore. Death is most welcomed. Extreme suffering turns a person in on himself/herself completely; it destroys his/her ability to communicate.

Only the suffering that can be changed and from which we can learn is potentially meaningful. Potentially meaningful suffering is one that is not completely passive. What a person does when he/she suffers is the active dimension of suffering. It is in the doing that meaning can be given to suffering; and the doing is in the interpersonal realm. The doing involves the opening of the sufferer's horizons and the transcending of self to the other. /33/

Suffering leads an individual to reality. M. de Unamuno writes: "Suffering tells us that we exist; suffering tells us that the world in which we live exists..." /34/ In suffering a person reaches his/her extreme limit, the decisive question of personal identity, of the meaningfulness or futility of existence, of reality as a whole. Suffering proves to be the ongoing test of reality. Suffering challenges basic trust in reality and existence. It is through suffering that we begin to answer the question "Who am I?" The possibility of a heightened self-consciousness accompanies suffering. /35/ Lavelle writes about suffering: "It gives us an extraordinary intimacy with ourselves, it produces a form of introspection in which the spirit penetrates to the very roots of life, where it seems that suffering itself will be taken away. It deepens consciousness by emptying it of all the preoccupying and distracting objects that had hitherto sufficed to fill it." /36/

What is most important about the experience of suffering is that it leads one to the acceptance of self as limited and the other as other. It leads to the fundamental acceptance of interdependence of the for-otherness and from-otherness of personal existence. We do not experience directly the radical dimension of our finitude. What we experience directly are particular expressions of our finitude such as suffering, the death of someone else, the other's needs and our needs of them. We only become more aware of the radical dimension of limitedness after reflection upon these particular events. There is a movement from the particular to the universal, from the concrete to the more abstract; from the immediate and specific experiences, the individual person universalizes about his/her total situation.

E. Suffering and Self-transcendence

Suffering leads to reflection upon the deepest dimension and depth of our existence. And because of its interpersonal dimension it can reveal not only our finitude but also the dialogical nature of our existence. Suffering can be an experience of self-transcendence and as such discloses to us the deepest dimension of our existence, its communal dimension supported essentially by love. Victor Frankl wrote, in describing his experience in a Nazi concentration camp: "In a position of utter desolation, when man cannot express himself in positive action, when his only achievement may consist in enduring his suffering in the right way - an honourable way - in such a position man can, through loving contemplation of the image he carries of his beloved, achieve fulfillment." /37/ As G. Marcel writes: "A complete and concrete knowledge of oneself cannot be egocentric; however paradoxical it may seem I should prefer to say that it must be hetero-centric. The fact is that we can understand ourselves by starting from the other, or from others, and only by starting from them." /38/ Suffering can lead to a discerning of the vicariousness of interpersonal existence. Since suffering is basically caused by the breakdown of interdependence, that interdependence may be restored vicariously by someone not responsible for the original breakdown. And this is because vicariousness is a fundamental characteristic of interdependence. Personal life is vicarious in that it involves living from and for others. Vicariousness is not something esoteric but the fundamental principle of all personal life. When interdependence has been broken and affliction and alienation have resulted, the breakdown can be remedied by someone not involved in the original breakdown. Interdependence is broken by self-centering. Vicariousness involves self-giving. Vicarious suffering is but one category of the larger and more general principle of vicariousness. It does not stand alone but presupposes the give and take of ordinary relatedness.

The acceptance of fundamental interdependence is a basic ingredient of love. To love is to accept one's dependence upon the other. To love is also to accept another who makes his/her own decisions. In loving one makes the history of another's freedom one's own history. The refusal to accept the other's freedom to be and to decide is a failure in love. The most profound level of love is the acceptance of the other without regard for one's own well-being; this demands a radical self-emptying. Here love and suffering coinhere. Interdependence that is abused is traumatic and leads to suffering. It is the cessation of self-giving which leads to the breakdown of interdependence. The restoration of interdependence involves the restoration of self-giving.

F. Compassion

Accepted suffering leads one out of oneself towards the other. It invokes love and compassion; it implies growth in self. It ultimately brings about real communion, solidarity. It can occasion the beginning of a new life where isolation is removed. Life comes forth from the fellowship of the suffering. Out of compassion for one another love becomes flesh. Those who come together in mutual vulnerability in authentic compassion become one body and are strengthened by a new force. M. de Unamuno writes: "For men love one another with a spiritual love only when they have suffered the same sorrow together, when through long days they have ploughed the stony ground bowed beneath the common yoke of a common grief." /39/ Solidarity with the suffering other leads to a compassion and to the elimination of isolation of those who suffer more than us.

There is no love without compassion. The compassionate manifests his/her human solidarity by crying out with those who suffer, by feeling deeply the wound of the other. Compassion invokes the consciousness and awareness of the oneness of the human race, the knowledge that all people, wherever they dwell in time and space, are bound together by the same human condition. This is the meaning of the statement: "Nothing human is foreign to me." P. Ricoeur writes: "My humanity is my essential community with all that is human outside myself; that community makes every man my like." /40/ The sense of self here is not based on an understanding of how and where we differ, but on being the same. Personal identity is found in the common experience of being human, in compassion, in suffering with others, in real love. Compassion does not lead to commiseration, to mutual despair, but to comfort, to being strong with the other. /41/

Shared suffering has the potency to create communities of understanding and mutuality. Shared suffering is possible if suffering has been given meaning and if it is communicated to and heard by the other. The sharing must occur in some form of dialogue, through communication. Language as sign has an ontological as well as a descriptive purpose. It extends our vision of reality and initiates a process of fuller realization of self. Processes of self-understanding and self-realization are intertwined. Self-realization can be realized even when the context of self-understanding is obscured. The escape from meaninglessness is achievable through the transcendence of the act of dialogue. The importance of the dialogue is that it brings into consciousness a sense of the actuality of suffering and reveals possibilities that interact in the future determination of that actuality. Dialogue introduces additional possibilities for the determination of the deeper understanding. In dialogue there is a reaching out for a plenitude of meaning in suffering. The phase of dialogue cannot be skipped as it if were possible to do away immediately with the suffering. Without dialogue there can be no change; causes of suffering can be eliminated from the outside, but not suffering, since it is by essence interpersonal. In dialogue the sufferer finds solidarity, and solidarity is already a victory over suffering. /42/

This solidarity is not simply a present reality. There is an historical dimension to it. While solidarity constitutes an ongoing community of interpretation, it is also constitutive of an historical community of interpretation which transmits present interpretation to future generations. Past sufferings are not remedies for themselves but give the ongoing community new hope in the present and for the future. Past memories are not simply recalled but they are re-interpreted, reconceived, accepted and lived and within the present. J. B. Metz speaks of this memory as a dangerous and liberating memory. /43/

G. Conclusion: Personhood, Suffering and the Idea of God

The realities of personhood and suffering disclose a dimension of transcendence, transcendence to the other. They reveal the openness of all human existence, radical finitude and yet transcendence. Personhood and suffering pose the fundamental question about the existence of meaning, about ultimate reality. While the experience of personhood and suffering is not necessarily religious, it can be disclosive of a religious dimension of our existence. Not only are they a source of self-understanding but also a way to the discovery of God.

According to de Unamuno, "...suffering has its degrees, according to the depth of its penetration, from the suffering that floats upon the sea of appearances to the eternal anguish, the source of the tragic sense of life, which seeks a habitation in the depth of the eternal and there awakens consolation; from the physical suffering that contorts our bodies to the religious anguish that flings us upon the bosom of God, there to be watered by the divine tears." /44/ Suffer- is a fundamental experience that awakens us to our own mystery and to the mystery of God. From the standpoint of the Bible it is the experience of suffering which turns individuals to God. "...in their distress they seek me..." (Hos. 5:15) "Before I was afflicted I went astray; but now I keep your word (Ps. 119:67).

It is primarily in connection with questions about human suffering and limitation that speech about God and another world emerged and has been used. According to G. Kaufmann: "Such speech appears, within the context of man's sense of limitation, finitude, guilt and sin, on the one hand, and his (man's) question about the meaning or value or significance of himself, his life, and his world, on the other." /45/ Again Kaufmann writes: "If there were no experiences within the world which brought us in this way up against the limit of our world - then there would be no justification whatsoever for the use of God-language." /46/

PERSON AND SUFFERING: KENOTIC ANTHROPOLOGY

In the context of a limit situation, the idea of God functions as a limiting concept, a concept that does not necessarily have a context in its own right, but refers to a reality not fully known in itself yet apprehended as the ultimate limit of our experience. God is the symbol here for our unending capacity to love.

E. Becker writes: "The person reaches out naturally for a self beyond his own self in order to know who he is at all, in order to feel that he belongs in the universe." /47/ While Freud thought that man's search for God was based on everything that was immature and selfish in man (fear, helplessness, greed), Otto Rank, in Becker's view, "...understood that the idea of God has never been a single reflex of superstition and selfish fear as cynics and realists have claimed. Instead it is an outgrowth of genuine life - language, a reaching-out for a plenitude of meaning." /48/

NOTES

1. J. M. Laporte, "Kenosis: Old and New," The Ecumenist, Vol. 12, No. 2 (1974) pp. 17-21.

2. J. Macmurray, The Form of the Personal, Vol. 1: The Self as Agent, (London: Faber, 1957); The Form of the Personal, Vol. 2: Persons in Relation, (London: Faber, 1961).

   There are several other important works:

   Reason and Emotion, (London: Faber, 1935);
   The Structure of Religious Experience, (London: 1936);
   Religion, Art and Science, (Loverpool: Liverpool University Press, 1961).

   For a complete bibliography of J. Macmurray's work consult: T. E. Wren, ed., The Personal Universe. Essays in Honor of John Macmurray, (Atlantic Highlands: Humanities Press, 1975) pp. 109-111.

   Cf. C. Davis, Body as Spirit, (New York: Seabury Press, 1976) pp. 78-97.

3. J. Macmurray, The Self as Agent, op. cit., p. 71.

4. J. Macmurray, Persons in Relation, op. cit., p. 80.

5. Ibid.

6. Ibid., 24

7. Ibid., 61.

8. J. Macmurray, The Self as Agent, op. cit., p. 98.

9. In a dialectic the word "contraplete" is used to refer to one or both of the original terms suggesting that the terms stand in some sense over each against each other, yet need each for a statement of the complete truth. Cf. John W. Buckman, "Contrapletion: The Values of Synthetic Dialectic," The Personalist Vol. XXVI (1945) pp. 353-366.

10. Cf. J. Macmurray, Persons in Relation, op. cit., p. 79.

11. Ibid., p. 28.

12. Ibid.

13. Ibid., p. 80.

14. Ibid., p. 169.

15. The identity of a person is relational; it is constituted through interaction with speaking and thinking subjects. Self-identity is mediated through symbolic systems, like language and culture. The attainment of I-dentity involves socio-linguistic competence.

16. Cf. J. Macmurray, Persons in Relation, op. cit., p. 221.

17. Ibid., p. 221.

18. J. Macmurray, The Self as Agent, p. 148.

19. J. Macmurray, Persons in Relation, op. cit., p. 223.

20. Ibid., p. 223.

21. J. Macmurray, The Self as Agent, op. cit., p. 134.

22. J. Macmurray, Persons in Relation, op. cit., p. 66.

An analysis of human nature which presupposes the primacy of action rather than of reflection shows that the secular concept of man and woman as autonomous could hardly be further from the truth. Individual independence is not appropriate for persons.

When J. Macmurray discusses Freud's view of religion he agrees that Freud's primary assertion - that religion is a development of the child's experience of family life - must be accepted. But the conclusion that religion is therefore illusory so that the acknowledgement of continuing dependence on God as Father should be outgrown

by "man come of age" is quite false. Macmurray writes: "We have seen that the form of the child's experience is dependency on a personal Other, and that this form of experience is never outgrown, but provides the ground plan of all personal experience, which is constituted from start to finish by the relation to the Other and communication with the Other. It is this form which finds expression in religion, no doubt, but there is nothing illusory about this. The adult who endeavors to create or discover, in the context of mature experience, the form of positive personal relationship which he experienced as a child, is not indulging in phantasy, but seeking to realize his own nature as a person. Phantasy as Freud recognized is the result of a failure to grow up properly...the wish to destroy the father and take his place is one of the common phantasies of childhood. Would it be as good an argument as Freud's then if we were to conclude that adult atheism was the projection upon the universe of this childish phantasy?"
Persons in Relation, pp. 154 ff.

23. J. Macmurray, Persons in Relation, op. cit., p. 211.

24. Ibid.

25. G. W. F. Hegel, Lectures on the Philosophy of Religion, Vol. 3, (London: 1932) pp. 24-25.

26. Cf. E. Moberly, Suffering: Innocent and Guilty, (SPCK, 1978).

27. P. Ricoeur, Fallible Man, trans. C. Kelbley, (Chicago: Henry Regnery, 1967) p. 27.

28. Ibid., p. 196.

29. L. Lavelle, Evil and Suffering, trans. B. Murchland, (New York: Macmillan, 1963) p. 32.

30. B. Wolf, Living with Pain, (New York: Seabury Press, 1978).
F. J. J. Buytendijk, Pain and Experience, (Chicago: University of Chicago Press, 1962).

W. J. De Sauvage Nolting, "The Meaning of Suffering," Existential Psychology VI: xxviii (1970) pp. 75-86.

31. L. Lavelle, op. cit., p. 65.

32. Cf. D. Soelle, Suffering, trans. E. R. Kalin, (Philadelphia: Fortress, 1973) p. 68.

33. All suffering, even the potentially meaningful, seems to have certain characteristics which the individual alone can experience. "You cannot imagine how I suffer or the nature of my suffering."

Suffering is seen by many of us as a very solitary act. In a very definite way we are alone in our suffering. Lavelle writes: "The existence revealed to me in suffering is that of the individual self in its unique and most privileged aspect, at the moment when it ceases to communicate with the world which is now felt as an oppression that turns the self back upon itself." Op. cit., p. 61.

34. M. de Unamuno, Tragic Sense of Life, trans. T. E. Crawford Flitch, (New York: Dover Publications, 1954) p. 207.

35. Psychiatrists are astonished at the amount of suffering people will bear unnecessarily. We cling to our suffering as guaranteeing our identity. Our sufferings are ourselves. The self wants to hold on to anything which makes self-recognition possible rather than move toward an unknown experience. This is pathological and a misunderstanding of the real nature of self-identity. Suffering is both an identification of present being and the possibility of becoming. And both of these dimensions are simultaneously necessary.

36. L. Lavelle, op. cit., p. 33.

37. V. Frankl, Man's Search for Meaning, (New York: Washington Square Press, 1963) pp. 58-59.

38. G. Marcel, The Mystery of Being, (Chicago: Regency Press, 1951) p. 28.

39. M. de Unamuno, op. cit., p. 135.

40. P. Ricoeur, op. cit., p. 93.

41. Ibid., p. 42.

42. H. G. Gadamer writes: "...Language has its true being only in conversation, in the exercise of understanding between people. The process of communication is not a mere action, a purposeful activity, a setting-up-of-signs through which I transmit my will to others... It is a living process in which a community of life is lived out ... All forms of human community of life are forms of linguistic community; even more they constitute language. For language in its nature is the language of conversation, but it acquires its reality only in the process of communicating." In Truth and Method, (New York: Seabury Press, 1975) p. 404.

43. Cf. J. B. Metz, Faith in History and Society, (New York: Seabury Press, 1980) pp. 88-136.

44. de Unamuno, op. cit., p. 205.

45. G. Kaufmann, "On the Meaning of God: Transcendence Without Mythology," in H. Richardson and D. Cutler, Transcendence, (Boston: Beacon Press, 1969) p. 118.

46. Ibid., p. 120.

47. E. Becker, op. cit., p. 152.

48. Ibid., p. 153.

CHAPTER 8

THE SUFFERING HUMANITY OF JESUS CHRIST. KENOSIS AND CROSS

A. Introduction: Humanhood and Transcendence

A kenotic Christology is not viable unless there occurs a shift in process: its starting point is not "from above," but "from below." A Christology "from below" directs itself to the historical man Jesus; it views the life, ministry, passion, death and resurrection of Jesus as the locus for the revelation of God's self-giving love. What is being affirmed in a Christology "from below" is that God as God is revealed in Jesus as human, from the manner of "his being-human." The true face of God is unveiled in the human face of Jesus. A Christology "from below" poses in a unique way the basic question about the nature of human transcendence which is also the question about human nature, about what it means to be human.

While Jesus' humanity in its concreteness is unique, it is not essentially different from our humanity. While one should not approach Jesus' humanity with an a priori anthropology, it is not possible to abstract from what we know about authentic humanity. In order to understand Jesus' humanity and to discover what is deepest and most revealing of God, it is necessary that we understand what is deepest in our own humanity; the question of human transcendence must be posed. In accepting in faith God's radical salvific presence in Jesus, we cannot simply affirm our own idea of what humanity is as a norm and criterion for Jesus' own humanity. We must approach Jesus' humanity with openness, as a possible revelation about our own human nature. As Schillebeeckx writes: "Going to Jesus in order to find in him salvation is to approach him in a state of ignorance, or better, of 'open knowledge,' of what 'being man' properly means." /1/ This does not mean that our previous knowledge of what it means to be human is unnecessary. A grasp of the basic universal structure of humanhood can serve as a point of encounter between Jesus Christ and ourselves. In some way Jesus' uniqueness can only be grasped fully when such fundamental and universal structures have been understood.

The fundamental structure of humanhood is that of transcendence and radical openness. This becomes evident in two fundamental dimensions of human reality - that of personhood and suffering. We detect here the basic nature of human transcendence as that of interdependent solidarity and radical co-existence, the essential necessity of the "other" for the "significant other." Human existence as personal is an "existence-through-others." Human essence as destined for the other, is disclosed concretely in his/her "yes" to the other. The execution of this "yes" is fundamentally through an act of love. This love is the acceptance, the intending and supporting and fostering of the other's personhood. The execution of love, of "being-for the other," and "having-to-be-for-the-other" is the expression of authentic humanhood. Interdependence is the fabric of human existence.

B. The Paschal Mystery

It would be surprising if such a disclosure would not be perceived in Jesus. Christian faith claims that Jesus is unconditionally grounded in God. This unconditional grounding must be revealed in Jesus' life and death. The question then arises: in what way is the transcendent grounding of Jesus' human life manifested; what does this mean for Jesus' mode of being human? The other question that needs to be asked is: what does Jesus' humanity reveal about God's being as God?

The core of the early Church's kerygma is the Paschal Mystery, "that Christ died for our sins in accordance with the Scripture, that he was raised on the third day." /2/ The Paschal Mystery is also the core of a kenotic Christology. The term pascho, from which the term Paschal originates, means basically to experience something "which comes from without and which has to be suffered." /3/ In the Gospels we find two kinds of reference to pascho as regards Christ, one to the "death" of Jesus (Lk. 22:15; 24; 26; 46) and the other to his suffering in general, though not exclusive of death.

It is interesting to note that out of the thirteen usages of the word pascho or pathein in the Synoptic Gospels, seven are in the gospel section of the three predictions of the Passion and Resurrection which are interpretations of the meaning of the Passion for Jesus and his disciples. The Paschal Mystery is one of life and death and resurrection, but the emphasis is on the crucified Jesus.

C. The Centrality of the Cross

Paul, in the last two chapters of I Corinthians, argues that the Cross cannot be understood as one theologumenon among others which can be leveled into a chain of saving events, but rather as the center and horizon of theology as a whole: "I decided to know nothing among you except Jesus Christ and him crucified." /4/

To understand the primacy of the Cross in the Paschal mystery it is important to realize that after the initial theology of the Resurrection and the experience of the Spirit, the early Church returned to the earthly Jesus and his death on the Cross. According to Moltmann, it was this reaching back that gave rise "...to the new literary category of a gospel, in the synoptic sense." /5/

In fact, coming to terms with the Cross was a question of life and death for the early Church. At a very early stage the Church tried to proclaim the scandalous Cross as God's will and God's deed. They first did so by way of Scriptural proof "in accordance with the Scriptures." /6/ The Cross is not an absurdity but God's decree and will. God's command of events is stressed, and it is felt as an enigmatic and harsh necessity. The first prophecy in Mark (8:27) speaks of a "must" (dei) in relation to the Passion of Jesus. "The Son of Man must suffer many things and be rejected." The verb dei expresses a necessity, a must which an event has, without, however, specifying the reason for it. The reason can only be inferred from the relation this event has with the power which lies behind the necessity. In the Synoptics and especially in Luke, the term dei is often used to express the will of God. This will is a salvific will; in this context, the Passion and death of Christ are seen as having their basis and origin in the saving will and plan of God.

The New Testament underlines the voluntary dimension of Jesus' death, his self-surrender. /7/ The epistle to the Hebrews presents Jesus as pleading to be spared death (5:7) but his voluntary acceptance of it was included in his own career, as fidelity to God the Father. Jesus' death is represented by the authors of the New Testament as the action where he comes to the uttermost limits of his obedience to his vocation. According to P. Schoonenberg:

> "Only when the opposition grows and these opponents develop a truly deadly hatred of him, there dawns upon him the significance of the violent death which awaits him. Now he recognizes from these circumstances that his Father's will for him is to fulfill the function of the Servant of Yahweh to the end, to die in order to bring the many to righteousness. Thus his horizon broadens out from the lost sheep of Israel to Jew and Gentile, and his mission develops from that of a prophet proclaiming salvation to that of victim bringing salvation." /8/

While there are certain affirmations that could be challenged here, the fact that Jesus re-understood his mission, faced it and accepted it is what the New Testament writers witness to. Jesus' death is not the surprise ending but the capstone of a career. In his own career, in his fidelity to Father, his voluntary acceptance of the Cross is included.

We must not view Jesus' death on the Cross as something which overtakes him extrinsically, either at the hands of men or by the hands of God. Jesus' death was necessary but not as having been chosen by God as one of several options for our redemption. In his message and in his very person, Jesus was a threat both to the Jewish leaders and the Roman authorities. Jesus' death was necessary because his life was one of complete dedication to the Father and to the oppressed. As Dorothy Sölle put it: it is not that love requires the Cross, but _de facto_, it ends up on the Cross. /9/ It is not that the Father needs the suffering of Jesus; the Cross is above all a symbol of reality. In this world, it is the necessary end to a life of free, total self-abandonment to the Father in the love of mankind.

In the past there has been an ongoing tendency to isolate the Cross from the rest of Jesus' ministry. According to V. Harvey, "...the Cross at once symbolizes

God's sovereignty, which appears as weakness in the eyes of men, as well as the cruciform character of Jesus' ministry." /10/ The isolation that occurred can be traced to the interpretation of Jesus' death as a foreordained event and to an overemphasis on its nature as a necessary vicarious sacrifice for sin. The Cross must not be understood in isolation but in connection with Jesus' earthly ministry. The Cross can be rightly interpreted only in the context of all that Jesus said and did before his death. The saving significance of this particular death can be understood only from the significance of the particular life that preceded it of which it is the final act. The Cross can be rightly interpreted only in the context of the total event of Jesus' history. Jesus' whole life is the interpretation of his death. The death was the end-product of the radicalization of his message and his life-style; his pro-existence (his being-for-the-other) and his unconditional obedience to God's will.

D. The Redemptive Meaning of Jesus' Death

According to Rahner, because man is a union of nature and person, death has two dimensions, a personal and a natural one. /11/ Because man and woman always appear within a spatio-temporal world, over which he/she has no absolute control, his/her death will always have a natural aspect. Death is something which happens to us. Biologically, the human organism wears out. It weakens and collapses, or it is destroyed. In its personal aspect, death is something active and performed, not simply passive and suffered. Because a person is free, he/she has the ability to dispose of himself/herself. In its personal aspect, then, death can be the culmination of a personal history of freedom. As a person, one can assume a stance at the end of one's journey, a stance of acceptance or of rejection.

But because of the limited nature of human existence, death always has an ambiguous character; even though death remains outside the realm of control in its natural aspect, in its personal dimension, it can be the free disposition of a person. /12/ Jesus' death as a human death has a natural and personal dimension. It also has an ambiguous character. On one level it remains outside the realm of his control and manifests Jesus' helplessness and powerlessness. Jesus was done violence to; he was killed on the Cross. /13/ But there is a personal dimension to this death. Jesus' life, his twofold solidarity with the Father and with the outcasts led to his condemnation. Precisely because of his double solidarity, Jesus was condemned and executed. Jesus' self-identity had to offend both the religious and political leaders. Jesus' life was one of dedication to the Father and dedication to the neighbor. /14/ His life was one of self-outpouring; his death is the definitive act of this self-outpouring. Christ in freedom pours himself out in loving surrender to the Father and in solidarity with the outcasts, even to death on the Cross. /15/

Jesus' death is his final act of obedience, whereby he acknowledges the rule of God and establishes the right relationship between God and man, the relationship of Creator and creature, of Father and Son, of word of God and word of faith. Jesus' obedience acknowledges God to be creator and man to be creature. Obedience is the sign of regained creaturehood, of regained humanity. It is an expression of radical interdependence. Käsemann regards obedience as the central motif in Paul's theology of the Cross. /16/ Paul designates Jesus as the obedient one, because by his death he restores man to the righteousness of true obedience - an obedience that acknowledges God to be Creator and man to be creature, a creature who renounces all pious and rebellious attempts at self-salvation. For in Paul, obedience is the sign of a humanity re-established in the proper order. For Paul, Jesus' life and death are expressions of his obedience.

The radical obedience of Jesus to his Father which led him to his death on the Cross expresses not only who he is but also manifests the radical integrity of his life to the extent that he was killed for being who he was. Jesus' solidarity with the Father, expressed in his obedience, and his solidarity with the outcasts, the rejected, manifested by his concern and care for them, constitute his self-identity, his personhood. Here Jesus' cause and mission and his personal identity are one.

The redemptive and salvific interpretation of Jesus' death has its foundation in Jesus' life and message and death. The atoning effect rested upon his willingness to give his life in solidarity with God's salvific purpose and human suffering. While Paul and Hebrews see Jesus' death and resurrection as being redemptive, the redemptive force of Jesus' death and resurrection lies in his solidarity of love. Here the redemptive dimension of Jesus' suffering does not lie with the negativity of death as such but with the positiveness with which it is accepted. In a sense redemption occurs not "because" of Jesus' death but despite it.

In the same way that we can discern some basic elements of Jesus' own message in the Gospel, there are also present in that message some clues on how Jesus understood the implication of his message and mission for his own destiny. Jesus was among his disciples as one who serves. /17/ Love of the neighbor, of the enemy, living for others, is the way Jesus preached and lived. A life such as this is one of radical poverty; /18/ it involves being prepared for anything; it demands leaving everything, /19/ even one's own life. /20/

Jesus' death, be it political or religious, is not at all in contradiction to the rest of his life, to what we can discern from that life, and from his message. Unless we are willing to separate radically the order of acting from knowing, we somehow must affirm that Jesus accepts knowingly his own death; not necessarily as universally redemptive, but as essentially in line with his mission and total dedication to the Father. It is not a question of having Jesus seek his own death as a violent death. Accepting his death was simply another form of self-surrender, self-gift.

E. The Implicit Soteriology in Jesus' Life and Death

There is an implicit soteriology in the life, ministry, and message of Jesus. A totally unintended death would simply imply that a meaningless death is given meaning totally from outside, from God. It would mean that Jesus' death is simply chosen by God as redemptive. Another important element here is the kind of death Jesus accepted as his. The Pauline and deutero-Pauline letters speak in a particular, even technical, way of Jesus' death as being a death on the cross and not simply any kind of death. This aspect is seen in Phil.

2:6-11 where Paul adds to the hymn the gloss "even death on the cross." The gloss underlines the extraordinary dimension of Jesus' suffering and death, the dimension of rejection. Crucifixion was a form of death reserved for criminals and sinners. This is emphasized in Galatians 3:13. The Old Testament considers anyone who was crucified as under a curse and excluded from a covenantal community with God. We have here the criminal dimension of the death on the cross and the forsakenness by God. The crucified one died "outside the camp" /21/ and was reckoned with transgressors. /22/ According to Pannenberg, Jesus "died as one expelled, expelled by the entire weight of the legitimate authority of the divine law, excluded from God in whose nearness he had known himself to be in a unique way the messenger of the immanent kingdom of God." /23/ While suffering can be celebrated and admired and bring about compassion, rejection in the words of Moltmann "takes away the dignity from suffering and makes it dishonourable suffering." /24/ To have suffered and died on the cross meant rejection for Jesus. D. Bonhoeffer writes: "In the Passion, Jesus is a rejected Messiah. His rejection robs the Passion of its glory." /25/ This rejection is expressed by the word paradidonai, to be delivered up. Jesus is to be "delivered up" in the hands of sinners. /26/ This "being-delivered-up" is also attributed to the Father. /27/ This last dimension of Jesus' rejection is the most mysterious and radical one. /28/ Jesus suffered and died alone. /29/

In the earliest Passion narrative, Jesus' death is reported without any embellishments: "Then Jesus uttered a loud cry and expired." /30/ This cry, which is an expression of fear before death, is later on toned down. Luke adds the words "Into thy hands I commend my spirit," /31/ and John, "It is consummated." /32/ The words, as recorded by Matthew and Mark, seem nearer to the reality: "My God, my God, why have you forsaken me?" /33/ Jesus' cry of God-forsakenness is undoubtedly both the literary and historical climax of the Passion narratives. The quote from Psalm 22:1 is an expression of deep anguish. It is a cry that sums up the entire crucifixion event. It expresses the agony, despair, estrangement and isolation of death. It is the quintessence of the event of death itself, insofar as death is an experience undergone by man. The cry is an appeal to God; it implies that death is not simply accepted patiently, but endured. The cry described the starkness and darkness of Jesus' death. There is no mention of serenity, of superiority. Jesus offers no remedy for death in his cry from the cross. The man who saw his relation to God as one of closeness and his mission as that of proclaiming this closeness dies without apparent ratification from his God.

As L. Keck writes: "By sundown all three men on their crosses were equally dead. The God who, according to Jesus, sends sun and rain on the just and unjust alike did not give Jesus preferential treatment either. Jesus dies without a word or a wink from God to reassure him that, whatever the gawking crowd might think, he knew that Jesus was not only innocent but valid where it mattered." /34/

Jesus' death on the cross appears as an alienation from men and women and from God. It is important here, in order to understand the full symbolism of the cross, to realize how death is understood in the Old Testament. /35/ Schillebeeckx writes:

> "However, this religious insight into the connection between living communion with God and life after death had a long history in Judaism. In a religious, and above all Jewish, religious understanding of _life_, death is not merely a departure from the earthly sphere of life, a separation from close friends, and loved ones, but the end of everything and thus, by nature, a separation from God. It is the end of a living communion with God and, therein and consequently, of all inter-personal relations and enjoyment of creation." /36/

To understand the nature of death for the Old Testament one must understand in what way the Old Testament values life. Life is the highest good; its source and fountain lie in Yahweh. Man and woman live because and to the extent that God stands in relation to them. In the Old Testament, "life" means to have a relationship, above all to have a relationship to God. Death is relationlessness. The dead person is forever alienated from God and from others. Death hopelessly alienates the person from God and from one another. Death is the most intensive experience of

God's absence, the final evidence of human powerlessness and finitude. It is the deadly alienation of God and the human which constitutes the real mystery of death. "For Sheol cannot thank thee, death cannot praise thee: those who go down to the pit cannot hope for thy faithfulness. The living, the living, he thanks thee as I do this day." /37/ In the Old Testament the truth about death means to be forsaken by God. G. von Rad writes:

> "...death begins to become a reality at the point where Jahweh forsakes a man, where he is silent, i.e., at whatever point the life relationship with Jahweh wears thin... The decisive declaration about the state of the departed, which keeps recurring, is against theological: 'Thou rememberest them no more, and they are cut off from thy hand' (Ps. 88: 5,6)... The dead stood outside the cult and its sphere of life. Properly, this was what constituted their being dead. In death there is no proclamation and no praise (Ps. 88:11,12; Is. 38:18); the dead stood outside the action of Jahweh in history (Ps. 88:9,10,11), and for Israel death's real bitterness lay in this exclusion." /38/

We have here the reason why Jesus faces death with every expression of the most profound horror. It is because of Jesus' closeness to God his Father. The death of Jesus on the cross is not distinguished from other deaths except as seen in the light of his closeness to the Father experienced during his life and the sense of abandonment by the same Father on the cross. According to Moltmann, "The torment in his torments was this abandonment by God." /39/

Jesus' death within the Old Testament context meant an exclusion from a God whose nearness can be experienced most deeply to the degree that one is aware of God's nearness. According to Pannenberg:

> "In the usual course of everyday human life we human beings do not live

> in God's nearness, but that nearness is hidden by the involvement with finite things that surround us, in happiness as in suffering. Therefore, we experience only rarely being closed to God as the real suffering in our life... Only in the light of God's nearness would that closedness, after it has become incapable, become absolute torment." /40/

This would be hell in a classical understanding. According to Pannenberg, "...this element agrees remarkably with the situation of Jesus' death, or as the one who pardoned and lived the eschatological nearness of God, Jesus dies the death of one rejected." /41/ Again Pannenberg writes:

> "Death, not only as a final biological fact but also as a rejection from God's eternal life - this is the death of the sinner, the seal upon his having closed himself to the creative origin from whom he once received life and whom he has to thank for it from moment to moment. In closing oneself to the origin toward which human life is directed in its openness beyond itself, death is included in the sense in which no animal dies, namely as a contradiction to human longing and destiny. Jesus dies this death as the sinner because his death on the cross sealed his exclusion from God's nearness." /42/

According to Küng:

> "The unique communion with God which he (Jesus) had seemed to enjoy only makes his forsakenness more unique. This God and Father with whom he had identified himself to the very end did not at the end identify himself with the sufferers... He who had announced the closeness and the advent of God his Father publicly before the whole world dies utterly forsaken by God and was thus publicly demonstrated as godless before the whole world, someone judged by God himself, disposed of once and

for all." /43/

While the full soteriological dimension of Jesus' death was worked out after the Resurrection event, its foundation lies in Jesus' life, suffering and death. Otherwise the core of the Gospel message would come close to being simply a subjective interpretation. The basic theological interpretation of Jesus' death is found in the affirmation that "Christ died for our sins." We find in Paul such an interpretation: "Jesus died for our sins." /44/ The "pro nobis" formula used to interpret Jesus' death has its roots in Jewish expiation theology. But for Paul the ideas of sacrifice and substitutionary punishment are not significant. Rather Jesus' death was a matter of his dedication to God and neighbor. /44/ According to Käsemann:

> "...love for Paul means the demonstration of existence for others, concretely and especially emphatic, particularly in death. Paul gives a distinctive and for theology important nuance to the formula when he speaks of death for the ungodly and for sinners in Rom. 5:6ff., for the Christian brother in Romans 14:15 and for all men in II Corinthians 5:14. The 'for us' remains always the central motif. It encompasses the two meanings, 'for our benefit' and 'in our place' and the reciprocating interpretations characterize its intensity and range." /45/

F. Jesus' Compassion

In the Synoptics Jesus' obedience to God and responsibility for the world are co-constitutive themes. While the word "responsibly" is not used in the Gospels, the Gospels do make use of a similar comment to characterize the action of Jesus - "to have compassion," which is a stronger term than Love, and more commonly associated with Jesus. /46/ To have compassion means to be moved from the viscera as from the heart. In K. Barth's words, "the expression is a strong one which defies adequate translation. Jesus was not only affected to the heart by the misery which surrounded him, but it went right into his heart, into himself, so that it was his misery. It was more his than that of those who suffered it. He took it from them and laid it on himself... He humbled himself in their place." /47/

THE SUFFERING HUMANITY OF JESUS CHRIST. KENOSIS AND CROSS

The term "to have compassion" is used by Jesus himself in three of the most significant parables. It describes the action of the Good Samaritan in Luke 10:33 ("he had compassion"), of the father of the prodigal son in Luke 15:20, and of the king in the parable of the unforgiving servant. It was used three times in association with acts of healing, where Jesus is "moved by compassion" to perform the deed of healing in question. Both forgiveness and reconciliation underline the dimension of solidarity of God and us.

This concept of solidarity is expressed clearly in the Letter to the Hebrews: "Therefore he had to be made like his brethren in every respect, so that he might become merciful... For because he himself has suffered and been tempted, he is able to help those who are tempted." /48/ "We have not a high priest who is unable to sympathize (sympathein) with our weakness, but one who in every respect has been tempted as we are." /49/ Jesus is the one for others, the one who identifies with others.

This concept of solidarity is also enlarged to mean representation. The concept of representation is employed by the New Testament to explain salvation history. /50/ The term also occurs five times in Matthew and Mark as part of a formula which describes Jesus as he is moved with compassion for the crowds. The expressions "in our place" and "on our behalf" which designate the deepest meaning of Jesus' compassion also anticipate the oldest soteriological category for interpreting the death of Jesus, a category taken over and refashioned by Paul: "But God shows his love for us in that while we were yet sinners Christ died for us." /51/ Jesus' compassion is possible because of his solidarity with us. According to Paul a real exchange has happened in Christ: "Though he was rich, yet for your sake he became poor, so that by his poverty you might become rich." /52/ "Who, though he was in the form of God, took the form of a servant." /53/ For Paul this exchange, this solidarity is a reconciliation, a katallage, which means "a becoming other." Reconciliation implies a forgiveness. Both forgiveness and reconciliation underline the dimension of solidarity of God and us.

Representation is not substitution. Substitution

very often renders the other superfluous; representation, solidarity, takes nothing away from the other. It simply opens possibility for the other. Representation and solidarity unite the other to the same reality. Representation and solidarity have an hermeneutical function. Because of the possibility of representation and solidarity, man and woman can understand, experience what they personally have not experienced. The phenomenon of death is indicative of such an hermeneutical function. It is the other's death that leads us to understand the dimension of death in our own lives: the death of another can move us deeply and affect us existentially. In death something happens unconsciously for others; no one dies fully for himself/herself but always for others, too.

G. The Vicariousness of Jesus' Death

Jesus' death on the cross was vicarious. In the Cartesian concept of person, the ideas of solidarity and representation seem strange. But in a different understanding such as John Macmurray's human solidarity is a must. Here the person can develop only in an atmosphere of acceptance, in love and trust. W. Kasper writes: "Human language especially shows that human subjectivity exists only in intersubjectivity in men's existence with one another, as oriented to one another and for one another." /54/

Personal being is essentially being in relation, not being in isolation. The fundamental form of human existence is not individual isolation, but "togetherness." There can be no I without a Thou; they exist in mutual interdependence. All real life is meeting; to be a person means to be in relation to other persons. Man and women can exist only as a complex of social relationships. It is in this context that human freedom is possible; the "other" is not simply a limit to freedom but its condition. Again, according to Kasper: "The freedom of the individual is the freedom of all, and the freedom of all, of course, presupposes that the freedom of each individual is respected." /55/ Representation is essential to human development and to freedom.

Vicariousness and representation are basic dimensions of human interdependence, of human inter-subjectivity. All human life is vicarious because it involves basic freedom for others. Vicariousness is not something esoteric but the fundamental principle of all personal life. The self-giving demanded by vicariousness is not something necessitated by the condition of a sinful world, but is characteristic of the interdependence of human existence. Vicarious and representational suffering is but one category of the larger and more general dimension of vicariousness. Vicarious suffering does not stand above but presupposes the give and take of ordinary relatedness.

In Jesus Christ, the saving nearness of God was made present through a historical life of care for men and women. The death of Jesus on the cross was vicarious because it occurred in solidarity with us. Theology cannot neglect the circumstances of Jesus' death and consider that death in and of itself and ascribe to that death a universal, saving meaning. Without the specifics of Jesus' life, his life is deprived of its saving significance and has to be given a meaning elaborated in mythological terms. The salvific meaning of Jesus' death is rooted in the salvific meaning of his life, in the radical dimension of his love. Jesus' love is radical in the sense that he was no longer concerned with the consequences of this love for his own life. The vicarious death of Jesus is an instance of the law of love. Love is a personal relationship; it presupposes the distinctness of the persons concerned. But it is the very nature of love to transcend the boundaries of personal distinctness and to weld the person together in a unity in which it is the most natural thing for one to act vicariously for another. There is no need to refer Jesus' death to an arbitrary decision on the part of the Godhead; it has its sufficient basis in the love with which and in which Jesus identified himself with us. Jesus' whole life is the interpretation of his death. The very substance of salvation is present to that life and in that sense Jesus' death is tied in with his mission of salvation. In his life Jesus showed what love brings about - relief of physical suffering, the healing of illness, the abolition of hunger and discrimination. Through Jesus' love the depth of interdependence in reality is revealed to us: "No man has ever seen God; if we love one another, God abides in us and his love is perfected in us." /56/ One cannot say that God required the death of Jesus as compensation for our sins. It is not possible to make God responsible for what human injustice has done to Jesus. We should not look for a divine reason for the suffering and death of Jesus. /57/ As a matter of history, Jesus' death comes as a reaction to his life and ministry, as the consequence of his love.

Seen in itself, alone and isolated from Jesus' life and from the Resurrection, the death on the cross appears as the ultimate absurdity. There could hardly be a more convincing symbol of the absurdity of human existence, of the uselessness of human passion, than the cross. In light of the Resurrection what appeared to be absence and abandonment on the part of God becomes presence. In light of the Resurrection, the utter futility of death as expressed in the Old Testament is shown to be false. Death cannot destroy an authentic, living communion with God. Life with God is stronger than death.

H. The Meaning of the Resurrection

Jesus on the cross cannot be isolated from the life and mystery of Jesus, nor can it be isolated from the Resurrection. And in the same way that the cross cannot be isolated from the life and ministry of Jesus, the Resurrection cannot be isolated from the entire life of Jesus which is gathered up on the cross. Easter was the outcome of Jesus' life and death. /58/ Cross and Resurrection are bound together most closely, distinguishable but never separable. Between the event of Jesus' death and the event of his Resurrection from the dead there prevails a unique relation which forbids that one event be viewed in isolation from the other. The themes of crucifixion and resurrection must be drawn together into the closest unity possible. This is evident in Paul's writings. /59/ E. KÄSEMANN comments: "only the Crucified is risen, and the dominion of the Risen One extends only so far as the Crucified is served." /60/

The Resurrection does not do away with the cross. On the contrary, it is the manifestation and confirmation of what happened on the cross, and therefore of what happened in the life of Jesus. It is not a question of choosing between two different interpretative contexts - Jesus' life or his Resurrection. No dichotomy must be imposed between Jesus' life, ministry and death, and his Resurrection. /61/

THE SUFFERING HUMANITY OF JESUS CHRIST. KENOSIS AND CROSS

To understand the cross Christologically is to see it as the cross of the one Jesus who lived, suffered and died and was risen from the dead. /62/ According to Moltmann, "The historical Jesus is not 'half Christ' nor is the risen Christ the other half of Jesus. It is a question of one and the same person and his unique history. The risen Christ _is_ the historical and crucified Jesus, and _vice versa_." /63/ There is real continuity between the life, death and the Resurrection of Jesus and therefore a real continuity in the faith of the disciples before and after Jesus' death. /64/

Jesus' death must be understood as the determinative free act which gathers up the entire human life of Jesus in its utter abandonment to the Father. And the Resurrection must be understood as the Father's simultaneous, irrevocable acceptance of Jesus' life and death. The Resurrection is the significance of Jesus' life and death accepted by the Father and set free to work. It is the Father's yes to the person and the life of Jesus. The Resurrection of Jesus is not just another event after his passion and death. It cannot, therefore be isolated from the cross simply as another event in its own right. Rather, Good Friday and Easter should be seen as two separate aspects of a strictly unitary event of the existence of Christ which are essentially related to one another. The Resurrection reveals Jesus precisely as the Crucified Lord. The cross remains the signature of the risen one. /65/ The Resurrection is simply the "other side" of Jesus' death, the definitive acceptance by God of Jesus, his activity and preaching, his self-awareness, in short, of his life of filial obedience. The confession that Jesus is risen can and must be determined in light of his ministry and death. The Resurrection does not give meaning to the life, ministry and death of Jesus, but confirms their validity in the face of rejection.

While Jesus seems to have experienced a real abandonment on the cross, the Resurrection reveals that the Father was present. In fact, on the cross God identified himself with a dead man. In the Old Testament perspective, death means relationlessness. While in the Old Testament God is understood as standing at an infinite distance from death, wholly untouched, in the death of Jesus he endures contact with death.

By identifying himself with the dead Jesus, God truly exposed himself to the alienating power of death. He exposed his own divinity to the power of negation. And he did precisely this in order to be God for all men.

God himself bears the relationlessness of death which alienates man from him. In doing this God reveals himself as God of life. In the light of the Resurrection the death of Jesus appears as not having been in vain. God who seemed to have left him without support in the public gaze did, in fact, sustain him through death. While seeming to have been abandoned, yet Jesus had not been forsaken. Küng writes: "Suffering and death are encompassed by God; suffering too even though it seems like being forsaken by God, can become the point of encounter with God." /66/

On the cross, God takes upon himself the relationlessness of death itself, and in doing so reveals himself as a God of love. The Paschal Mystery reveals the triumph of self-giving love, of radical kenosis. The Paschal Mystery reveals God's nature as one of self-giving love. Only as the very substance of God could he proceed to such an identification with human reality.

Jesus' death for us includes the meanings "for our sake," "to our advantage," and "in our place," "as our representative." These various meanings underline the depth of the formula. It underlines the fact that salvation is a gift, that we are saved through God's love. That God's love is one that gives life to the dead and calls into existence that which does not exist. The cross reveals that God is the one who raised Jesus from the dead. Salvation is always resurrection of the dead since it is God's work for us. The Resurrection of Christ reveals the realities to which all the work of God has tended and reveals what his works have meant in every age. On the cross, God took upon himself the relationlessness of death itself, and in doing so revealed himself as a God of love.

In the same way, the Resurrection means the death of death. The Resurrection does not mean that Jesus who suffered death now leaves death behind and returns to life. The Resurrection of Jesus is not a resuscitation as that of Lazarus. Lazarus who returned to life, still has death before him. The death of Jesus in which God himself shares, is the transformation of death itself. As Paul wrote: "For we know that Christ being raised from the dead will never die again; death no longer has dominion over him. The death he dies he died to sin, once for all, but the life he lives he lives to God." /67/ P. Hodgson writes: "God puts death to death by taking it up into his own being, his own life. Thus death is deprived of its essential character as negativity, estrangement, absence, and is converted into presence, the presence of the living God." /68/

In light of the Paschal Mystery, suffering and death take on a different meaning. Yet suffering and death still remain impenetrable. Jesus' resurrection is the object of our faith, of our hope. As Schillebeeckx writes:

> "our faith in the Resurrection is itself still a prophecy and a promise for this world - <u>qua</u> prophecy unsheltered and unprotected, defenceless and vulnerable. And so the life of the Christian is not visibly 'justified' by the facts of history... The servant is not greater than his Lord. Just as Jesus did, the Christian takes the risk of entrusting himself and the vindication of his living to God; he is prepared to receive the vindication where Jesus did - beyond death." /69/

The absence of God is what we experience daily.

Jesus' Resurrection is a promise that ultimately we will not be abandoned, but not a promise that God will remove our suffering, pain and death. Jesus offers no palliatives for death in his cry from the cross. Even in the context of hope in the Resurrection, death is recognized to be death. Death is a negative reality and this includes Jesus' death.

I. Salvation in Solidarity

We can now ask in greater depth to what extent and in what manner is Jesus' death for us? Are we spared anything because of Jesus' death? Yes, we are spared having to be in complete rejection, but we are not spared death and suffering. We are not spared from working out our salvation in fear and trembling. We cannot collapse the eschatological dimension of the cross into a salvation already realized and brought about. Pannenberg writes: "Whoever is bound up with Jesus no longer dies alone, excluded from community with God, above all no longer as one who is divorced from community with God and his future salvation... Whoever is bound up with Jesus dies, to be sure, but he dies in hope of the life of resurrection from the dead that has already appeared in Jesus." /70/

Solidarity with God in Jesus means salvation ultimately from death. It means salvation for all. It is in this sense that Jesus' death has vicarious significance for all humanity. In the crucified Jesus, God has revealed what authentic salvation is - God's unconditional grace which brings justice to those who have been oppressed, and makes righteous the unrighteous. Like the parable of the prodigal son, the cross shows God's love as not conditioned on whether or not it is reciprocated. "If you love those who love you, what reward have you?" /71/ In the parable of the prodigal son, the father forgives and condones without exacting suffering and pain. The father's forgiveness wipes away the guilt and there only remains the fact and memory of having sinned. The Father did not need to be placated. Before the son "came to himself" the father was already awaiting and desiring his return. "This parable," according to J. Macquarrie, "stresses the unchanging character of God's attitude and work, which is always one of reconciliation...no historical event changes God's attitude or makes him from a wrathful God into a gracious God, or allows his reconciling work to get started." /72/

Paul, who perceived the shocking dimension of the cross, emphasized its paradoxical saving significance in the fact that God gives himself away to the sinner, to the Godless - to the enemy. On the cross God's law is manifested as breaking through narrow national boundaries. Salvation is extended to all, Jew and Gentile alike. The universal dimension of God's love as expressed on the cross is emphasized according to Moltmann in the fact that it happened outside the gate of the city of Jerusalem with its temple, its legal tradition. He writes:

> "It happened on the boundary of human sanity where it does not matter whether a

> person is Jew or Gentile, Greek or barbarian, master or servant, man or woman, because death is unaware of all these distinctions. So the crucified one does not recognize these distinctions either. If his death is proclaimed and acknowledged as the death of the Son of God 'for many' as by the centurion, then in his death God's son has died for all, and the proclamation of his death is for all the world. It must undermine, remove and destroy the things which mark men out as elect and non-elect, educated and uneducated - those with possessions and those without, the free and the enslaved." /73/

The proclamation of the cross is Christianity for all the world. Therefore, the theology of the cross is the true Christian universalism.

Universal salvation in Jesus Christ is through solidarity with God, an emancipative solidarity /74/ from injustice, evil and death. God's solidarity, while eschatological, is emancipative in nature and involves the past, the present, and the future. As Kasper writes:

> "If the sufferers of the past remained unconsoled and the wrong done to them were unatoned, the murderer would triumph at the end over his victim. Then the right of the strong would finally count in history and history would be purely a history of the victory. A solidarity restricted to the present and the future would be a further wrong-doing to the victim of the past." /75/

Absolute solidarity is possible only with God; only God can call back the dead and emancipate from the suffering of the past.

J. The Revelation of God in the Paschal Mystery

In the "for us" of Jesus' death, God reveals himself but identifies and defines himself. Paul can say:

"God was in Christ." /76/ According to Moltmann, "God is on the cross of Jesus 'for us' and through that becomes God and Father of the godless and the godforsaken." /77/ The Paschal Mystery underlines the critical dimension of Jesus' life and death. What is at stake in the Paschal Mystery is God, our God. Who is this God who seems to be free to keep silent while Jesus hangs upon the cross? Can we accept such a God? A God who is free to keep silent even in the midst of our suffering?

Because of the life Jesus lived, his death faces us with a fundamental question about God. We are obliged to radically revise our understanding of God, our own ideas of God - God of whom Jesus spoke as being utterly reliable is either a tragic farce or we are invited to commit ourselves to this God of Jesus. The Paschal Mystery is a challenge to go on trusting in God. As Schillebeeckx writes: "Thus Jesus' message, becoming the signature of his death, calls upon us to revise our self-understanding by speaking of God who silently reveals himself in Jesus' historically helpless failure on the cross." /78/ The Christian conviction is that in the selfless service of Jesus towards his fellow men, a man who is rejected by others, God reveals himself most deeply, fundamentally, and finally as God.

The emphasis and revealing nature of the Paschal Mystery is on God's saving action in Jesus of Nazareth: God has assumed the aspect of the crucified and risen Christ. In Christ, God has the last word. Although history goes on much as before, God's definitive saving action has been accomplished in Jesus of Nazareth. The reality of the human and personal mode of being of Jesus Christ is the very thing needed to make the depth of the redemptive self-giving of God comprehensible while not imprinting alienation, suffering, and death to God. We cannot look for the ground of suffering in God, nor follow Moltmann in "eternalizing" suffering in God. /79/ God is absolute positivity; he wills life and not death. God is a fellow sufferer; the Resurrection is a corrective, a victory over the negativity of suffering and even death. The cross, then, is not an event between God and God; it is what needs to be opposed. It is overcome through affinity with God. Redemption occurs not "because of" death, but despite it. /80/

THE SUFFERING HUMANITY OF JESUS CHRIST. KENOSIS AND CROSS

Since the Resurrection reveals the triumph of self-giving love, of radical kenosis, in some real and paradoxical way the death of death means the making presence of absence. The cross reveals God's nature as one of self-giving love; the Resurrection is the vindication and the revelation of this self-giving love. Everything is recapitulated not in the elevation of the world toward God but in the descending of God into the world. In the Paschal Mystery we have the revelation of God's solidarity with a suffering humanity. Jesus' total participation in our finite powerlessness, suffering and death is the central, interpretative principle of God's nature. In the cross we discover the fundamental law of the divine life itself: "Power is to be found in weakness." And when the crucified Jesus is called the image of the invisible God, the meaning here is that the cross is the symbol, the ideograph of God's action and being. God is not greater than he is in this humiliation. His glory is the glory of self-surrender; his power, that of helplessness.

G. Kaufmann writes: "God as it were, 'turns the other cheek' and 'goes the second mile': he loves his enemies and in this way wins them. God does not strike back vengefully or in any other way retaliate: on the contrary, he deigns to suffer whatever wrong his creatures inflict on him, that he might in this way rescue them from the mess they have made of history." /81/

Bonhoeffer writes that the cross shows God to be the one who "...is weak and powerless in the world, and that is exactly the way, the only way, in which he can be with us and help us." /82/ The cross must be understood as the most profound symbol of God's being and action; of the fact that God's power is love and therefore that our God is a suffering God." As N. Berdyaev writes: "God the Creator...is powerless to conquer evil by an act of power. It is only the God of sacrifice and love who can triumph over evil, the God who took upon himself the sin of the world, God the Son who became man." /83/

The only God who is trustworthy is the one who does not interfere to protect the pious but who is present in the thick of darkness. Divinity consists supremely and essentially in self-giving and letting-be. God, in the powerlessness, suffering, and death of

Jesus Christ reveals himself as against those who use their power to lord it over others and to destroy their freedom. It is not therefore an unequivocal revelation, but in hiddenness, as nothingness or powerlessness. Powerlessness implies that one is subjected to forces over which he has no control and therefore powerlessness means suffering (pascho). According to L. Gilkey, "In revealing his judgment on all human power through his powerlessness, God in Christ shows not only how the suffering and death of our brother arises from our grasping for power, but he also reveals his willingness to subject himself to fate, to suffer with those who lack power, and to die with those who die." /84/

The cross is the symbol of the radical dimension of God's kingdom, God's presence and love for poor and outcast. According to W. Kasper this love of God is one "which endures and reconciles the paradoxicality without minimizing it, for it is the pecularity of love to establish unity in the midst of diversity. Love means unity and fellowship with the other person, who is affirmed in his otherness, and thus unity and reconciliation in persistent duality." /85/

K. Our Compassionate God

God is a redeeming God, because he is a compassionate God. It is of God's nature to be compassionate. The word compassion means literally "to suffer with." There are three basic elements to compassion: solidarity, consolation, and comfort. To be compassionate, God must be and is in solidarity with us. God's compassion is made possible because of his solidarity with our human reality. God does not refuse identity with us. God participates in our humanity to its full depth. What happens when one is in solidarity with another? One really shares in the life of the other person, although not in the same way. The Father's suffering is of another kind than Jesus', than ours. Moltmann and Rahner have underlined this aspect./86/Through love, God suffers in the other. Love saves both aspects - identity and non-identity, true presence of the same suffering, but in another manner, freely taken up out of love. In no event does he who suffers wish the pain of the other or deliberately cause his pain. We cannot take over the bodily pain or the death of another, but we can assume the anguish and pain that is bound up with it. We can suffer for others but we cannot accept their pain for them. This is still clearer in the case of sin. We can carry with someone his guilt without willing the fault itself, and we certainly can suffer the depravity and loneliness of sin with the other.

God suffers - because he is love. Love, however, does not want suffering. Love seeks for happiness and struggles against evil. One may say that God's suffering exists in the love relationship on the condition that the term relationship provides no occasion to undervalue or to deny the hard reality of the pain of the one whose pain is shared. God himself has entered into our realm, into the realm of suffering, has identified himself with a dead person. That identification does not take away the stark and naked reality of suffering and pain now; but it renders it ultimately powerless. In solidarity with us God has freely accepted the limitations of pain and death. This acceptance renders pain and suffering ultimately powerless. The key word here is ultimately. God's suffering with us is a suffering freely accepted. In this sense it can be called kenotic suffering.

This brings us to the second element of compassion: consolation, to be alone with the other (cum solo). Compassion, to suffer with, does not imply the covering up of pain, but the deepening of pain to a level where it can be shared. Consolation implies the willingness to be alone with the other, where the other is in his suffering, powerless with the powerless. Jesus' saying, ""Come to me all who labour and are heavy laden, and I will give you rest," /87/ was not merely an offer of an easier way, but was a self-conscious "yoking" of himself to us. He stands where we stand. Bonhoeffer has described this dimension of God's compassion in the following manner: "The God who lets us live in the world without the working-hypothesis - and is the God before whom we stand continually. Before God and with God we live without God. God allows himself to be driven out of the world on to the cross. He is powerless and weak in the world, and that is precisely the only way that he is with us and helps us." /88/

Comfort is the third element of God's compassion. Solidarity in suffering and the willingness to share the other's pain without taking it away leads not simply to commiseration but to comfort, which means "strength together." Through solidarity and consolation, the one who is suffering no longer feels isolated and alone. While comfort does not take away suffering nor dispel basic human loneliness, it does give new strength. As in Christ, God participates in our weakness, sin, suffering and death, so through our participation in his weakness, humility, suffering and death we are given new strength. We are able to accept our finitude and our sinful denial of it, because God participates in it and gives us the courage, the confidence, and the power to be what we are.

Because of God's compassion, we are assured not only that we are accepted despite these conditions but are also made one with God. God, in becoming weak and vulnerable, frees men and women from the quest for powerful idols and protective compulsions, and makes them ready to accept their humanity, their freedom, and their mortality. In sympathy with the pathos of God, they become open to what is other and new. The cross is the final answer to Job's dilemma. God does not instigate our suffering, nor did he decree the sufferings of Jesus. Rather, he participated in them. Our God, Jesus' God, is not the executioner but the fellow-sufferer.

L. Conclusion

During his life and his preaching Jesus proclaimed God as the Father of the outcasts; not as someone remote, but as someone close to human reality. Jesus' God is a God for us. The cross reveals God as a redeeming God, not as a cruel God demanding revenge, but a compassionate God. In Jesus' death on the cross, God reveals who he is, God-for-us. At the same time, he reveals who we are - the ones who can <u>be</u> truly, only inasmuch as we are for-this-God. The self-definition of God and the definition of men and women through God occur in the cross of Jesus Christ. /89/

Theology and anthropology are involved in a mutual relationship, not as identical, but as reciprocal. God is the situation in which we understand, develop and shape ourselves. If our God is a crucified God, a correspondening anthropology and ecclesiology will develop. As Moltmann writes: "In the sphere of the apathic God man becomes <u>homo apatheticus</u>. In the situation of the pathos of God, he becomes <u>homo sympatheticus</u>." /90/ Sympathy here implies the openness of a person to the presence of another. It has the structure of a dialogue. Sympathy is founded on solidarity - which is turn implies reciprocity. God's solidarity with us leads to solidarity with others. The compassionate God demands compassion on our part. Commitment to the crucified involves a radical conversion and that brings about a revolution in life - not a conformation of one's ideas and hopes, but a painful confrontation with truth. This confrontation with truth is not, as Moltmann writes, "positive and constructive, but is in the first instance critical and destructive." /91/ Initially a conversion to the crucified Christ brings no harmony in one's life, but contradiction within oneself and society. Yet conversion to the "crucified Christ" liberates and frees by confrontation with cultural and social illusions.

It frees from false needs, religious and others; it points to the disorder and depth of our alienation from our real selves. It questions our personal growth; not everything is O.K. True and authentic human personhood consists in self-giving, in being for others, in the continuing self-surrender to God in the radical obedience of ultimate faith, in the acceptance of one's finitude and relativity. Conversion to the crucified Christ is conversion to the crucified and risen Christ. The Resurrection underlines the need for radical obedience of faith and the acceptance of our own finitude and relativity. The decision for or against Easter faith has its foundation on the acceptance of one's own finitude and radical faith, on the determination of living not simply out of one's own potentialities but from the other who cannot be controlled.

Belief in the crucified and risen Christ is the assurance that the way of love is open to all men and women and that the effort to love one another as Christ did is not a hopeless one even though in this world such a love ends up on the cross. But for one who believes in the crucified and risen Christ, the cross and Resurrection are the foundation of hope, hope that life as a whole is meaningful and that it can ultimately be shaped in happiness and life. Conversion to the cross and Resurrection is the willingness to say yes to life. /92/ It is also the acknowledgment that suffering is a part of life and that God shares that life of suffering with us, that he is not distant from us. To accept suffering is to accept the truth of reality, and the prerequisite for such acceptance is a deeper love for reality, a love which avoids placing conditions on reality. /93/

The cross points beyond the growth and development of society. Gilkey writes,

> "In embodying powerlessness rather than power; in identifying with the outcast, the oppressed and the guilty against the creative, the significant and the distinguished; in identifying himself with suffering and death rather than with the power that contends against suffering and death, Jesus revealed the alienation of even the creative world from its true self, from the kingdom to be preached." /94/

As a revelation event, the cross touches fundamental human realities. It can symbolize the necessary self-emptying as a path to new life, the very suffering of God which can lead to important ways of seeing human reality. In the cross we discover the fundamental law of the divine life itself: "Power is to be found in weakness." Christology must begin at the cross; it must take with utmost seriousness the fact that God himself has entered the realm of human suffering and death, while remaining identical to himself.

Kenosis, the self-emptying and self-giving that is love's essence, and that characterizes Jesus' life, is above all to be understood as characteristic of the life of God. Kenosis should be seen as characteristic of the very being of God and therefore it is a characteristic of God's action vis-a-vis created being.

THE SUFFERING HUMANITY OF JESUS CHRIST. KENOSIS AND CROSS

NOTES

1. E. Schillebeeckx, Jesus - An Experiment in Christology, trans. H. Hoskins, (New York: Seabury Press, 1979) p. 604.

2. I Corinthians 15:3-5.

3. Cf. W. Michaelis, "Pascho" in TDNT, Vol. V, p. 904.

4. I Corinthians 2:2.

5. J. Moltmann, The Crucified God, (New York: Harper & Row, 1974) p. 74.

   On the passion in the New Testament, consult:
   E. Käsemann, "The Pauline Theology of the Cross," Interpretations 24 (1970) pp. 151-177.
   G. S. Sloyan, Jesus on Trial: The Development of the Passion Narratives and Their Historical and Ecumenical Implications, (Philadelphia: Fortress, 1973).
   J. Guillet, "Les Recits de la Passion," Lumiere et Vie 23 (1974) pp. 6-17.
   R. E. Brown, "The Passion According to John," Chapters 18 & 19, Worship 49 (1975) pp. 126-134.

6. Mark 14:21.

7. Cf. I Thessalonians 5:10; Colossians 2:20; Matthew 20:28.

8. P. Schoonenberg, "The Kenosis or Self-Emptying of Christ," Concilium, Vol. I, No. 2 (1966) p. 35.

9. D. Sölle, Suffering, (Philadelphia: Fortress Press, 1975) p. 163.

10. V. A. Harvey, The Historian and the Believer: The Morality of Historical Knowledge and Christian Belief, (New York: Macmillan, 1966).

11. K. Rahner, On the Theology of Death, (New York: Herder & Herder, 1965).

12. Cf. K. Rahner, "Ideas for a Theology of Death," Theological Investigations XIII, (New York: Seabury Press, 1975) p. 179.

13. M. B. Chambers, "Was Jesus Really Obedient Unto Death?" Journal of Religion 50 (1970) pp. 121-138.

14. John 4:34.

15. W. Pannenberg, Jesus - God and Man, (Philadelphia: Westminster, 1968).

16. E. Käsemann, op. cit.

17. Luke 22:27.

18. Cf. J. Moltmann, The Crucified God, op. cit.

19. Mark 10:28.

20. Mark 8:34-35.

21. Hebrews 13:12-13.

22. Luke 22:37.

23. W. Pannenberg, op. cit., p. 263.

24. J. Moltmann, op. cit., p. 53.

25. D. Bonhoeffer, The Cost of Discipleship, (London: SCM, 1959) p. 76.

26. Mark 14:41-47.

27. Romans 8:32.

28. Cf. L. Mahieu, "L'Abandon du Christ sur la Croix," MSR II (1945) pp. 209-242.

    M. Rehm, "Eli, Eli Lamma Sabacthani," BZ 2 (1958) pp. 275-278.

    J. Gnilka, "Mein Gott, Mein Gott Warum Hast Du Mich Verlassen?" Mark 15:34, BZ 3 (1959) pp. 294-297.

U. von Balthasar, Le Mystere Pascal, Coll. Mysterium Salutis, Vol. 12, (Paris: Ed. Du Cerf, 1972) pp. 119-122.

29. Cf. E. Schillebeeckx, Christ, the Experience of Jesus as Lord, (New York: Seabury Press, 1980) pp. 298-299.

30. Mark 15:37; Matthew 27:50.

31. Luke 23:46.

32. John 19:30.

33. Mark 15:34.

34. L. E. Keck, A Future for the Historical Jesus, (London, SCM, 1972) p. 229.

35. Cf. E. Jungel, Death: The Riddle and the Mystery, trans. I & U. Nicol, (Philadelphia: Westminster Press, 1974) pp. 59-95.

36. E. Schillebeeckx, Christ, the Presence of Jesus as Lord, op. cit., p. 798.

37. Isaiah 38:18 ff.

38. Cf. Gerhard von Rad, Old Testament Theology, Vol. I, trans. D. M. G. Stalker, (Edinburgh: Oliver & Boyd, 1962) pp. 388-389.

39. J. Moltmann, op. cit., p. 149.

40. W. Pannenberg, op. cit., p. 270.

41. Ibid., p. 271.

42. Ibid., p. 270.

43. H. Küng, On Being a Christian, trans. E. Quinn, (New York: Doubleday, 1976) p. 342.

44. Galatians 1:4; 2:20; II Corinthians 5:14-15.

45. Quoted by P. Hodgson, op. cit., p. 208.

46. Cf. G. S. Hendry, The Gospel of the Incarnation, (Philadelphia: Westminster Press, 1958) pp. 100-107.

47. K. Barth, Church Dogmatics, Vol. IV, Part II, p. 184; cf. also Vol. III, Part II, p. 211.

48. Heb. 2:17 f.

49. Heb. 4:15.

50. Mark 1:41; Luke 7:13; Matthew 20:34.

51. Rom. 5:8.

52. II Cor. 8:9.

53. Phil. 2:6-11.

54. W. Kasper, Jesus the Christ, (New York: Paulist Press, 1976) p. 222.

55. Ibid.

56. I John 4:12.

57. E. Schillebeeckx, Christ, the Experience of Jesus as Lord, op. cit., pp. 726-729.

58. Cf. K. Rahner, "Resurrection," Encyclopedia of Theology: The Concise Sacramentum Mundi, (New York: Seabury Press, 1975) pp. 1436-1442.

59. Cf. Romans 4:25; 8:35; I Corinthians 15:3-4; II Corinthians 5:15.

60. Quoted by P. Hodgson, Jesus - Word and Presence, An Essay in Christology, (Philadelphia: Fortress Press, 1971) p. 216.

61. Cf. J. B. Metz, Faith in History and Society, (New York: Seabury Press, 1980) p. 113.

62. Cf. J. Moltmann, op. cit., p. 113.

63. Ibid., p. 160.

THE SUFFERING HUMANITY OF JESUS CHRIST. KENOSIS AND CROSS

64. According to R. Pesch, the foundation of the Church's faith in the Resurrection is not to be found in the historical Jesus, and not in the events that followed Jesus' death. Cf. "Zur Entstehung Des Glaubens An Die Auferstehung Jesu," TQ 153 (1973) pp. 201-228.

65. Cf. Romans 4:25; 8:34; I Corinthians 15:3-4; II Corinthians 5:15.

66. H. Küng, op. cit., p. 434.

67. Romans 6:9-10.

68. P. Hodgson, op. cit., p. 215.

69. E. Schillebeeckx, Jesus. An Experiment in Christology, op. cit., p. 643.

70. W. Pannenberg, op. cit., p. 194.

71. Matthew 5:46.

72. J. Macquarrie, Principles of Christian Theology, (New York: Charles Scribner's Sons, 1966) p. 283.

73. J. Moltmann, op. cit., p. 194.

74. F. Fiorenza, "Critical Social Theory and Christology: Toward an Understanding of Atonement and Redemption as Emancipatory Solidarity," CTSA Vol. 30, pp. 108-110.

75. W. Kasper, op. cit., p. 224.

76. II Corinthians 5:19.

77. J. Moltmann, op. cit., p. 192.

78. E. Schillebeeckx, Jesus. An Experiment in Christology, op. cit., p. 638.

79. E. Schillebeeckx, Christ, the Experience of Jesus as Lord, op. cit., p. 738.

80. Ibid., p. 729.

81. G. Kaufmann, Systematic Theology. A Historical Perspective, (New York: Charles Scribner's Sons, 1968) p. 220.

82. D. Bonhoeffer, Prisoner for God, (New York: Harper, 1952) p. 248.

83. N. Berdyaev, The Beginning and the End, (New York: Harper, 1952) p. 248.

84. L. Gilkey, Reaping the Whirlwind. A Christian Interpretation of History, (New York: Seabury Press, 1976) p. 282.

85. W. Kasper, op. cit., p. 168.

86. Cf. K. Rahner, "On the Theology of the Incarnation," Theological Investigations IV (London: Norton, Longman and Todd, 1966) p. 113.

87. Matthew 11:38.

88. D. Bonhoeffer, Letters and Papers from Prison, ed. E. Bethage, trans. R. H. Fuller, (New York: Macmillan, 1972) p. 360.

89. Cf. L. Malevez, "Anthropologie Chretienne et Theologie de la Croix," in Nov. Rev. Theol. 92 (1970) pp. 449-467.

90. J. Moltmann, op. cit., p. 272.

91. Ibid., p. 39.

92. D. Sölle, Suffering, op. cit., p. 108.

93. Ibid., pp. 91-92.

94. L. Gilkey, op. cit., p. 269.

CHAPTER 9

THE GOD OF JESUS. A GOD-WITH-US

A. Introduction - The Immutability of God

From what can be discovered about Jesus' own message, it is apparent that he was all about God and God's kingdom. Jesus was a pointer to the Father and to the Kingdom of the Father. As Jesus is confessed to be the Christ by the early Church and becomes the focus of its preaching, the centrality of the Father is not forgotten. God the Father still remains the focus of the New Testament. /1/ The basic question in Christology is the question about God; more specifically it is the question about God and the human. It is the question about the transcendence and immanence of God, God being fully God and the human being fully human.

The tradition expressed this basic mystery in the symbol of the Incarnation. This symbol can already be discerned at work in the New Testament even if the language is not specifically its own. /2/ At Chalcedon the symbol of the Incarnation attained classical formulation in the notion of hypostatic union. While there has been a marked tendency in recent Christologies to abandon this symbol, /3/ the question about Jesus the Christ still remains a question about God and the human. As a theological symbol, Incarnation speaks in a very specific way of God's presence and initiative, of God's saving graciousness and self-communication in Jesus Christ. The specificity of the symbol has been described as a "from above" approach to the mystery of the self-communication of God in Jesus Christ. /4/ While this approach may prove to be problematical, the primary question in any Christology remains that of the relationship of God to the human, the unity of God and the human, the transcendence and immanence of God. In its theological meaning the symbol of Incarnation says that God belongs to the world of his creatures; the Incarnation is a characteristic of God's being with us. God's transcendence is not from another world. It is a transcendence for men and women. The Incarnation as a symbol expresses something decisive about God's self-communication to the total creation. It also expresses something decisive about the relationship of the human to God, and this specifically in Jesus Christ. /5/ For the Christian community, God is present in Jesus Christ as a saving mystery and definitively reveals himself. Theologizing about Jesus becomes a real discussion about God, about God who has joined himself at a particular point in time with the earthly corporeality of the man Jesus. /6/

The primary function of Christology is that of illuminating our experience and understanding of God. God remains the one absolute mystery which defines all other mysteries including that of Jesus Christ. While the person of Jesus Christ leads us into the mystery of God, he is himself defined by God. The underlying and critical question in Christology is the question of God, of God's agency and causal relation to his creation, to the human reality of Jesus. Is a human history capable of mediating the action and presence of God? Can the history of the man Jesus be at the same time the history of God? W. Kasper sees the primacy of God in Christology in terms of the fundamental problem of freedom. Human freedom that is not grounded in the freedom of God is destined to self-destruction. The question of the unity of God and man in Christ has to be rethought in such a way as to show that the unity is not the antithesis of human emancipation, but the condition of its possibility. /7/ The underlying question in Christology then is that of the causal agency of God upon his creation and specifically upon Jesus. Any approach to the specific Christological question must at the same time say something about God's causality.

In elaborating their doctrine about Jesus Christ, the early Christian theologians were faced with the question of the relationship of God and the world. This question had been given an earlier solution in the thought of the Greek philosophers. When Plato had been faced with the question of the relationship of God and the world, his answer had been expressed in terms of a dramatic imitation. The world includes the image of God and imitations of his ideas but never God himself. The Church fathers struggled to express their conviction that in Jesus of Nazareth men and women were confronted with the definitive instance of God's immanence, of God's presence. Yet it would seem that because of the theological framework they inherited they were not able to express consistently what they wished to say. /8/ What the Fathers wished to express was the unity of the person of Jesus without obliterating the distinction between the divine and the human. With their doctrine of God, inherited from Greek philosophy, that became a difficult task. For, according to J. Pelikan, "the early Christian picture of God was controlled by the self-evident axiom, accepted by all, of the absoluteness and the impassibility of the divine nature." /9/

The philosophical tradition posed and attempted to answer the basic question: how is God related to the world? God, being perfect in form and substance, undifferentiated and indivisible in himself, impassive and unaffected by anything external, could really have no involvement. For the Fathers, God was eternal, without change and impassible. Such a conception of God had a great and determining influence upon what the Church Fathers could say about the suffering of Jesus and thus affected their understanding of the Incarnation. Their struggle with the issue of Jesus' suffering provides a clear example of the way in which the theology of God influenced their understanding of the Incarnation. If the Son is consubstantial with the Father, and therefore inherently perfect and incapable of change, progress and suffering, how is He truly one with us, consubstantial with us, authentically a mediator? The Christological controversies that took place in the early Church were concerned with the seemingly insoluble problem of how the eternal Logos, incapable of change or suffering, could be incarnate at all. The two major opponents in the controversy that finally led to the formula of Chalcedon were both unable to solve the problem. Since the Logos, like God, could not really be involved in the world, the Antiochenes insisted on the difference between the two natures and had real difficulty in accounting for the unity between them. Although the Alexandrians stressed the oneness of the Logos enfleshed; nevertheless, the Logos could not suffer on the cross. /10/

Because the problem was posed in a framework not conducive to a real solution, the solution attempted at Chalcedon was unsatisfactory. The definition defines in a negative way by excluding the extremes of the opposite approaches. The definition affirms parameters beyond which discussion is no longer within the realm of orthodoxy, yet does not offer any positive Christological understanding. The basic understanding of God's unchangeability and freedom from suffering remained operative in the formula. And therefore the becoming of God remained problematic.

B. God and History

In a kenotic Christology it is essential to ask: with what conception of God do we attempt to approach the Incarnation? The main differences in Christological doctrines are rooted in different conceptions of the nature of the God-head. As we have already indicated, a kenotic Christology cannot be viable if expressed in the traditional patterns of thought about God. Kenotic Christology implies a major reconstruction of the doctrine of God. Traditionally the doctrine of God is elaborated independently of Christology. As a result this Christology presupposes the Trinity and develops its own understanding of the Incarnation within this setting. Yet it is only as Christians that we can hope to understand the Incarnation. Christianity's God is accessible only through the historical man Jesus. We can only know the God of Jesus Christ by starting from the particular history of Jesus. A Christology "from below" sees the historical Jesus as the place of God's revelation.

Jesus is the decisive revelation of what God is always about - love. Classical Christology sees the Incarnation as an historical explanation of God's love. But it perceives God in a totally ahistorical way. Now the basic Christological question has always been: can the transcendence of God be understood in an historical form?

The God who revealed himself in the history of Jesus participated in that history in a most profound way in the passion, cross and resurrection of Jesus. It is in Jesus' suffering that the real nature of God is revealed, that God is not dispassionate and aloof, but involved and caring. Jesus leads us to the realization that God is love. A revision of our concept and understanding of God's nature must be undertaken in light of God's presence to Jesus Christ at the cross and resurrection. The mystery of the Incarnation cannot be approached from any understanding of God that is not gained from the unique history of Jesus. This does not mean that any extra-Christian understanding of God should be excluded or is not valid. For Christians the definitive revelation of God is Jesus Christ. "He is the image of the invisible God" as Colossians puts it. Jesus is the criterion or the model in terms of which we need to establish our understanding of God and in light of which we may approach the Incarnation.

The cross and Resurrection reveal God's nature and Trinitarian existence. The death of Jesus is first a statement about God before it is an assurance of salvation for us. To ask "Who is the crucified God?" is simply to ask "Who is God?" And this necessarily entails a "Christology from below." A "Christology from above" can never be anything more than an exercise in begging the question. That approach presumes that there is no problem whatever about the word "God," that everyone knows precisely what divinity means.

In the Old Testament and in the New Testament, God's nature is not deduced a priori, from a metaphysical understanding of God; it is deduced from the type of dialogue he has initiated with his people, from the covenant he has established. The question about God's attributes is a question about how God behaves in relation to his creation. In a real sense, then, it is the personal God in the concreteness of his free activity that is the source for our discussion of his nature. The experience of God's free personal activity within history is the source of whatever attributes are given to Him. It is from God's deeds that we know of his virtues, his attributes.

One of the fundamental Biblical truths is that God is present in the theater of human history. The Old and New Testaments are concerned with the nearness of God. The various affirmations in the Old Testament concerning God's nearness to men and women are deeply rooted in the emotional language of human suffering. The experience of the pathos of God in the Old Testament is the presupposition for the understanding of the history of his "passion" in the New Testament. In Exodus, God is "merciful and gracious, slow to anger, and abounding in steadfast love and faithfulness." /11/ In the New Testament God is the Father who has given up his only Son for our salvation and redemption.

Such an historical understanding of God cannot easily be reconciled with the affirmation that God is "unchangeable," that God is "immutable." The acceptance of the apathetic God into classical Christology led to insoluble theological difficulties. Qualities such as pity, compassion and love appear incompatible with absolute "immutability." Impassibility and immutability belong to the order of being which has nothing to do with the order of becoming, with our world. According to Aristotle, God the First Mover causes change without itself being changed, without having any potentiality. The First Mover rules the world from the outside and has no interaction with the world of humanity. As *actus purus* God is pure causality and cannot be the object of suffering.

C. Love as Constitutive of God's Being

The Incarnation as revelation of God brings us to an ontological ultimate which a purely rational ontology cannot express. It demands a willingness to strain our imagination for viable symbolization. We are grappling with a new and totally different notion of transcendence, one which involves a different concept of becoming. It is a transcendence of love. God's love and the suffering of his Son, Jesus, as an expression of that love shatter philosophical expressions and common symbolization.

Love must be understood not as something about God but rather as God's very definition. Love cannot be conceived as an accidental or contingent accretion; it is rather constitutive of God's very being. That God is love we know from the Word of the Cross (I Cor. 1:18; Rom. 1:16 f.). In the crucified Jesus, God exists within us in the fullness of his essence. In the New Testament the event of Christ's death is summed up in terms of an event of God's love: "God loved the world so much that he gave his only Son, that everyone who has faith in him may not die but have eternal life." (Jn. 3:16). What happens in the Son's self-offering on the Cross is the revelation of the nature of God himself. The Cross is the central interpretative principle of God's nature. The Christian doctrine of the Trinity did not arise from Greek metaphysics but from the experience of God in the crucifixion and Resurrection.

If we view the cross/Resurrection event as revealing God's Trinitarian love, there is one basic quality of that love that appears and is predominant; it is a kenotic love. God manifests and reveals Himself as "powerless" in the finitude, weakness, suffering and death implicit in the Incarnation and explicit in the actuality of the cross. As in Christ, God participates in our weakness, suffering and death. In light of the Cross, divine love must be viewed as a pure agape that empties itself into the world in such a way as to become vulnerable to all the negativity of that world. God's omnipotence is seen as effective and actual, not primarily in expressions of power but in apparent weakness. God's vindication of what is weak and frustrated is not a renunciation of his true nature; it is its clearest expression.

D. God as Personal Agent

Kenotic love as found in God transcends the distinction between agape and eros. It is altruistic and simultaneously involved and caring. It is neither the divine transcendence without immanence nor the divine immanence without transcendence, but their inclusive unity. This kenotic dimension of God's love as revealed in Jesus Christ must be the starting point for any understanding and symbolization of God as he relates to us in his action, and as he is in himself. A loving God must necessarily be understood as personal agent. What is drastically needed in Christology is a perception of God as personal agent. The foundations we need for this new perception must be discovered in our knowledge of persons as agents.

John Macmurray has provided us with a model of the person primarily as agent. His model takes into consideration the historical and dynamic nature of personal identity. The unity of the personal is not primarily substantial but dialogical and it is characterized by interdependence. The classical view of God has made him absolutely independent. God is said to be totally independent with no real relation to any other realities. God is a substance and substance has been defined as "that which required nothing but itself to exist." Descartes applied this definition to three kinds of substances: God, finite minds, and finite bodies. While, according to Descartes, finite minds and bodies are not substances in the same way God is, yet they, too, are self-sufficient. It is no surprise that Western culture is characterized by individualism and isolation.

When one predicates the terms "person" and "personal agent" of God, one is using analogous language. Yet this analogous language should not be understood simply as a language that exists at a midpoint between univocation and equivocation. In fact, because we are characterized by transcendence and that transcendental experience is the very condition of any knowledge of individual and categorical reality, that which is analogous expresses what is most radical and original in our knowledge. Analogy according to Rahner is "the tension between a categorical starting point and the incomprehensibility of the holy mystery; namely, God." /12/ In a sense, we exist analogously since we are grounded in this holy mystery which is God. To speak of God as person is to speak of him analogously. But as Karl Barth wrote, God is the supreme person; men and women are persons only in a limited or derived sense. The true meaning of personhood can only be found in God; it exists, therefore, as mystery and can only be mediated to us through created reality. As analogous the reality of personhood as attributed to God works in two directions, it moves from man to God and from God to man. What we have grasped about human personhood we attribute to God; but what God has disclosed about himself in the person of Jesus Christ reshapes our own understanding of what personhood means and is.

What has been grasped about personhood and attributed to God over the centuries has varied. Most contemporary theology is founded on the Cartesian-Kantian model of the person. This has led to the impossibility of understanding God as a personal agent. It has led to stress on subjectivity over against objectivity, and has established a strong dichotomy between the two. We have established that our model of the person would be that of John Macmurray. John Macmurray has outlined a world-view where men and women are seen primarily as personal agents. His understanding of the person sheds new light on the possibility of understanding God as personal agent. Also, according to Macmurray, in personhood alone do we find the possibility of juxtaposing subjectivity and objectivity. Personhood is that pole of being in which the poles of subjectivity and objectivity cohere.

Although the Biblical testimonies do not use the term "person" as such, they make it clear that any thought about God is obliged to use the category of the personal. In the Bible, we have an ongoing dialogue with God. According to H. Küng:

> "from the first to last the Bible means by God a true partner, friendly to man and absolutely reliable: not an object, not a silent infinite, not an empty unechoing universe, not an indefinable nameless depth in a Gnostic sense, not a dark, intermediate void interchangeable with nothingness, least of all an anonymous interpersonal something which could easily be confused with man and his (so very fragile) love." /13/

Israel understood God as a "Thou" and understood itself as relating to a Thou. While God is not a person as we are persons, he is the infinite in all that finite, the ground of all that is grounded, he is not less than a person as we know person; he is not a thing that can be controlled, manipulated; he is not subpersonal even if beyond our grasp of his personhood and therefore beyond the personal.

The one essential difference between God's personhood and ours is that while we are created as persons, God is an uncreated person; we are dependent upon others to become persons; we receive our personhood; we depend on that which is other to become ourselves. God cannot be dependent on the other; he must be his own other. As creatures we constantly experience the tension of being-for-ourselves, and being-for-others. In God there is no such tension. In order to become persons we must risk being assimilated into the horizon of another person. God does not need the world; thus he is free to be radically for the other.

It is as a person that God is transcendent. The transcendence of God means nothing else than that God is person, radically for himself and radically for other. God is transcendent because he can be totally for others yet without risking to be absorbed by others. To understand God as personal agent is not necessarily to reduce God to the level of an object at the disposal of man's thought. As personal agent God is the subject who confronts us in the midst of our earthly historical reality. The reality of God is his reality as subject who stands over against us. God's objectivity can be understood in terms of his "standing-over-against us." In the concept of person as agent both the subjective and objective poles can be simultaneously affirmed.

When God is considered as person with action as the primary mode of his being, his correlate cannot simply be the material or the organic world but a personal world. As a personal agent, God does not exist in a personal sense in isolation nor does he lose his "wholly otherness." Personhood implies the "openness of being" and even more than that the exstasis; i.e., a movement toward communion.

While not receiving his personhood from an "other," the main thrust of calling God person is that we perceive him as relating to us as a personal agent whose activity manifests a definite personal character. Yet one of the most acute problems confronting contemporary theology is that of the possibility of attributing action to God; it is also the question of the nature and the discerning of God's action in history. The ultimate problem of modern theology is not really the problem of God and his existence; it is the problem of God as a personal agent. Does God himself act? Has he acted in the past, in history, and can he act today? Can one speak of act as the fact of God unless God is perceived as a personal agent? Can there be such a thing as an act unless there is a personal agent with purpose and intention?

Starting from Descartes's thinking subject, from the initial presupposition that man as person is basically thinking subject, with the world as the object of thinking, it is impossible without logical inconsistency to reach the conclusion that man is also an agent, free and able to act in and make purposeful changes in the world. If God is conceived in the same way as primary subject and not agent the same impossibility also applies to him. But if we accept with Macmurray that person is primarily characterized as agent, then it is possible to understand that God as person is one who acts, that in fact God's transcendence is in his action. There can be no division between the divine being and the divine action, between the inner life of God and God's action. God does not stand apart from his action, for God's being is being-in-act.

John Macmurray has underlined that what characterizes human action is intentionality. An action is a succession of activities ordered towards an end. Its unity consists in an intention to realize a goal. An action can be specified only by its purpose, by its intentionality. While action involves causality, the unity of action is one of intentionality. Actions need to be interpreted and a personal agent always transcends any single action and is never fully expressed in any series of actions. Gilkey writes:

> "In history, therefore, the conformation of effect to cause, of event to the factors that brought it about, is never totally determined. For, as we showed, no factor is a cause in history until it elicits a human response, and that invariably involves human interpretation, intentions, norms, judgments and decisions. Thus history is a process of centered decisions in which there is an unremoveable 'given," a destiny, but in which also freedom and spontaneity--and so contingency and purposes--are at work. This is also true for the entities of historical life; what is effected and affected, what in turn has effect, namely, groups, communities and cultural entities, are likewise multi-dimensional. Consequently, as our own analysis has shown, action in history takes place on many different levels of changes which help to effect fundamental historical transformations." /14/

E. God's Transcendence as Self-Communication

This understanding of a human agent as developed in John Macmurray can be applied to God as personal agent. In seeing God as agent we must stress his intentionality rather than his causality. At the same time, seeing God as agent implies that there are other agents. As agent, God's relation to the world is not an organic nor mechanical one as if the world were God's body, but it is personal, dialogical. It is as personal agent that God's transcendence can be understood. Transcendence can be defined not in terms of one substance existing beyond the reach of another, but in terms of the act by which a personal agent moves beyond his own self-existence and confronts and interacts with an other. Transcendence is not associated with a mode of being as such, but with a personal agent who acts as such in a particular mode of being. God's transcendence is the act by which he interacts with his creation. Transcendence is the reality of God in his action. Transcendence is not that which is predicated about the reality of God from the standpoint of the created but is rather that which God as personal agent predicates about reality.

For God, transcendence is self-communication. The maximum of transcendence is in the terms of self-communication. In his maximal self-giving, God becomes man. God's transcendence is his act which constitutes the reality of that which is other to him. Yet God's transcendence cannot be set over against his immanence. The transcendence of God is God's placing of himself into concrete historical relation to his creation as the limiting reality of creation's authentic existence. Through his self-communication God as personal agent brings into existence a possibility by actualizing it in time and space. God as personal agent through his actions makes himself accessible while at the same time preserving his freedom. God in his transcendence creates space for our transcendence over against him and at the same time creates the possibility for reciprocity and communion.

While man is "other" than God, free, and in a responding situation, this otherness is constituted by the transcendence of God himself, in such a way that God does not have to renounce or restrict his transcendence in order to himself become that "other," that is, to become man. /15/ It is in light of this transcendence that we can understand and speak about a special intervention on the part of God such as the Incarnation. Rahner writes:

> "A special 'intervention' of God, therefore, can only be understood as the historical concreteness of the transcendental self-communication of God which is already intrinsic to the concrete world." /16/

God always intervenes from the openness of matter and of spirit. Again according to Rahner every intervention of God "...is always only the becoming historical and becoming concrete as that 'intervention' in which God as the transcendental ground of the world has from the outset embedded himself in this world as its self-communicating ground." /17/ As personal agent, God is immanent and transcendent. God is the personal source of a person's free act; human transcendence is constituted by God's self-communication; God's self-communication is mediated by human historical transcendence. The event of God's self-communication which is transcending and in itself trans-historical belongs simultaneously to our history and takes place within it. This self-communication is also an act of disclosure, a revelation, never simply a matter of fact. In this act of disclosure God reveals to us our own reality as well as the reality of the other. Revelation is intrinsic to the act of a personal agent.

God's causality is covenantal; it is ultimately that of self-communication. God is not one cause among others; nor does he exist along other causes; nor does he replace created causes by intervening in their place. God caused the world but is not _a_ cause in the world. God must be in all history as its personal ground. The finite world and we who are in it cannot be outside God. The boundary between us and God is only our boundary, not God's. While God's causality is covenantal because fundamentally self-communication, God is not one who reaches out to his creatures out of loneliness. His immanence precedes his condescension. /18/

F. The Mutability of God

While John Macmurray has provided us with a model of person as agent which can be analogously affirmed of God, process theology has given us a valuable way of understanding the nature of God's activity. Process thought rejects static actuality as applicable to process and change. /19/ Process theology provides us with a way of recovering the conviction that God acts in the world, and of understanding this activity as the expression of divine love. For Whitehead, love, which neither rules nor is unmoved, is the starting point for an understanding of God. For Whitehead, it is love which must be perfect in God. And precisely because of this, God cannot be thought of without relating him to the world in which his created goodness is concretized.

Traditionally, theism has portrayed God as the absolute controlling power. The doctrine of divine omnipotence meant that God controlled every detail of the world process. The notion that God knows the world, and that this knowledge is unchanging, suggests that God determines every detail of the world, And yet, God in his omnipotence remains unrelated to the world. The act of knowledge and will which he is, is infinitely actuated in his perfect self-possession in self-knowledge and self-love, and so that act is in no way determined or specified by the finite objects whose radical source he is. According to Thomas Aquinas, "God's temporal relation to creatures are in Him only because of our way of thinking of Him; but the opposite relation of creatures to Him are realities in creatures." /20/ God is uniquely stable and immutable. God is seen as pure being, as changeless. The key contrast between God and his creation is that between the changeless and the changing.

Process thought has a different understanding of perfection. In the world there is not only being but also becoming; there is the subsistence and identity of beings but also their internal relation to other beings; there is both individuality and sociality, activity and receptivity. These are all perceived as perfection and therefore attributable to God. In light of this, God is considered as di-polar, as having a "primordial and consequent nature." /21/ The fullness of God demands both poles which represent transcendence and immanence, eternity and temporality, impassibility and passibility. This di-polarity is also reflected in the two fundamental symbols of the Christian faith - the cross and the Resurrection. The cross implies that God truly suffers; the cross speaks of his power to change reality and transform death into life. Yet God is God no less on the cross than in the Resurrection. While God is active in his primordial nature creating or at least ordering and leading the world, he is receptive in his subsequent nature receiving and prehending the fruits of the world's history. A. N. Whitehead writes: "Viewed as primordial, he is the unlimited conceptual realization of the absolute wealth of potentiality." /22/ The primordial mode of God's nature is free, complete, and eternal; the consequent nature of God is determined, incomplete. In some way God becomes actualized. The di-polar understanding of God insists that God is both absolute and supremely relative, both ground of all realities and affected by all reality.

In both "poles" of his reality God alone is

supremely perfect. In his primordial nature, in his abstract pole, God alone among all realities is not dependent on others for existence. In his consequent nature, in his concrete pole, God is relative to all other beings, he affects and is affected by all others. The di-polar God is both absolute and supremely relative: as a loving God he is related to all. God, as the eminently relative one, is the perfect expression of creative becoming.

The divine creative activity is understood in terms of a responsiveness to the world. It is such because this causality is grounded in love. God's activity in the world is a persuasive activity which always involves a creaturely response. The power of persuasion is the power of love; it resides in love's ability to evoke a response while respecting the integrity of the other. While traditional theism affirms that God is essentially love, this love is subordinated to the divine power which is understood as a dominating control. In process thought, God's power is persuasive, not coercive. God's activity does not frustrate human activity but opens it up to new possibilities. There is a shift here from the consideration of a God who has control over the world to a God who is an ongoing creative relationship of love with a world in process. As MacGregor writes:

> "The power of God is not to be conceived as an infinite degree of power understood as the ability to do everything (omnipotere) or to control everything (pantokratein). The unintelligibility of an infinity of such power has been more than once demonstrated by contemporary critics. The divine power should be conceived as, rather, the infinite power that springs from creative love. That is the power that is infinite, being infinitely creative and therefore infinitely sacrificial. The power that is at the heart of all things, transcending all, has been called by some agapistic. It is the power of sacrificial love. God does not control his creatures; he graciously lets them be. That need not mean he exercises no providential care over them. What it does mean is that the divine almightiness consists, not in God's possession

> of an unlimited ability to do what he pleases but of unlimited capacity for creative love, so that not only does he bring creatures into being to let them be; he creatively restores whatever seeks such restoration, so that the redeemed might indeed well be called a new creation, that is, a re-creation. /23/

Love is the abdication of power; in a real sense God is he who abdicates. In the words of Simone Weil, "Love consents to all and commands only those who consent. Love is abdication - God is abdication." /24/

This understanding of God does not mean that God is turned into a finite struggling God: it is simply the recognition that God's omnipotence is qualified by the creation which he has himself brought about. This understanding is a corollary of the character of creation and Incarnation: God must be seen as deeply involved in time and history which cannot be considered as external to him. While God transcends history, yet history is important to him and makes a difference. He is not simply above history, unaffected and unchanged by it. There is, therefore, a helplessness in God that is corollary of the character of Creation and Incarnation. This helplessness is freely chosen and is not ultimate. Divine omnipotence is defined as the ultimate triumph of his unchanging will of love. The key word here is ultimately. God has freely accepted temporal helplessness in the interest of open personal relation with his creatures. There is real interdependence and reciprocity between God and the world. This interdependence does not spring from the limitation of his essential being, but from voluntary self-limitation.

G. The Kenosis of God

There is a basic principle of self-limitation, a kenosis that applies to God in relation to finite being. The nature of God's being as personal agent is a letting-be, an enabling to be. Letting-be is also self-giving or self-spending so that God's creative work is a work of love and self-giving. Creation is not so much an exercise of power as rather an exercise of love and generosity, an act of self-limitation.

Creation is an act, not of self-expansion but of self-limitation. While it is true that creation does not mean a lessening of the divine life, yet through creation God enters a new limiting relationship. Through creation, God brings about an "other" who is free. In creating, God has surrendered his triumphant self-sufficiency and brought about his own need. He has done this freely out of love. Because in his transcendence God is free _from_ the world that has been brought about, he is also radically free _for_ the world. As Hodgson writes:

> "God is free to enter into communion with the world, free to be conditioned by his relationship with human beings, free to co-create the historical future with them without ceasing to be the Creator, free to liberate his creatures through their own personal and social struggles for freedom such that his grace does not cancel but rather undergirds their humanity, free finally to suffer to be crucified in history without thereby giving himself up." /25/

Creation is never from nothing but out of God himself. Creation is through a self-bestowal; it is an act in which God communicates his own reality. In creation, God gives of himself. The doctrine of creation _ex nihilo_ has often inserted an infinite gap between God and man, a gap that could be bridged only by another action of God - by redemptive Incarnation. The danger of this approach to creation is its underlying presupposition that man has his roots in nothingness. What creation "out of nothing" means to say is that creation is totally from God and therefore totally and radically dependent upon God. Through his creation God establishes reality truly as different from him, although always from him. God gives of himself in such a way that what is established is established in its difference from himself. Creation as a self-limiting act on the part of God is the establishment by God of what is other precisely as other.

The power of self-communication is the root of God's power to create and creation is the constitution of the context needed for the self-expression of God. God's self-communication consists precisely in the fact that God really arrives at man, really enters into man's situation.

There is a sacrificial nature to creation; it is intrinsically a self-humbling, self-restraining, self-limiting act. "The creation of heaven and earth," writes S. Bulgakov, "...is a voluntary self-diminution, a metaphysical kenosis, with respect to divinity itself." /26/ Creation is an act of kenosis in that God allows other beings besides himself. In order to understand how a unique God brings about an other as an other, some dimension of self-limitation must be attributed to God. This is even more so the case when the other is given the specific possibility of freedom and personal relation. In creating not only does God allow for the existence of a reality other than himself, but he actually gives a created being the possibility of choosing to respond to the Creator. By giving to creation a measure of independence, the possibility of loving, God limited himself, and in a real way rendered himself vulnerable. Creation is the work of authentic love and is not simply the effortless expression of the divine will. God's creative activity sets no limits to its own self-giving. It seeks constantly to enlarge the "other's" capacity to receive. In creating God holds nothing back.

Creation as self-bestowal may be termed an omnipotent act of God; but this power is not power as we commonly understand it in human affairs. Power is commonly understood as a controlling domination, the control of things, events, and other persons. MacGregor writes: "God does not wield power over his creation; on the contrary, he exercises it in the creative act, and the exercise of it is the exercise of his love." /27/ God's omnipotence is characterized and marked by the fact that God's power is to be grasped in the same sense that God's power is effective even in apparent weakness. In God, power and love are simply the two sides of the same reality. Because God's creative power is the power of love, his creating is a letting-be. Love does not only allow the other his or her otherness but actually makes it possible and requires it. The desire to make certain of the other, to guarantee the other's response, is in fact a violation of otherness and love. This can amount to little more than an attempt to control and hence to reduce the other to an instrument of one's interests and purposes.

Creation understood as a kenotic act on the part of God implies that there is a basic principle of the self-limitation of God in relation to finite being. A kenotic approach to creation implies the radical rejection of extrinsicism. The infinite is immanent in the finite not by absorbing or destroying it but by assuming its finitude and existence. The infinite is in and through the finite, but never identical with it. The mode of God's immanence is not identity, but transcendence. God's transcendence consists in the fact that he does not remove the difference between himself and what is other, but rather accepts the other precisely as different from himself. God frees human beings to be human and the world to be secular. As Kasper writes: "The intensity of creation's independence grows in direct and not inverse ratio to the intensity of God's action." /28/

H. Creation and God's Immanence

We cannot view God and man/woman as two beings, competing with each other. The real distinction between God and man/woman is in the fact of their finitude. Men/women have their permanent and ongoing origin in God. Created reality and, in a special way, human reality find their own authentic existence, freedom, and autonomy insofar as they live out their dependence upon God, their radical poverty. This radical poverty is the very nature of created reality; it is the orientation of created reality to the incomprehensible mystery that God is. And it is because creation is an act of self-bestowal on the part of God that creation and in a special way the human reality have that openness: there is an immanence of God which belongs intrinsically to creation; God bears a fundamental relationship to the world as such. Rahner writes: "the existence of God bears a quasi-formal relationship to the world such that the reality of God himself is imparted to it as its supreme specification." /29/ Because God creates through self-bestowal, God's self-communication as other is present in every person as the very condition for the possibility of personal acceptance. /30/ Man/woman is created as an otherness to whom God can communicate himself. Humanity is first of all a possibility for God. Through God's creative act, the human emerges as a way of being to which God can communicate himself without ceasing to be God. Humanity is a possibility for God to become other than

God, a possibility for Incarnation. /31/ God not only creates the world, he also gives himself to it as ground and ultimate goal, the historical manifestation of which is the Christ. /32/

Human nature is an active self-transcendence made possible by God. God, as the factor in the efficiency of the human and finite agent, enables the human agent to make a "quantum leap" to a higher nature. While creation through self-bestowal means that God is immanent to his creation, and that creation's nature is a for-Godness, it also means that God does not have to intervene from outside of his creation. The expression "from outside" applied to God's creating and even to God's revelation is not an adequate one. God never acts in anything really from outside because he is present in everything that exists distinct from him, as the deepest foundation of that existence, as Creator. He is not encompassed by what exists distinct from him, but he is certainly always more deeply present in it than that reality is to itself.

I. Our Suffering God

Because creation is an act of self-limitation, God in some mysterious way has put himself at a disadvantage - he has let himself be at the mercy of his own creation. Simone Weil has underlined this paradoxical nature of God's love: "A victim of misfortune is lying in the road, half-dead with hunger. God pities him but cannot send him bread. But I am here and luckily I am not God. I can give him a piece of bread. It is my one point of superiority over God." /33/ Divine creativity involves risk, the risk of being denied. The creating God is not, according to Küng, "a God of solitude, but a God of partnership, of the covenant. He is not an apathetic, unfeeling, impassible, but a sympathetic, compassionate God." /34/ The power of God resides in its ability to evoke a response while respecting the integrity of the other. In that process it opens itself to refusal and therefore to suffering.

The activity of God in creation must be precarious. It must proceed by no assured program. Each step is a precarious step into the unknown. If creation is the work of love, then its shape cannot be predetermined. God is determined to be God only in relationship to his creation. That is the risk of his infinite love. So eternal love can become suffering love because of its openness to be refused. As Moltmann writes: "God is not unchangeable if to be unchangeable means that he could not in the freedom of his love open himself to the changeable history of his creation. God is not incapable of suffering if this means that in the freedom of his love he would not be receptive to suffering over the contradiction of man and the self-destruction of his creation. God is not vulnerable if this means that he could not open himself to the pain of the cross. God is not perfect if this means that he did not in the craving of his love want his creation to be necessary to his perfection." /35/

According to Moltmann, God takes man so seriously that he suffers under the actions of man. /36/ The suffering of love is one in which one voluntarily opens oneself to the possibility of being affected by another. The justifiable denial that God is capable of suffering because of a deficiency in his being may not lead to a denial that he is incapable of suffering out of the fullness of his being; i.e., love. God suffers, contrary to Greek thought, not out of imperfection but out of the plenitude of his love. Suffering in God does not spring from the limitation of his essential being but from voluntary self-limitation and self-expression of his love for others. The suffering of God does not imply the limitation of his essential nature, but it rather signifies his strength to limit himself.

To say that God suffers is to say that God is actively engaged in dealing with a history which is real to him. At no point does God overwhelm human freedom. The genuine freedom of the created to do what God has not willed or done is guaranteed by the self-limitation of God in bringing freedom into being. It is thus that freedom is real, and the future open, that history is history. God acts in the future through our freedom and is limited by our freedom. The future is undecided, open, and so is unknowable in principle even to God. God as the eternal one does not merely establish time by creating it, but freely assumes it as a specification of his own self. As D. Dawe writes:

> "In creation, God accepted the limitation
> of co-existence with man and the world,

> which have their own creativity and freedom. Hence as long as there is a real human history in which men are acting freely and as long as God is concerned with men, there is some aspect of the divine being that is only potentially perfect. If God has a relationship with creation, and the created order has some measure of freedom, then there is an element of openness or incompleteness in the divine being." /37/

J. The Mutability of God

God is free to act in any and all ways. Yet that freedom is anchored in love and there is therefore an unchangeableness about God, his unswerving faithfulness to his covenant. The unchangeable quality in God is his will to love. God's immutability cannot be understood primarily in a static way. God's immutability is dynamic and historical and it implies the dynamic capacity for infinite responsive change in the interests of his fixed purpose of love. God has unlimited "ego strength" in his relation to his creation. In his "holy mutability" he has the ability to stay integrated in the fulfillment of his fundamental purpose of love. God's selfhood remains unimpaired no matter how deeply and intimately he becomes involved with his creation, with his people. If anything is immutable in God, it is the completeness of his love for us, which must include responses to our ever-changing needs.

The change that is denied to God is a change that rests on the incompletion of the subject, whose potency is not yet fully actualized. If God is God then such a mutability cannot be predicated of him. But does change always involve imperfection, a transition from potency to act? The whole question here consists in the nature of perfection. The problem is how to conceive the perfection of God properly. How can God be understood as the perfect reality and yet open to change and growth? Immutability, changelessness, are static attributes. They may be useful in describing the being of God; they do not provide a useful understanding of God in his relatedness. The Bible pictures God as involved with his creation, and creation as a kenotic act of God cannot be understood through static metaphors. Biblical thought is dominated by a highly personal conception of God. This personalism is best characterized by the attribute of freedom given to God. He is not determined by some abstract metaphysical necessity.

God is immutable in his divine being and mutable in his self-communication which coincides with his being. God's becoming is not the fulfilling of a need because of which he should be dependent on others, but it is the communication of God's richness by which he, in complete freedom, makes himself dependent on an other. God does not change nor is he changed by his own fulfillment. But we are saying too little if we make him a mover who himself always remains unmoved. He changes in the causing of being and becoming of the realities he has created and he does so in a fully divine way without compulsion, from freedom, from love. The immutability of God is a dialectical truth like the unity of God.

Rahner has attempted to explain this dialectic in the following fashion: although God "is immutable in and of himself, he himself can become something in another." /38/ According to Rahner, this possibility is not rooted in an imperfection, "but the height of his perfection. This perfection would be less perfect if he could not become less than he is... The absolute, or, more correctly, the absolute One in the pure freedom of his infinite unrelatedness, while he always preserves, possesses the possibility of himself becoming the other, the finite." /39/ This possibility is the possibility of kenosis: the other is established as his own reality through a dispossession of himself, through a giving away of himself. While in creation this kenosis is not complete, not full, and therefore the other established by God is not fully himself, still creation is the becoming of God in the other. God as personal agent is changed and affected existentially, not structurally, by the constitution of the other. The change is dialogical; God's personal being is enriched or depleted by the character of our relationship with him. God has willed to be God not for himself alone but also for us and this decision affects God's own being.

Hodgson writes: God will not be the same God upon the consummation of all things and their return to the Father as he was prior to the act of creation. In this sense he will have 'become' something 'other' and will have experienced something 'more' than was the case when God was God for himself alone." /40/

K. Kenosis within the Godhead. The Trinitarian Mystery

God is revealed in the history of Jesus as a loving God. This love determines the realm of creation: creation is a kenotic act. In creating God has freely accepted limitations in the fulfillment of his loving will for fellowship with others. The history of Jesus, the Paschal Mystery points inward into the very heart of God. The self-limiting nature of God as revealed in the Paschal Mystery and in the act of creating extends to the inner life of God. Self-limitation in creating and in the Incarnation is based on the very nature of God. Creation and Incarnation are the results of a movement of divine compassion in the very heart of God. God's kenosis in creating and the Incarnation did not begin there but within the eternal Godhead. Divine passibility, the ability to remain other while being present totally to the other, does not begin with the act of creation or with the sending of the Son; they are the results of an eternal passibility. Creation and Incarnation are not the beginning of divine passibility but the continuation of it with an intensification in time and space. Creation and cross are the projection on the plane of history of that which is eternally true about God's nature. /41/ In creating and in the "becoming flesh" God has revealed himself as dynamic, as the "One who has freedom absolutely," as "the one who constitutes himself and the world through an organic dialectic of relationships *ad intra* and *ad extra*." /42/ The Johannine statement that "God loved the world so much that he gave his only Son," (Jn. 3:16) seems to imply that there is within the Godhead a kenosis, an act of self-emptying that results in a letting-be, in the enabling of another to be. Kenosis in the Godhead means that there is "otherness" within God. God is triune because he is love. As Jüngel writes, "love is an ever greater selflessness in the midst of ever greater self-possession, freely going out from self and bestowing self." /43/ God as personal agent exists in self-dedication to the "other" and he does so within himself. God's "relativity" is in the first instance vis-a-vis himself. /44/ The begetting of the Son and the Spirit is a kenosis, a process of self-giving to the other. /45/

THE GOD OF JESUS. A GOD-WITH-US

According to E. Jüngel,

> "the grounding of trinitarian dogma on the act of Jesus on the Cross has hardly been sought in the theological speculation on the Trinity. The principle of immutability in the metaphysical conception of God, and the rule devised for avoiding tritheism, ('the actions of the Trinity outside God are undivided') led to the distinction between 'theology' and 'economy' and the corresponding separation of the 'immanent' from 'economic' Trinity." /46/

Historically, the dogma of the Trinity arose out of the original necessity in which Christian thought found itself at once of distinguishing Jesus Christ from God and of identifying him with God. This necessity in its turn arose out of the Christian experience itself, that is, out of the impression which Jesus Christ, in his life, death and Resurrection
of his disciples. Theologically speaking, we might almost say that it was in order to make intelligible the experience of the Incarnation and the atonement that the doctrine of the Trinity was formulated. Therefore, we ought to test the truth and significance of our doctrine of the Trinity by our apprehension of the truth and significance of the Incarnation, and not to limit the significance of the Incarnation by the supposed demands of the doctrine of the Trinity.

What seems clear to contemporary theologians is that the divine Trinity should not be conceived of as a closed circle of perfect being in heaven. This was, in fact, the way in which the immanent Trinity was conceived in the early Church. In contrast to this, though, one should think of the Trinity as a dialectical event, indeed as the event of the cross and then as "eschatologically open history." /47/ Karl Rahner has proposed the thesis that: "The 'economic' Trinity is the 'immanent' Trinity and the 'immanent' Trinity is the 'economic' Trinity." /48/

The unity of the Trinity is the unity of reciprocal self-dedication, a unity that comes into existence through the power of reciprocal dedication. By surrendering himself, God shows his divinity; the way of humanity is not only that of the Son but also that of the Father.

THE GOD OF JESUS. A GOD-WITH-US

NOTES

1. On this point E. Martinez writes: "Jesus did not proclaim himself, his whole life was a proclamation of the Father and the coming of the Kingdom of God his Father. Faith in God the Father who saves is what Jesus proclaimed and this shines through all the expression of his teaching. After Jesus' Resurrection the early Church did not change this emphasis: the disciples proclaimed the God who has raised up Jesus." "The Identity of Jesus in Mark," Communio 4 (Winter, 1974) p. 342.

2. Cf. J. Knox, The Humanity and Divinity of Christ, (New York: Cambridge University Press, 1967).

3. Cf. J. Hick, ed., The Myth of God Incarnate, (Philadelphia: Westminster Press, 1977).

4. W. Pannenberg, Jesus - God and Man, (Philadelphia: Westminster Press, 1977) pp. 33-37.

5. Cf. K. Rahner, Theological Investigations V, (Baltimore: Helicon Press, 1966) p. 176.

6. To concentrate too exclusively on the Christ-event and not on what the Christ-event reveals about God is to run the risk of reductionism. Such a concentration gave rise to the death-of-God theology.

7. W. Kasper, Jesus the Christ, (New York: Paulist Press, 1976).

8. Cf. R. A. Norris, God and the World in Early Christian Theology, (New York: The Seabury Press, 1965) p. 28.

9. J. Pelikan, The Christian Tradition. A History of the Development of Doctrine, Vol. I: The Emergence of the Catholic Tradition (100-600), (Chicago: University of Chicago Press, 1971) p. 52.

   Cf. also H. Chadwick, "Philo and the Beginnings of Christian Thought" in A. H. Armstrong, ed., The Cambridge History of Later Greek and Early Medieval Philosophy, (Cambridge: Cambridge

University Press, 1926).

10. Cf. J. K. Mozley, The Impassibility of God. A Survey of Christian Thought, (Cambridge: Cambridge University Press, 1926).

11. Exodus 34:6.

12. K. Rahner, Foundations of Christian Faith, (New York: Seabury Press, 1978) p. 73.

13. H. Küng, On Being a Christian, (Garden City: Doubleday, 1974) p. 304.

14. L. Gilkey, Reaping the Whirlwind. A Christian Interpretation of History, (New York: Seabury Press, 1976) p. 244.

15. Karl Rahner writes: "and this possibility (of God becoming other) is not a sign of deficiency, but the height of perfection, which would be less if in addition to being infinite, he could not become less than he always is." On the Theology of the Incarnation, op. cit., p. 114.

16. K. Rahner, Foundations of Christian Faith, op. cit., p. 87.

17. Ibid.

18. P. Schoonenberg writes about prayer: "Prayer is speaking to God, certainly, but it is not speaking to someone who is simply the other over and against us. Praying is raising one's heart to God, certainly, but also knowing that he is present in the depth of our heart. When we pray, we make ourselves open to the God who is already penetrating us everywhere and who wants to fill us more and more. Praying is opening ourselves to the Other, who in his freedom is never our possession, but who hears us in his love. Prayer is directing ourselves toward the one who is over and against us and who is already present in our subjectivity, because his Spirit prays in us with sighs too deep for words." "God as Person(al)," in A Personal God? (New York: Seabury Press, 1977) pp. 90-91.

19. Cf. W. A. Beardslee, A House of Hope: A Study in Process and Biblical Thought, (Philadelphia, 1972);

D. Brown, et al. (ed.), Process Philosophy and Christian Thought, (New York, 1971);

J. B. Cobb, Jr., God and the World, (Philadelphia, 1969);

E. Cousins (ed.), Process Theology: Basic Writings (New York, 1971);

D. Griffin, A Process Christology, (Philadelphia, 1973);

J. E. Barnhart, "Incarnation and Process Philosophy," Religious Studies, Vol. II (April, 1967) pp. 225-232.

For a critical evaluation: L. Gilkey, "Process Theology," Vox Theologica, Vol, 43 (1973).

20. Thomas Aquinas, Summa Theologica I, q. 13, a. 7 and 4;

Cf. A. Krempel, La Doctrine de la Relation Chez Saint Thomas, (Paris, 1952).

21. A. N. Whitehead, Process and Reality: An Essay in Cosmology, (New York: Macmillan, 1967) p. 520.

22. Ibid., p. 524.

23. G. MacGregor, He Who Lets Us Be. A Theology of Love, (New York: Seabury Press, 1975) p. 15.

24. Quoted in G. MacGregor, op. cit., p. 120.

25. P. Hodgson, New Birth of Freedom, (Philadelphia: Fortress Press, 1966) p. 336.

26. Quoted by G. MacGregor, op. cit., p. 104.

27. G. MacGregor, op. cit., p. 25.

28. W. Kasper, Jesus the Christ, (New York: Paulist Press, 1976) p. 95.

29. K. Rahner, "Christology in the Setting of Modern Man's Understanding of Himself and of His World," in Theological Investigations Vol. XI, (New York: Seabury Press, 1974) p. 225;

On the concept of formal causality see K. Rahner, Foundations of Christian Faith, op. cit., p. 120ff.

30. K. Rahner, "Dogmatic Reflections on the Knowledge and Self-Consciousness of Christ," Theological Investigations Vol. V, (Baltimore: Helicon, 1966) p. 209.

31. Cf. K. Rahner, "On the Theology of the Incarnation," op. cit., p. 116.

32. Cf. K. Rahner, "Christology in the Setting of Modern Man's Understanding of Himself and of His World," op. cit., p. 200.

33. Simone Weil, First and Last Notebooks, trans. R. Rees, (London: Oxford University Press, 1970) p. 297.

34. H. Küng, op. cit., p. 308.

35. J. Moltmann, The Church in the Power of the Spirit, (New York: Harper & Row, 1975) p. 62.

36. "The more the covenant is taken seriously as the revelation of God, the more profoundly one can understand the historicity of God and history in God. If God has opened his heart in the covenant with his people, he is injured by disobedience and suffers in the people. What the Old Testament terms the "wrath of God" does not belong in the category of the anthropomorphic transference of lower human emotions to God, but in the category of the divine pathos. His wrath is injured love and therefore a mode of his reaction to men. Love is the source and the basis of the possibility of the wrath of God. The opposite of love is not wrath, but indifference. Indifference towards justice and injustice would be a retreat on the part of God from the covenant. But his anger is an expression of his abiding interest in man. Anger and love do not therefore keep a balance. 'His wrath lasts

for the twinkling of an eye,' and, as the Jonah story shows, God takes back his anger for the sake of his love in reaction to human repentance. As injured love, the wrath of God is not something that is inflicted, but a divine suffering of evil. It is a sorrow which goes through his opened heart. He suffers in his passion for his people."

J. Moltmann, The Crucified God, (New York: Harper & Row, 1975) pp. 271-272.

37. D. Dawe, The Form of a Servant, (Philadelphia: Fortress Press) p. 189.

38. K. Rahner, Foundations of Christian Faith, op. cit., p. 221.

39. Ibid., p. 222.

40. P. Hodgson, Jesus - Word and Presence. An Essay in Christology, (Philadelphia: Fortress Press, 1971) p. 128.

41. Cf. J. Moltmann, The Crucified God, op. cit.

42. P. Hodgson, New Birth of Freedom, op. cit., pp. 336-337.

43. E. Jüngel, "The Relationship between 'Economic' and "Immanent' Trinity," in Theology Digest 24, No. 2 (1976) p. 182.

44. E. Jungel, The Doctrine of the Trinity. God's Being is Becoming, (Grand Rapids: W. Eerdmans, 1976) p. 182.

45. This aspect of the inner life of God has been developed by S. N. Bulgakov. He writes: "The Sonship is already an eternal kenosis... because the Word seems to become wordless (in Himself) and makes Himself the Word of the Father ... If, on the side of the Father, there is self-negation in begetting of the Son, the Son is thoroughly emptying Himself when He accepts the passive state of the One who is begotten." Quoted by N. Gorodetzsky, The Humiliated Christ in Modern Thought, (London, S.P.C.K., 1938) p. 162.

46. E. Jüngel, "The Relationship Between 'Economic' and 'Immanent' Trinity," op. cit., p. 180-181.

47. J. Moltmann, *The Crucified God*, op. cit., p. 255.

48. K. Rahner, *The Trinity*, (New York, 1970) p. 23.

49. K. Rahner has been criticized for his position by G. Lafont. Lafont objects to Rahner's *Grundaxiom* because this seems to posit necessities within the Godhead. Cf. G. Lafont, *Peut-on Connaitre Dieu en Jesus Christ? Problematique*, (Paris, 1969) pp. 220-222.

CHAPTER 10

JESUS CHRIST: GOD-FOR-US

A. Introduction

In a kenotic Christology or in any other Christology, the basic question and problematic is that of the living unity of God and man in Jesus Christ with the continuing differentiation of the two: the personal unity of God and man in Jesus the Christ. This unity has been understood in classical Christology as the hypostatic unity; this doctrine, as laborious and involved as it is, is simply an attempt at a conceptual and ontological expression of the New Testament affirmation that God has manifested himself with eschatological finality in Jesus Christ. The development of this conceptual model has been dominated by the "God-man" formula, the two natures/one person approach. /1/
The major opposition to the traditional understanding of the hypostatic unity is that its initial approach is ontic. The two natures/one person approach often leads to seeing the hypostatic unity primarily as a synthesis. The ontic approach does not take as its starting point the unity of the concrete person Jesus of Nazareth, but the difference between the human and divine natures. According to Pannenberg, "The pattern of thought thus moves in the opposite direction from the formula, _vere deus, vere homo_. Jesus now appears as a being bearing and uniting two opposed substances in himself. From this conception, all the insoluble problems of the doctrine of the two natures result." /2/ Jesus cannot be understood as the synthesis of the human and the divine, of which only the human side can be seen.

The unity of God and man in him is much more intensive than any form of synthesis could ever express. At the same time one cannot speak of two persons in Christ; no dialogue can be assumed between the divine and the human person within the one Christ such as between Christ and the Father.

The unity of Jesus with God can be found only in the historical existence of Jesus in his message and actions. Our starting point for the question of the hypostatic unity is the history and destiny of Jesus of Nazareth, his relation to the Father in dedication and obedience.

A Christology that begins with the historical sonship of Jesus cannot appeal to the eternal sonship to establish the transcendence of Jesus' human existence. A Christology from below must establish Jesus' transcendence of Jesus' human existence. /3/ A Christology from below must establish Jesus' transcendence precisely in his manhood. In the Incarnational model, there is a danger of removing the transcendence of Jesus from his humanity. As Schoonenberg affirms, "One need not worry then about Jesus' humanity, seeing that the second person of God's Trinity stands 'behind' it with his divine nature." /4/

B. Jesus' Personal Unity with the Father

The unity of Jesus Christ with God is primarily a personal community with the Father, one expressed in total dedication and obedience. While our initial categories are historical and existential, ultimately they must open up into more ontological categories. /5/ The ontological questions arise when the question about the ground of Jesus' historical dedication to the Father is posed. Is the personal community of Jesus with the Father also a community of essence? The question can also be asked in the following way: Is Jesus the eternal Son of God?

The Resurrection reveals that Jesus' life was grounded in God himself. The personal community of Jesus with the Father is not simply accomplished through Jesus' dedication to the Father but it is given, it is from the Father. The basis of Jesus' unity with the Father does not reside simply in Jesus' humanity; it can only be sought on the side of God. Here the Incarnational model is correct in affirming that the unity of Jesus with the Father was already consummated in the beginning. The Incarnation underlines the fact that in the life of Jesus, from the beginning there is no independence from God. What is true from the perspective of the Resurrection is true for the totality of Jesus' person from the beginning. Jesus' unity with God is one of total dependence expressed historically in dedication and obedience. The Easter event revealed the truth about Jesus' unity with the Father, about Jesus' nature; it was not constitutive of it. /6/

God's acceptance of Jesus from the very beginning is the expression of God's fatherhood towards Jesus. This is what the Resurrection reveals about God's relation to Jesus. Jesus' dedication and obedience to God can be characterized in terms of sonship. As the one fully obedient and responsive to the will of God, Jesus is the one in whom the fullness of divinity dwells, the one to whom God is fully present.

According to Pannenberg, "Such personal community is at the same time essential community. It is so first of all in the sense that it is the essence of the person itself to exist in dedication... To be submerged in the 'Thou' means at the same time, however, participating in his being. Thus the divinity of Jesus as Son is mediated, established through his dedication to the Father." /7/ "Through personal community one achieves a share in the essence of the other in spite of the continuing personal distinctiveness. An 'essence' common to both emerges in the course of their interaction." /8/ Thus Jesus' unity with the Father and his identity with the eternal Son of God is dialogical. This unity and identity emerges fully only in the history of Jesus' existence.

In a Christology that centers itself on the Incarnation the unity of the man Jesus with the eternal Son of God is the starting point. It is a given. In a Christology that begins with the historical particularity of Jesus' sonship to the Father, there is no such given. Nor can Jesus' sonship be related to the eternal sonship as one person to another person.

Pannenberg sees the unity of Jesus to the eternal Son by way of a detour - through Jesus' dedication to the Father. "Only the personal community of Jesus with the Father shows that he is himself identical with the Son of this Father." /9/ Again, "In the execution of this dedication, Jesus is the Son. Thus he shows himself identical with the correlate Son already implied in the understanding of God as the Father, the Son whose characteristic it is not to exist on the basis of his own resources but wholly from the Father." /10/ "Nonetheless, with the special relation to the Father in the human historical aspect of Jesus' existence, his identity in the other aspect, that of the eternal Son of the eternal Father, is given." /11/ It must be emphasized that the possibility of moving from Jesus' historical dedication to God his Father, to affirming that through this dedication he is identical to the eternal Son, implies and demands the possibility of historical transcendence. Jesus' dedication must have a depth, a God-given depth that makes the transition possible.

To say that the unity of Jesus with the Father can be found only in the historical participation of the man Jesus is to say that transcendence is fully situated in the human. In some way, the experience of the historical Jesus must be so profound and radical that it becomes the experience of the transcendent in our midst. Jesus' personal community with the Father can be said to be a community of essence only if Jesus' dedication to the Father is rooted in a transcendence characterized by self-emptying love. This community must be seen as the coming together of God's self-emptying and Jesus' acceptance. Without the divine self-communication and Jesus' receptivity there would be no Incarnation. Two activities, one requiring and complementing the other, are indispensable to the full and irrevocable coming together of God and man. It is impossible for God to become incarnate apart from human response and human responsibility, and therefore human transcendence expressed in self-emptying.

C. A Dialogical Unity

A dialogical unity between God and man demands a line from below: the open transcendence of the human subject as spiritual being oriented to the absolute being of God. The essence of man as openness for and toward the other constitutes in its own way the presupposition for an incarnation. God's self-communication constitutive of Jesus' humanity establishes the necessary condition for the acceptance of such a gift. According to Rahner, "...God's self-communication or offer is also the necessary condition which makes its acceptance possible." /12/ The offer of the gift is already an orientation, an openness to the gift, a God-given openness. It is also the source of man's radical poverty: fulfillment can only be from God. As Rahner writes: "...in our poverty we are oriented toward the mystery of fullness." /13/ "All beings and above all the created spirit in its transcendence towards absolute being, partake of the mysterious character of God insofar as all beings are referred to God and cannot be adequately understood without this relationship and hence without the term of this relationship." /14/

Human nature needs to be understood as "emerging." As John writes, "It does not yet appear what we shall be." /15/ The finite is capable of the infinite because the infinite is present to the finite as gracious offer. According to Rahner, "...the finite itself has been given an infinite depth and is no longer a contrast to the infinite, but that which the infinite himself has become, to open a passage into the infinite for all the finite, within which he himself has become a part..." /16/

The essence of man as openness for and toward the other constitutes in its own way the transcendental presupposition for an incarnation. Human nature, because created through God's self-bestowal, must be conceived as an active transcendence, as an opening ultimately toward God. /17/ Humanhood, therefore, and Godhood cannot be taken to be fixed natures infinitely far apart. Rather humanhood is an open, emerging reality transcending towards God, because created as such by God. The human reality from the very depths of its God-given being is an openness to God perpetually opened by God. That openness is the openness for God's self-communication as the possible but free and radically highest answer of God to what the human reality itself is. In the Incarnation God does not enter a realm foreign to himself; human finitude does not exclude God. Men and women exclude God from their lives through sin. The human limitations do not of themselves alienate the human from God. This is his world. The uniquely full relation between God and man seen in Christ is grounded in God's initial relation to all mankind.

In the Incarnation God's self-communication is the communication of a personal agent to a personal agent. What is communicated is not a thing but a self, God's own personal being. In this self-communication, God posits Jesus fully in his own intrinsic humanity as a human person, as a personal agent free and able to respond "yes" and "no."

Jesus stands before God in free human obedience. He is Mediator, according to Rahner,

> "not only in virtue of the ontological union of the two natures, but also through his (Jesus') activity, which is directed

> to God (as obedience to the will of the Father) and cannot be conceived of simply as God's activity in and through a human nature thought of as purely instrumental, a nature which in relation to the Logos would be ontologically and morally purely passive." /18/

D. Unity Through Self-Emptying

In the mystery of the Incarnation the decisive question is not primarily that of the otherness of creation; it is the question of the unity of God with the other. To see creation as a kenotic act through which God posits what is differentiated from him through a self-giving is not yet to see God's unity with what is differentiated from him. Yet that act is the very foundation of any such unity from God's side. The possibility of creation is grounded in the fact that God has within himself the possibility to give himself to what is not God, which is the very possibility of the Incarnation.

In a kenotic approach, both creation and the Incarnation are understood as two phases of "the one process of God's self-giving and self-expression." /19/ God is already in a self-limiting relation with the whole of the created order. The kenosis in Jesus the Christ is the ultimate expression of God's kenotic love for his creation. The uniquely full relation between God and man in Jesus is grounded in God's initial relation to all mankind. Kenosis means that there is a humanward movement in the divine life that is expressed in creation and finally consummated in the Incarnation.

In a kenotic Christology, God is considered as absolute letting-be, as self-giving, as self-spending. Kenosis is seen as the way God relates to the world; his creation is a work of love, of self-giving, into which he has thrown himself. A kenotic Christology is built on that fundamental conception of God's nature as eternal _agape_. God's love expressed in his self-giving, while manifested in his creation, is supremely manifested in Jesus Christ. In a kenotic Christology, God poses the humanity of Jesus as other, through his own self-emptying. God in his absolute freedom has the possibility within Himself of becoming the other without danger to his own identity. The other is brought about, constituted, as God's own reality by an act of kenosis, by a dispossession on the part of God, by a giving away of himself.

Here the Incarnation is not seen as an assumption of a human nature on the part of the eternal Logos but as a self-emptying on the part of God. In a kenotic understanding of the Incarnation, the personal humanity of Jesus is not prior (therefore we do not have adoptionism) but comes to be and is constituted in essence and existence when and insofar as God empties himself.

We have here not an impersonal humanity but the full humanity of Jesus as the proper vehicle for divinity in the space-time context, and this without eliminating the distinction between God and man. Through God's self-communication as constitutive of Jesus' humanity, Jesus belongs to the divine mystery rather than to himself, but he does so through his own human acceptance. While Jesus exists as the kind of person he is only in and because of his relationship to that mystery which God is, yet his unity with God is understood primarily in terms of his human dedication to the Father and to the neighbor, a dedication that comes to fulfillment only in the crucifixion. The person of Jesus is constituted by a twofold movement of God to Jesus, of Jesus to God. The person of Jesus does not result from the synthesis of two static natures. We have here a unity of agency rather than of substance, of activity rather than natures, a *homo-praxis* rather than a *homo-ousia*, a personal and dialogical unity. The locus of unity is the self-emptying of God that is essentially a letting-be of Jesus as Jesus and the corresponding self-emptying of Jesus which is also a letting-be of the Father as Father. When the capacity for self-emptying and letting-be is raised to an absolute level, a particular personal being can be of one essence with the Father, the primordial being. Here personal community is also essential community. The unity is dialogical. /20/

The mystery of the Incarnation as understood kenotically implies that when God gives of himself, even fully, he does not do violence to the other, but gives it full authenticity. Jesus is the one who sees himself

and the whole of his life in the context of receiving and giving. Receiving is the fundamental expression of his being. In self-surrender, in self-emptying, in accepting to be fulfilled by God, Jesus posits his own existence. This is actualization by letting-go. In Jesus we have the affirmation that the more deeply one is accepted by God and is taken into his own existence, the more he discovers himself, the more radically he is made free for his own possibilities. Being accepted and independence are not opposed but they correspond to one another. Jesus of Nazareth is the one who, from the very depths of his being, has surrendered himself to God and has been accepted by God. Jesus lived his life in complete dependence on his Father.
such dependence does not destroy human personality. Man is never so truly and fully personal as when he is living in complete dependence on God. This is how human personality comes into its own. This is not impersonal humanity, but humanity at its most personal, since what appears to be radical dependence upon God is in fact interdependence.

Because receiving is Jesus' fundamental nature, his life is lived out in giving, in a pouring out of self, and ultimately in a complete giving, his dying on the cross. Jesus' answer to God's self-emptying is in his own self-emptying. By emptying himself, Jesus participated fully in the life of God, the plenitude of being. Self-emptying, the principle of the kenotic Being of God, became the law of Jesus' own life. Jesus universalized this law: "Whoever would save his life shall lose it, and whoever loses his life for my sake and the gospel will save it" (Mk. 8:35; John 12:24). All personal reality must go out of itself in order to preserve itself. The "I" must empty itself at a "Thou" in order to gain itself in the other. Whatever exists finds its identity not through an absolute, aloof being-in-itself, but concretely, and only through a relationship. Jesus does not find his nature in
a self-subsistence, which has always been regarded as the highest perfection; instead it is his nature to exist for others, it is self-surrender, self-abandonment; he is the one who steps aside, who stands up for others and identifies with others. Jesus' personhood possesses both passive and active qualities. On the one hand, and this is primary, it contains the element of surrender or self-negation, in relation to the Father; on the other hand,

it invites a dedication to the neighbor. The Thou of the Father and the thou of the neighbor are constitutive of Jesus' own personhood. The depth of Jesus' personhood is measured in terms of his relation to God and to the neighbor. These relations determine the concrete essence of his person. Jesus' "ego" comes not from himself, but from beyond himself, from the Father and from the neighbor. To be constituted by these singular relationships is to be unconditionally responsive. In being fully responsive to the Father and to the oppressed, Jesus is the Son of God. Jesus' divine sonship is his humanness to the utmost. Jesus is the Son of God.

E. Jesus as Eternal Son of God in History

Is this doctrine consonant with what tradition affirms about the eternal pre-existent Son of God? In Jesus we do not have two persons: the person-ness of the divine Son and the person-ness of the man Jesus. What is being affirmed in our kenotic Christology is that the unity of the personal cannot be thought of as the form of an individual self, but only in the mutuality of personal relations. The eternal Son does not stand alongside Jesus as another person. Anything said about the eternal Son can only be fully said when reference is made to the man Jesus; anything said about Jesus can be fully said only by recourse to the eternal Son. We must remember here Hegel's words; "It is the essence of the person to acquire an identity by losing it in and for the other." In the economy of salvation, in the event of the Incarnation, the abstract personality of the eternal Son became concrete through a limitation, through a free self-limitation. There is no Son of God apart from the Son of flesh. This is not made explicit prior to the Incarnation, but the inner logic is there in God's self-communication in Creation and to Israel. Through an identification with a creature, God introduces within himself a real opposition and the possibility of inter-personality. The Incarnation as a kenosis is what allows God to become existent in the world in such a radical sense.

The <u>egeneto</u> of John's gospel carries the force of an historical existence. <u>Egeneto</u> is the predicate which by essence belongs to creaturehood; it now exists as the predicate of the Creator. It is not simply that the eternal Son has become conditioned in some manner by flesh, as though the flesh were an external and temporary condition of the eternal Son. But the eternal Son has become truly flesh, has entered into the experience and existence of creaturehood. The transcendence of God has become historical. /21/

God's transcendence is the act by which he moves outside and beyond his own immanent freedom. The transcendence of God is God's placing of himself into concrete, historical relation to his creature. Transcendence means that God can become for another because the power of becoming belongs to his own being in his own inner, kenotic act. Kenosis means that there is a humanward movement in the divine life that is expressed in creation and consummated in the Incarnation. Christhood may be understood as that point at which humanhood and Godhood come together and in which Godhood is manifested and mediated in God-manhood. John Macquarrie writes: "So we can understand how it is that Christ has a complete human nature and what was meant by saying that at the limit of existence, that is to say, at the furtherest point along the road toward fulfilling or unfolding the "nature" (existence) he manifests divine Being." /22/ Christ is the chief exemplification of God's gracious giving of himself and the actualization of man's own response. In Jesus we have the unique culmination of creation's own response. In Jesus we have the unique culmination of the general creator-creation relationship. In his personal unity with God, Jesus is the fulfillment of the human destiny. /23/

Human destiny is to have its origin permanently in God, to be permanently grounded in absolute mystery; to be radically different and yet one with God. Being from God and being totally dependent upon God in no way cancels out human personhood, individuality or independence. The deepest self of man is constituted by its relationship with God. This is directly related lated to man/woman's capacity for the infinite. The actualization of that capacity through God's graciousness constitutes the deepest dimension of a person's self-being. The more a creature participates in God's being, the more the creature is somone itself. To think of God or the creature as threatening the other is to fail to think of "in itselfness" and "for the otherness" as mutually fostering, mutually inclusive. In other words it is a failure to think dialogically.

In a kenotic framework the divinization of Jesus, the _gratia unionis_ is a humanizing action; the greater the proximity to God, the greater the intrinsic reality of the human being. The greater the unity, the more a distinct reality is posited. Genuine independence and self-coherence increases in direct and not in inverse proportion to radical dependence upon God. Jesus is autonomous because of and real in spite of total dependence on the Creator. /24/

What we have in the person of Jesus as the Christ is intensified creation. In Jesus Christ the dimension of creatureliness is not eliminated but sharpened. As J. B. Metz writes: "The human nature of Christ is not "lessened" by being taken up into the divine Logos, made simply into a dead tool, a mere accessory, a gesture of God within the world, but given its hitherto unsuspected full, human authenticity: Jesus Christ was fully man, indeed, more human than any of us." /25/ Being "accepted" by God is a freeing act since it is fundamentally a kenotic act. Again Metz writes: "God's divinity consists in the fact that he does not remove the difference between himself and what is other, but rather accepts the other _precisely as different from himself_." /26/ To be accepted by God is to be set free to be oneself.

F. Jesus as Eschatological Revelation of God

Incarnation becomes, then, a characteristic of God's being with us. Incarnation as applied to Jesus is a specific case of what is true about God's presence. Incarnation expresses something decisive about God's self-communication to his total creation. Here the problem of Jesus' difference from the rest of us causes no embarrassment. The hypostatic unity is not so much intended as a quality which makes Jesus different from the rest of us, as it is understood as a decisive point in the history of God's gift of self to creation. The once and for all dimension of the Incarnation is to be understood eschatologically. Jesus is the eschatological fulfillment of God's involvement with his creation. As eschatological, the drama of the Incarnation is not yet over; God's presence is still withhheld in some respect, since it is given in a full, historical way; "having come about historically" is a characteristic of God's presence. God's presence is in the "form of a servant"; it is not absolutely transparent. While Jesus Christ is in glory, the world is not yet "resurrected," it is still on the cross, the Kingdom of God is still to come. As historical and eschatological, God's presence in Jesus Christ is essentially revelational.

Since Jesus is the self-utterance of God, and since God expresses himself when he empties himself, then Jesus as the Christ is the revelation of God. The presence of God in Jesus is dialogical and therefore revelational. And it is not in spite of being a human person but because of being a human person that God is revealed in Jesus Christ. Incarnation in a man is a mode of communication peculiar to the Logos. Human nature is specifically designed to reveal the eternal Logos. The flesh is not the veil but a revelation of the Logos. /27/

Since kenosis is necessarily a personal act, the most personal of all acts, then God's revelation occurs in Jesus as a person. In the person of Jesus, of Jesus crucified, God's Word comes to speech, not only comes to speech but is dependent upon this person for his Word to be spoken fully. God's Logos depends upon an embodiment for its coming to speech in the world. Jesus' humanity is God's self-interpretation. In Jesus' life of perfect obedience the Logos expressed himself. By definition, the Logos is that which in God is able to express God in that which is not God. The Logos is God's ability to express himself in history.

God's presence in Jesus is revelatory. Revelational identity while combining presence as appearance and substantial presence emphasizes presence as appearance. /28/ The human form of Jesus is the personal revelation of God and is therefore God for us. Here the "is" does not express a real identification in the content of subject and predicate as would be the case if one affirmed that John is a man. Relative to his humanity, Jesus "is" not God, nor "is" God, relative to his divinity, Man in the sense of real identification. As revelational and concrete expression of the divinity, Jesus in his human personhood is a symbol. For any concrete assertion about God must be symbolic. Jesus the Christ, insofar as the unconditioned transcendent is envisaged in him, is a symbol. In his human personhood Jesus Christ is an historical symbol; and only as such is it appropriate to manifest and reveal a kenotic God.

According to J. Macquarrie, Jesus Christ "...is for Christian faith the decisive or paradigmatic revelation of God...we can call him the 'symbol of being'...in using the word 'symbol' no diminution or unreality in Christ's relation to Being is intended." /29/ According to Macquarrie, God is present and manifest in Christ. This expression "present and manifest" is peculiarly appropriate when we think of Christ as the revelation or the revelatory symbol, of God: for "presence" in Greek is parousia, and "manifestation" is epiphaneia and these are precisely the words that have traditionally been used for the revelation of God in Christ - "advent" and "epiphany." In Christ takes place the "advent of God, his coming to be present or his dwelling among us; and there likewise takes place the "epiphany" of God, the manifestation or showing forth of his grace and truth. /30/

The understanding of Jesus as the symbol of the Godhead or the revelation of God is not incompatible with the affirmation that in Jesus Christ, God has acted decisively and once and for all. To speak about the presence of God in Jesus Christ as revelational and of Jesus Christ as symbol of God is simply to unfold the kenotic nature of God and Jesus Christ.

In an important essay written in 1959 Rahner elaborated an understanding of symbol that sheds light on what we have just now affirmed. According to Rahner, "All beings are by their nature symbolic, because they necessarily express themselves in order to attain their own nature." /31/ The primary function of the symbol is to make another to be present primarily for itself and also for others. Because of the unity and multiplicity of being, one thing can be the expression of another. This is even true for God, since God is revealed as a distinction of persons in his own simplicity. Plurality in unity is not a deficiency. While unity precedes plurality and plurality is the consequence of an original unity, yet for a being the condition for the possibility of its self-possession in knowledge and love is the act of constituting itself as a plural. Self-presence or self-realization is the "coming to itself" of a being in its expression, its emergent and intrinsic plurality. Every being is primordially symbolic to the degree of self-possession. /32/

For Rahner, a being "comes to itself in the measure in which it realizes itself by constituting a plurality." /33/ This means that each being is itself primarily symbolic. "It expresses itself and possesses itself by doing so. It gives itself away from itself into the other and there finds itself in knowledge and love, because it is by constituting the inward 'other' that it comes to its self-fulfillment, which is the presupposition or the act of being present to itself in knowledge and love." /34/ Strictly speaking, then, the symbol is the self-realization of a being in the other. "Where there is such a self-realization in the other - as the necessary mode of the fulfillment of its own essence - we have a symbol of the being in question." /35/ For Rahner the notion of symbol highlights the characteristic of entities which requires that they express themselves in order to be themselves. Reality is symbolic because by essence it is kenotic: "self-possession" is attained through self-expression. It is the very essence of personal reality to express itself in the other. In order to be oneself, personal identity is always realized in and with the other.

The Logos, as already mentioned, is the expression, image and word of the Father. The Logos is the symbol of the Father, both in the inner life of God and in the world. "It is because God 'must express' himself inwardly that he can also utter himself outwardly; the finite created utterance _ad extra_ is a continuation of the immanent constitution of 'image and likeness' ..." /36/ So the Logos is the expressive presence of the Father in the world. In the Incarnation, the humanity of Jesus is the appearance, the symbolic reality, the genuine self-disclosure of the Logos. The Logos' humanity is not alien to the Logos; it does not function simply as a sign. If this humanity were alien and simply a sign, "The Logos would make himself audible and perceptible through a reality which was of itself alien to him, had intrinsically and essentially nothing to do with him and could have been chosen at random from a whole series of such realities." /37/

The humanity of Jesus as expressive of the Logos, is constituted by the Logos as he exteriorizes himself. /38/

Humanity can be understood as the symbol which emerges when God expresses himself outside of himself. In its quality as symbol, such a humanity possesses an unfathomable depth which faith alone can sound. /39/ Christ is the expression of God's self-presence in that which has been constituted as the other. Because humanity constituted by God is also symbolic, Christ as symbol is the outward expression that calls to life and feeds what is already part of our own inner dispositions. It shows us what we are and thus enables us to actualize our potentialities as sons of God. The truth of human existence is expressed in Jesus Christ. In the affirmation of Jesus as Christ we find the symbolic expression of the transcendent possibility of what it means to be fully human.

Christ is the eschatological symbol of the presence of the universal and eternal God in human history. Just as God's initiative in Jesus is part of a larger history of his self-communication, Jesus' acceptance is also part of a larger history of human response which both prepared the way for Jesus' acceptance and which is in part contradicted by Jesus' obedience. Jesus' human freedom is both rooted in and transcends the history of human freedom which precedes him. Incarnation is not simply an act of God but it is rather a cooperative act of God and man; a kenosis on the part of God and a kenosis on the part of man.

A KENOTIC CHRISTOLOGY

NOTES

1. For an influential criticism of this formula, cf. F. Schleiermacher, The Christian Faith, eds. H. R. Mackintosh and J. S. Stewart, (New York: Harper) Vol. II, pp. 392 ff.

   E. Brunner argues against the formula in the following way: "The doctrine of the Two Natures becomes the object of purely external, theoretical, semi-scientific discussion and explanation. Faith becomes intellectualized, and it is henceforth possible to discuss the Deity of Christ in the same way that a physical phenomenon could be discussed," The Mediator, trans. O. Wyon, (Westminster, 1967) p. 341.

2. W. Pannenberg, Jesus - God and Man, (Philadelphia: The Westminster Press, 1964) p. 284.

3. P. Schoonenberg, The Christ, (New York: Herder & Herder, 1969) p. 90.

4. Ibid.

5. Cf. K. Rahner, "Current Problems in Christology," in Theological Investigations, Vol. I, (Baltimore: Helicon, 1965) p. 117.

6. This is in opposition to W. Pannenberg, "Apart from Jesus' resurrection it would not be true that from the very beginning of his earthly way God was one with this man... Until his resurrection, Jesus' unity with God was hidden...because the ultimate decision about it had not been given." Op. cit., p. 321. For Pannenberg, the Resurrection is the ground of Jesus' personal unity with God. It is the Resurrection and nothing preceding it which decides Jesus' divinity. Here the future has ontological priority.

7. W. Pannenberg, op. cit., p. 336.

8. Ibid.

9. Ibid., p. 335.

10. Ibid., p. 336.

11. Ibid., p. 337.

12. K. Rahner, Foundations of Christian Faith, (New York: Seabury Press, 1978), p. 128.

13. Ibid., p. 217.

14. K. Rahner, "The Concept of Mystery in Catholic Theology," in Theological Investigations, Vol. IV, (New York: Seabury Press, 1974) p. 117.

15. I John 3:2.

16. K. Rahner, "On the Theology of the Incarnation," Theological Investigations, Vol. IV, (New York: Seabury Press, 1974) p. 117.

17. Cf. K. Rahner and H. Vorgrimler, Dictionary of Theology, (New York: Herder & Herder, 1965) p. 240.

18. K. Rahner, "Current Problems in Christology," op. cit., p. 161.

19. K. Rahner, Foundations of Christian Faith, op. cit., p. 197.

20. Cf. K. Rahner, Foundations of Christian Faith, op. cit., p. 202-203.

21. Cf. K. Rahner, "Theological Observations on the Concept of Time," Theological Investigations, Vol. XI, (New York: The Seabury Press, 1974) p. 290.

22. J. Macquarrie, Principles of Christian Theology, (New York: Charles Scribner's Sons, 1966) p. 274.

23. K. Rahner, Foundations of Christian Faith, op. cit., p. 218.

24. K. Rahner, "On the Meaning of the Incarnation," op. cit., p. 117.

25. J. B. Metz, Theology of the World, trans. W. Glen-Doepel, (New York: Herder & Herder, 1969) p. 26.

26. Ibid.

27. Cf. K. Rahner, "The Theology of the Symbol," Theological Investigations, Vol. IV, (New York: The Seabury Press, 1974) p. 237.

28. Cf. W. Pannenberg, Jesus - God and Man, op. cit., p. 133.

29. J. Macquarrie, Principles of Christian Theology, op. cit., p. 249.

30. Ibid.

31. K. Rahner, "The Theology of the Symbol," op. cit., p. 224.

32. Ibid., p. 230.

33. Ibid., p. 229.

34. Ibid., pp. 229-230.

35. Ibid., p. 234.

36. Ibid., p. 237.

37. Ibid.

38. Ibid., p. 239.

39. Ibid.

CHAPTER 11

THE HUMANITY OF CHRIST AND OUR HUMANITY

A. Introduction: Incarnation and History

In the mystery of the Incarnation, God, through an act of self-emptying, a kenosis, brings about the reality that Jesus is, a personal human reality. Since Jesus is brought about as person, the mystery of the Incarnation is not a one-sided mystery, totally on the part of God; Jesus' freedom, Jesus' acceptance is an important element. The symbol of the Incarnation points not only to God's self-communication, to God's kenosis, but also to Jesus' kenosis.

Christ is savior from inside. The appearance of Christ within human history is not simply a break-through from above. It does not simply touch from outside. Christ as the "Son of God" emerged from within history like any other person: "Born of a woman, born under the law" (Gal. 4:4). Jesus as the Christ, as the Son of God, was fully involved in the universal historical situation, which has been described by Paul as a state of accursedness, and which contemporary authors have described as one of alienation. /1/

There is a self-communication from the divine and human sides. In this sense the Incarnation is processive; it has a dynamic character. It is not a question of the Logos simply being implanted in a human reality at conception or at any other time for that matter. The moment of incarnation cannot be identified simply with the moment of conception. Conception and birth simply represent the beginning of the incarnational process; not a completed process. /2/ Personhood cannot be understood simply as a substance injected into a body at conception; personhood arises; it is brought about in the deeds and decisions of life; it is essentially historical. Personhood implies and demands an embodied existence in the world; an ongoing exercise of acceptance of freedom. Acceptance can never be understood simply as a once and for all act; it is essentially historical, always in process. The mystery of the Incarnation extends over the life history of Jesus, and over human history. In Jesus the divine is revealed in a human way; therefore, God's presence is still withheld in some fashion. The drama of Incarnation is not yet over; it has an eschatological dimension. The total life of Jesus, his ministry and death, are elements of God's incarnational act. Jesus' acceptance is sealed on the cross in an ultimate act of trust and acceptance of the Father's will. The Father's acceptance climaxes in the Resurrection of Jesus. /3/

Jesus' personhood and therefore his Christhood are realized progressively. There is growth and development. What is being affirmed here is that Jesus in all of his reality is marked by history. Not only does God enter into history, but he also accepts it and embraces it. John writes, "The Word became flesh and made his dwelling among us" (Jn. 1:14). The Savior is immersed in the full human condition. In the language of the Bible, "flesh" does not simply mean the material part of the person but the whole person as viewed in its wretchedness; God became not simply man but a wretched human being, fully subject to the human condition. God's way is the way of "enfleshment."

It is basically in denying Jesus' historicity that one attacks the full humanity of Jesus. A classical position relative to Jesus' humanity can be formulated in the following way: Christ is not an historical "person"; his person is the divine person, who assumes in himself all history, but who is not "exhausted" in time. History cannot be understood as accidental, extrinsic, adventitious to human existence. History is not simply an epiphenomenon of a human nature which remains static and totally unaffected; the human nature itself is historical. As historical, Jesus' existence is carried out in a situation which is defined and characterized by history. This situation makes some things possible and others impossible. It is essential that to be human, Jesus' history must be the result of his own personal decisions. These decisions conditioned by time and space, historical in their essence, have to be the source of Jesus' history.

From our classical Christology we have inherited that Jesus was simultaneously *viator et comprehensor*, earthly pilgrim and possessor of the heavenly vision. /4/ In this view, the pre-existent Second Person of the Trinity is understood as having chosen his own situation from all eternity. But if Jesus is characterized essentially by history there cannot be any pre-existent choice of the circumstances of his own life; these are given and brought about in time and space.

Pre-existent choices would nullify genuine human destiny and history; Jesus' history would be robbed of its actual source, the personal decisions of the man. It is not possible for Jesus to be simultaneously "completed" and "on the way" to completion, a pilgrim. These two are mutually exclusive. Any attempt to bring these two states together leads to a two-layer Christology. In an anhypostatic Christology the question of the full humanity of Jesus becomes problematical for the simple reason that the attributes of divinity are not simply different from those of humanity but are at times incompatible since the subject of both sets of attributes is the same subject, the second person of the Trinity.

B. Jesus' Knowledge

In traditional Christology Jesus has been attributed unlimited knowledge; he was given beatific vision from the very first moment of conception, and then all acquired knowledge and infused knowledge. /5/ He possessed a clear grasp of his identity as the second person of the Trinity and detailed knowledge about everything that would occur to him in his lifetime. Such declarations appear mythological and in real conflict with the way the New Testament describes the ministry of Jesus, where development in understanding and profession of ignorance, real suffering, and even abandonment are attributed to Jesus. /6/ According to Rahner, Jesus

> "...is shown as a man bearing the stamp of his times, as modern research into ancient religion and culture demonstrate clearly, and with ever-increasing precision. We almost have the impression that the only original thing about him was his own personality and the unique manner in which the influence of his milieu were concentrated in him - though every single human being is in his own way a unique sounding-board for his milieu." /7/

Medieval and later theology conceived the psychology of Christ as man not merely in ontological terms but also on the basis of the perfection that on *a priori* grounds were considered befitting a divine person. Today we have to attend more to the words of the Scripture (Heb. 4:15) as cited in the Council of Chalcedon, "similar to us in all things save sin." /8/ If we are to think of Jesus as truly a man we have to think of him as an historical being, as growing in wisdom, grace and age in a determinate social and cultural milieu or developing from below as other human beings and from above on the analogy of religious development.

Human reality as conditioned by history is a project into the future, a creative task, a dynamic movement made up of inward decisions and commitments, of outward behavior, actions and relations to others. Jesus is faced with the challenge of realizing his humanity. This realization can only occur in a human community. This is clearly expressed in the new emphasis on and evaluation of language. Self-consciousness arises only in the presence of and in dialogue with an "other," with a "Thou." Human life is only authentically human when it occurs in dialogue. J. Moltmann writes, "...subjectivity is always 'intersubjectivity,' and humanity, always co-humanity, and responsibility, the necessity of giving a response." /9/

As a human person, Jesus must be understood in his uniqueness - he must be understood not as contingently but necessarily in relation, as at the center of an infinitely complex network of relations, and he cannot be understood except in that complex. In a very special way it was as a Jew that Jesus trusted God, not as man in general, believing in the divine in general. Jesus cannot be emancipated from his Jewishness, for he cannot be emancipated from history. It follows that Jesus' mind was formed by the tradition he inherited and the particular culture he lived in. /10/ As a human person, Jesus is part of a moving flow of connectedness. As a movement, it is dynamic, it involves change. The human person is a mystery because its humanity is not a possession, not something which has already been attained. Men and women do not come into existence ready-made. They have their being only through a long period of growth and development.

This is most true in the realm of knowledge and will. Yet the concept of the human which lies at the foundation of the classical theory on Jesus' knowledge is most profoundly Hellenistic in nature. The perfection of man/woman is measured in terms of clear knowledge, of vision. Here history is perceived as accidental to human existence, as extrinsic to its substance; that which is permanent is of the highest importance. Development, movement, growth are imperfections.

In a situation where a person is marked and conditioned by history, knowledge and freedom are historical experiences. Knowledge and freedom are marked by the personal openness of human reality to the future. Because historical, all human knowledge is basically contextual and dependent on temporary processes and therefore developmental in nature. In human existence, a lack of knowledge is not merely a lack but the source for the venturing of one's own future. The whole scale of implicit consciousness, of questions, of provisional interpretations and decisions, are essential parts of this venturing. Rahner writes,

> "...risk is of the essence of the self-perfecting of the finite person in the historical freedom of decision. Risk is involved; committing oneself to what is not totally visible, the hidden origin and the veiled end - a certain manner of not knowing is essential to the free act of a man." /11/

If Jesus were omniscient he could not be "perfectly" human. /12/ Jesus' immediacy to God does not exclude that process of learning and risking.

Kenotic Christology has shown us that being from God determines the nature of every creature, and the more completely a creature is from God and therefore united with God, the more fully it is itself, the more it exists in its own particularity. The hypostatic union, therefore, far from excluding real humanity in Jesus Christ, on the contrary emphasizes that Christ possesses the perfection of real human existence to the highest possible degree.

Communion with God for Jesus can in no way be conceived in a nontemporal way which would impede the development of self. Jesus' understanding, his knowledge, the acceptance of his mission, his love of God, were shaped by the social context he found himself in and by the tradition he inherited. Jesus' immediacy to God does not exclude that process. Jesus' awareness of the "not yet decided" future is a condition of his human opennness and freedom.

In classical Christology it is affirmed that Jesus knew from the beginning what his destiny was to be; his death and resurrection in all their historical details and their redemptive efficacy were known and willed from the beginning. This robs Jesus of an authentic humanity, of the value of his sacrifice, and masks the revelation of God's love for us. On the cross Jesus still trusts in God and throws himself upon the loving power of his Father by unselfishly letting go of his own life. A full knowledge of the future, of his own resurrection, would render Jesus' sacrifice of self meaningless. Jesus faced his future as a mystery, and his death with dread yet in faith and hope. Jesus went to Jerusalem and to his death, with a human understanding and with human emotions. He did not perceive in advance everything that was to happen to him nor did he act out the script that he already knew by heart. Obedient to his vocation as he perceived it, Jesus entered into events, the shape of which were clearly perceived. While Jesus' death did not come upon him totally by surprise, yet his knowledge was a human knowledge.

C. Jesus' Self-Understanding

As an historical person conditioned by time and space, and in process of completion as person - in what way can we ask the question about Jesus' self-understanding? And more specifically ask the question about his knowledge of his relationship to God? Did Jesus know himself to be and call himself Messiah - Son of God? Can there be such a separation between the order of being and the order of identity? Bruce Vawter writes,

> "To say that Jesus in his earthly life knew and judged himself to be God's natural Son and very God is to assert the improvable, and from the perspective of the New Testament, the improbable. Had Jesus known such a thing he could hardly have contained his knowledge, yet the gospels are witness that his most

> intimate disciples did not recognize his essential relation to God prior to his resurrection." /13/

Contemporary theologians are not willing to give an unconditional yes to these questions. /14/ In light of the fact that Jesus is fully human with all the complexity of humanhood and its development nature, the answers to those questions have to be complex.

The process of self-understanding - and self-consciousness - occurs in one's own history, in interaction with others, in openness to what others have to say about one's own self. Self-awareness comes to realization in the process of a journey from inarticulation to articulation. Pannenberg writes, "The uniqueness and identity of a person is not constituted by an abstract self-consciousness, but by the particular character and unity of his life history." /15/

Rahner has attempted to construct a Christology based on the dimension of Christ's consciousness. According to Rahner, the unity of Jesus' humanity to the Logos is so radical that it must be conscious of itself, for the higher the intensity of being, the more intelligible it is, the more present to itself. The presence to self in Jesus is not the source of an objective knowledge but of unobjectified, unthematized consciousness. While the infinite horizon of the human spirit is fulfilled in Christ, yet there is still a need in Jesus for experiential fulfillment in the context of a genuine human history. /16/

D. Jesus' Freedom

Being limited in knowledge is an essential part of being human, since history is an essential part of the same humanness. The same limitations apply to freedom. Authentic freedom demands the possibility of choice in the context of unknown factors and finalities; one must entrust oneself to a variety of situations and possibilities and a future that is often unknown. Human freedom is always a freedom within a situation, within a context. Freedom, if it is to be authentic, implies the possibility to decide upon or to determine for ourselves a certain course of action within the context of certain external conditions. In fact, decision is an integral and foundational element of freedom. A person posits himself or herself through decisions. It is clear that the ability to decide is not simply a matter of sheer spontaneity. It is determined by inner motivation, and social and contextual conditions.

Rudolph Pesch writes in relation to a generally accepted opinion that Jesus was not free like other men but in some way pre-programmed:

> "...this is a false alternative - Jesus was not free like other people; he was freer to do or not do what he himself wanted, he lived in a liberated freedom, which he preached and passed on. Jesus was not pre-programmed like other people: a wider range of possibilities was open to his freedom because the institution of freedom is not a process which can be pre-programmed, but an endless task which demands inventive spontaneity, creativity, talent for innovation. His task made him free because it bound him completely to the cause of freedom. The "must" under the shadow of which his whole life, his journey to death (Mk. 8:31) was a tie to the will of the Heavenly Father who wanted men to be free. Freedom grows at the same rate as the tie to freedom, the tie to God as the source and guarantee of freedom." /17/

There cannot be for Jesus a pre-established plan that he simply fulfills; or a pre-existent choice of the circumstances of his life. These would nullify the reality of his freedom. The future cannot be for Jesus an open book. There could be no knowledge of the infallibility of his success. The future is always ambiguous and Jesus' freedom was conditioned by that ambiguity. The outcome of free decision is uncertain until the end of one's life. When the early Church understood sonship as expressing and symbolizing Jesus' relationship to God, we can accept this designation as referring to the humanity of Jesus in its process of completion in obedience and self-surrender to the Father. This self-surrender is the very nature of Jesus' sonship. It is in terms of this self-surrender that we may speak of Jesus' radical freedom. P. Hodgson defines radical freedom as a "...freedom which has its source in openness to the free, manifests itself in acts of liberation, and issues in a fulfilled subjectivity." /18/ Jesus' life was one of radical openness or obedience to God. Jesus' freedom is radical because in a fundamental way it is the freedom of God that is the reason and condition of Jesus' freedom. And as Kasper writes, "Only the bond with the infinite and absolute freedom of God as the ultimate ground and meaning of man makes the latter free from all dane claims to absoluteness and thus also free for engagement in the world." /19/ Jesus, because and not in spite of his unity with the Father, embodied the essence of human freedom. This embodiment is expressed in terms of his openness to the Father, in terms of his radical commitment and communion with the outcasts and the oppressed.

It is in this context that one must consider Jesus' sinlessness. The Scriptures speak about the sinlessness of Jesus - of his untainted and ongoing openness to God and to the neighbor. In classical theology the doctrine of the sinlessness of Jesus (Jn. 8:46, 14:30; 2 Cor. 5:21; I Pet. 2:22; Heb. 4:15) has its foundation on the doctrine of the hypostatic unity on the basic affirmation that there can be no separation from God for Jesus. Jesus' life is totally centered on God, in doing the will of God; it is a life of community with the Father; a community of will, of mind. The theological tradition affirms on this basis not only a factual sinlessness but also an essential sinlessness. /20/ Yet Jesus' sinlessness cannot be an a priori characteristic. This a priori would destroy the reality of his humanity. Sin is not a necessary characteristic of human nature; it is a possibility and a fact. Jesus because he is human shares with us the possibility of sinfulness.

Human fallibility is the underlying ontological constitution of human reality which establishes the possibility of faulted existence; but it is not to be simply identified to fault. Human fallibility implies that human freedom is always contextual, conditional and conflictual. Human freedom exists in the context of various polarities; it is marked by fragility. /21/ Polarities and tensions are not in themselves sinful. Yet unfaulted human existence is empirically impossible, although the roots of sin lie in an interior act of the will. In a sense fallibility is simply the susceptibility of human existence, of human freedom to fail. This susceptibility, this fragility, does not cause sin, it is the pre-condition, the possibility of sin. /22/ Sin is not necessary but it is inevitable. It is not necessary because it cannot be identified with the fallibility of human existence, but it is inevitable because it simply always happens.

E. Jesus' Sinlessness

The sinlessness of Jesus cannot be grasped as pertaining metaphysically to his humanity, but as a result of God's self-gift and Jesus' own response occurring during the full span of his life. In light of this, one can understand why it is possible to accept fully the affirmation of the Scriptures that Jesus was tempted, for it is characteristic of man to be tempted. Temptation is not sin, it is simply the condition of moral freedom; temptation is the external pre-condition of sin. While sinless in his own individual life, Jesus did not escape being caught up in the disorder of society. The temptations in the desert reflect this dimension. As P. Hodgson writes, "The situation for tension, anxiety, or disproportion becomes the occasion for sin only when it is falsely interpreted, which is not purely the product of human imagination but is suggested by a principle or force of evil antecedent to any individual human action." False interpretation of the sources of one's anxiety is the key to understanding temptation. /23/

F. Jesus, the Man for Others

When one has affirmed and accepted the full humanity of Jesus in all its finite and historically conditioned situations, one has not said enough about Jesus. Jesus' humanity is authentic as personal humanity. When we seek after Jesus' identity, when we ask who is this Jesus of Nazareth, we find that identity in the reality of his personhood. Jesus is the kind of person who lives only in and because of his relationship to God the Father and to the outcasts and the abandoned. A man and a woman reach maturity, discover the meaning of human existence through a steady increase of ever fuller and more authentic oblativity and selflessness. It is our discovery of others and our encounter with them which opens the closed world of our self-centered totalities to the infinity of the wholly other, to the one and unique mystery. Jesus does not belong to himself but to the other. He does not exist in and for himself but for the other; he has emptied himself for the sake of the other. It is in love and dedication that Jesus' personhood is brought about. Love means existing for the sake of the other, by means of which the identity of the individual self is not lost but fulfilled, taken up into a higher unity. In the case of Jesus, love assumed the form of suffering, self-giving and existence for others even unto death.

What characterizes Jesus' love for us is that it is without limitations; nothing is withheld - no greater sign than to give up one's own life. The cross remains the symbol of Jesus' limitless love; an attempt to express the depth of such love. What restricts Jesus' expression of love is our capacity to receive. The authenticity of Jesus' love implies a totality of giving - the giving of self. Jesus' self is that which is made available in his love. Because it is a total self-giving, Jesus' love is precarious; it can be frustrated; the greatness of what is offered is totally disproportionate to that which is received. Jesus dies abandoned, alone. Jesus accepts the fact that his love contains no assurance or certainty of completion. Jesus' love involves the hope that the other may receive; it also involves the possibility of failure.

The precariousness of Jesus' love is experienced in the passivity of "waiting." The apostles never understand, as we see so clearly expressed in the Gospel of Mark. They are blind; Jesus must "wait" for them, for their response of receiving which is the completion of his own activity of giving. Jesus' love is given to others. Jesus gives power over himself; the power to make him angry, to cause him grief and joy; to frustrate or fulfill. There is vulnerability in Jesus' love: he surrendered into other hands the issue and outcome of his own aspiration. Jesus' life is marked by interdependence. Jesus is not presented as a superman who deals with human misery out of power which very often creates new misery. Jesus transcends man by including himself in a humanity that is poor and suffering. His dominion is in no way similar to the domination of world-rulers; he dominates through service, love, and suffering. All force, all power will have to be judged by the way in which it deals with the powerless. As Moltmann writes, "His power is the impotence of grace, the reconciling force of suffering, and the dominion of self-denying love." /24/

THE HUMANITY OF CHRIST AND OUR HUMANITY

NOTES

1. W. Kasper, Jesus the Christ, (New York: Paulist Press, 1976), pp. 197-215.

2. Cf. K. Rahner, Theological Investigations, Vol. trans. by Cornelius Ernst, (Baltimore: Helicon Press, 1961) p. 155.

3. Cf. K. Rahner, On the Theology of Death, trans. W. J. O'Hara, (New York: Herder & Herder, 1965).

4. Cf. P. Schoonenberg, The Christ, (New York: Herder & Herder, 1971). pp. 105-176.

5. Pius XII in his encyclical Mystici Corporis wrote that Jesus had the beatific vision from the first moment of conception (DBS 3812).

6. Cf. E. Gutwenger, "The Problem of Christ's Knowledge" in Concilium I, No. 2 (1966) pp. 48-55.

7. K. Rahner, "Dogmatic Considerations on Knowledge and Consciousness in Christ," in Dogmatic versus Biblical Theology, ed. H. Vorgrimler (London: 1964) pp. 242-243.

8. Cf. R. E. Brown, Jesus, God and Man. Modern Biblical Reflections, (Milwaukee: Bruce Publ., 1967) pp. 39-103.

9. J. Moltmann, Man: Christian Anthropology in the Conflicts of the Present, trans. J. Sturdy, (London: SPCK, 1974) p. 81.

10. In the exegesis of the New Testament there must be an attempt, to use the words of Leander Keck, to free oneself from the "tyranny" of the negative criterion, according to which that which is "dissimilar to characteristic emphases both of ancient Judaism and of the early Church" is seen as most likely to be from Jesus. To apply this criterion in an absolute way is to isolate Jesus from his social and historical environment. Cf. Leander Keck, A Future for the Historical Jesus, (Nashville: Abingdon Press, 1971), pp. 33-35.

Cf. also Gerd Theissen, Sociology of Early Palestinian Christianity, trans. J. Bowden, (Philadelphia: Fortress Press, 1977).

11. K. Rahner, "Dogmatic Considerations on Knowledge and Consciousness in Christ," op. cit., p. 248.

12. Cf. Ibid.

13. B. Vawter, This Man Jesus. An Essay Toward a New Testament Christology, (New York: Doubleday, 1973) p. 134.

14. Cf. K. Rahner, op. cit., p. 262.

15. W. Pannenberg, Jesus - God and Man, (Philadelphia: Westminster Press, 1968) p. 304.

16. Cf. K. Rahner, "Dogmatic Reflections on the Knowledge and Self-Consciousness of Christ," Theological Investigations, Vol. V, (Baltimore: Helicon Press, 1966) p. 206.

17. R. Pesch, "Jesus: A Free Man," in Concilium, Vol. 3, No. 13 (1974) p. 68.

18. P. C. Hodgson, New Birth of Freedom. A Theory of Bondage and Liberation, (Philadelphia: Fortress Press, 1976) p. 217.

19. W. Kasper, op. cit., p. 213.

20. On this question, cf. J. A. T. Robinson, The Human Face of God, (Philadelphia: Westminster Press, 1973) pp. 68-98.

R. Niebuhr, The Nature and Destiny of Man, Vol. II, (New York: Charles Scribner's Sons, 1966) pp. 53-59.

21. Cf. J. Macquarrie, Principles of Christian Theology, (New York: Charles Scribner's Sons, 1966) pp. 53-59.

22. P. Hodgson, op. cit., p. 171.

23. R. Niebuhr distinguishes two pre-conditions for sin, one that is internal and the other, external.

He sees anxiety as the internal precondition and Jesus' injunction, "Therefore I say unto you be not anxious" as containing "...the whole genius of the Biblical view of the relation of finiteness to sin in man. It is not in his finiteness, dependence and weakness but his anxiety about it which tempts him to sin." The Nature and Destiny of Man, op. cit., Vol. I, p. 168.

It is Kierkegaard who has underlined the relation of anxiety to freedom and sinfulness. He writes: "Anxiety (angst) is the dizziness of freedom which occurs when the spirit would posit the synthesis of soul and body, and freedom then gazes down into its own possibility, grasping at finiteness to sustain itself. In this dizziness, freedom succumbs. Further than this, psychology cannot go and will not. That very instant everything is changed and when freedom rises again, it sees that it is guilty. Between these two instants lies the leap which no science has explained or can explain... Anxiety is the last psychological state out of which sin breaks forth with the qualitative leap." S. Kierkegaard, The Concept of Dread, trans. W. Lownie, (Princeton: Princeton University Press, 1946) p. 55. While anxiety is seen as a pre-condition for sin, it is not yet sin; it is an element of the disproportion of human reality, the polarity within persons of the finite and the infinite, of nature and freedom. Niebuhr writes, "Anxiety is the inevitable concomitant of the paradox of freedom and finiteness in which man is involved. Anxiety is the pre-condition of sin. It is the inevitable spiritual state of man, standing in the paradoxical situation of freedom and finiteness." Op. cit., Vol. I, p. 182.

Niebuhr affirms that anxiety is not yet sin for there is always the ideal possibility that faith "...would purge anxiety of the tendency toward sinful self-assertion. The ideal possibility is that faith in the ultimate security of God's love would overcome all immediate insecurities of nature and history." Op. cit., p. 183.

J. Moltmann, op. cit., p. 113.

CONCLUSION

When one confesses that Jesus is Lord, that he is the Christ, there is an understanding that this Jesus has universal significance. According to D. Tracy such an affirmation about Jesus implies that he "...is disclosive of all reality, is meaningful for our common existence, is central for a human understanding of the limitless possibilities of human existence." /1/ In Jesus is revealed what is meant to be fully human. Christianity proclaims that in Jesus Christ the human ideal for which all human beings strive has been attained in history and that unless one is human as Christ was human, one cannot be human at all.

Jesus Christ is not only the revelation of who God is but also the revelation of who man is. In him the question as to who is God and who is man are answerable only in their complementarity, not as two questions but as one. In its Constitution, Gaudium et Spes, /2/ the Church associates itself with a new humanism. The divine is not forgotten; it is understood as being implicit in man's growing responsibility for his brothers and for history. The question about God has become a question about God's presence in human life as creator and redeemer. Man's personal history is the "locus of the supernatural." According to G. Baum, "Christianity may be called a humanism, to be precise, a Christological humanism. For in Christ is revealed to us who man shall be or, more carefully, who the transcendent dynamism is by which, gratuitously, all men are summoned and freed to become more fully human. Divine grace recreates in men the perfect humanity revealed in Christ. Christianity is humanistic in the sense that it reveals, celebrates, and promotes the entry of all men into greater likeness to Jesus Christ." /3/

According to kenotic Christology what is remarkable about Jesus, the Christ, is his self-emptying for others. The special action of God in Christ is that of self-emptying; kenosis is actually plerosis, a positive expression of who God is. The form of a servant is the fullest expression of God's glory, and the ultimate significance of human existence. To the basic question posed by a hermeneutical approach to Christology: "Is there a distinctive Christian view of man?" or "In what way is Jesus Christ the true revelation of authentic humanity?" one must answer: in Jesus, kenosis is the revelation of that which constitutes a person's deepest nature, love surpassing itself and emptying itself. Jesus in his own life and death has universalized a fundamental law: "Whoever would save his life will lose it; and whoever loses his life for my sake and the gospel's will save it" (Mk. 8:35).

The Christological symbolism assures us that only through love can we do justice to the whole of reality, "for he who abides in love abides in God." In the kenotic way the crucial decision regarding God is made by men and women in their relationship to one another. The place for one's trusting surrender to God is the love of one's neighbor. In the kenotic way the "other" has been radicalized. When we read in the New Testament that one who loves one's neighbors has fulfilled the Law, this is the ultimate truth, because God has been one's neighbor. /4/

In the kenotic way, everyone is one's neighbor, whoever happens to be next to hand, unconditionally, without discrimation. /5/ This is why a kenotic love involves the enemy; it is that radical. Again Kierkegaard writes,

> "He who in truth loves his neighbour loves also his enemy. The distinction, friend or enemy, is a distinction in the object of love, but the object of love to one's neighbour is without distinction. One's neighbour is the absolutely unrecognizable distinction between man and man; it is eternal equality before God--enemies, too, have this equality." /6/

There is a permanence to such a love, an independence from changes occurring in the neighbor. Such a love is different from friendship and other forms of love. As Kierkegaard writes,

> "You can also continue to love your beloved and your friend no matter how they treat you, but you cannot truthfully continue to call them beloved and friend when they, sorry to say, have really changed. No change, however, can take your neighbour from you, for it is not your neighbour who

holds you fast...it is your love which holds your neighbour fast." /7/

Kenotic love is love of the unworthy, the worthless, the lost. The love of neighbour does not arise from nor is it proportional to anything one possesses or acquires. G. Outka writes that such a love "... is based neither on favoritism nor instinctive aversion. Its presence is somehow not determined by the other's actions; it is independent both in its genesis (he need not know who I am) and continuation (he may remain my enemy). One ought to be 'for' another, whatever the particular changes in him for better or for worse." /8/ There can be no exclusiveness, no partiality, no elitism. A kenotic love is characterized, essentially, by its universality; it is the foundation of interdependence. Interdependence is a way of being, of existing without mastery, without force, without difference in status. In interdependence whatever is superior demonstrates its superiority by its power to empty itself. The abundance of interdependence in reality is revealed in the humiliation of the exalted and the exaltation of the lowly.

The interdependent life is one of radical mutuality and reciprocity, of giving and receiving, of giving so completely from and for the other that nothing is left of self-centeredness. The deepest center of the self is always beyond the individual ego. Human subjectivity at its deepest is not the self-suffering of isolated monads.

A kenotic way of living usually ends in self-sacrifice in this life. Reinhold Niebuhr writes,

> "The perfect disinterestedness of the divine love can have a counterpart in history only in a life which ends tragically, because it refuses to participate in the claims and counterclaims of historical existence. It portrays a love 'which seeketh not its own.' But a love which seeketh not its own is not able to maintain itself in historical society. Not only may it fall the victim to excessive forms of the self-assertion of others; but even the most perfectly

> balanced system of justice in history is a balance of competing wills and interests, and must therefore worst anyone who does not participate in the balance." /9/

The self-sacrificing aspect of kenotic love is illustrated in the parable of the Good Samaritan (Lk. 10: 25-37). The Samaritan "was moved to pity at the sight" of the wounded traveler. A more literal translation of "being moved to pity" would be, he "was moved in his spleen." Pity here means compassion, "suffering with." It is not simply a question of understanding the other's suffering. It is a question of feeling the other's suffering in one's own guts.

Interdependence which can lead to self-sacrifice is possible only if God is present. Human interdependence is most truly realized when it is interdependence with God. Without interdependence restored there is the real possibility that human history could fail radically. That restoration is clearly not possible without God. The question of the reality of human interdependence poses in a radical way the question of the need, the reality and nature of God's presence. In the person of Jesus the answer to these questions has been given to us. What is revealed in Jesus is that chosen vulnerability in our relationship with one another will ultimately save us more than any dependence upon power. God has made himself powerless for us. In Jesus Christ God has revealed his solidarity with us, the full dimension of his presence as interdependence. Interdependence is possible in this world because of the loving God who first comes into the world to share in its burden. As Paul writes, "...it is no longer we who suffer, but God suffers in us." In Jesus Christ, God has communicated himself intimately to his creation; he has brought about an intimate partnership. God's omnipotence is not tucked away as a last-resort security blanket. Transcendence is not extrinsic but intrinsic to human existence, not a dimension super-added to life but rather the ground of its possibility. The "supernatural" is not alien to man, nor is it a perfection superimposed upon him. Within this viewpoint the frontiers between God's work and the human task become fluid. In Christ human existence and with it the total temporal structure in its very profanity become the objective expression of God's self-communication and the objective expression of the human response to that self-gift.

Rahner writes: "Cristianity does not add a vertical dimension of man onto the horizontal, nor does it divide man by placing two demands on him. In speaking of God, Christianity simply uncovers the radical meaning and dignity of man in relationship to his interpersonal "thou." In view of the mystery of the Incarnation, there can be no real love of God which in some way does not communicate its depth to this love given to man." /10/ The transcendental is not the infinite and unattainable, but the neighbor who is within reach in any situation.

The partnership and interdependence brought about by God's presence in self-emptying serves to reconcile the world through solidarity with the suffering and the oppressed. The only effective way to redeem people is the way of sociological incarnation, that is, by immersion in the wretchedness from which we are about to be liberated. This solidarity by immersion becomes emancipatory, because it is ultimately humanizing.

As disciples of the crucified and self-emptying Christ, we are drawn into his self-surrender, into his solidarity with the lost and into his public suffering. His self-emptying, his suffering is in this respect not exclusive and leads to compassion (Cf. I Cor 1:26-31). As Moltmann writes: "The fellowship called into life by Christ's self-surrender serves to reconcile the world through solidarity with the suffering of the people and through participation in the representative work of Christ in the Spirit. The Christian "being-there-for-others' cannot be separated from 'being-with-others' in solidarity; and being-with-others cannot be separated from being-for-others." /11/

This kind of compassion is inextricably interwoven with hope and justice. Compassion is not exhausted in the area of intentionality and demonstration but it demands efficacy. Such compassion has as its object and goal emancipatory solidarity. To identify with the crucified and compassionate Christ today is not to try to conjure up an emotional experience reproducing the suffering Jesus endured long ago. But it is to place oneself with the wretched of the earth today, those beyond human hope. Identification with the crucified Christ means solidarity with the sufferings of the poor and oppressed, those who have been abandoned.

Kenosis is a way of describing the divine being and the divine action in Jesus Christ. It describes not only who God is in Jesus Christ but also who the believer must be. Kenosis is the affirmation that chosen vulnerability in our relationships with one another will ultimately save us more than any dependence upon power. Kenosis, as a revelation of who God is and who we are is believable only within a kenotic community. The Church community of those who remember Jesus must have Jesus' vision and life-style. Apart from the ecclesial community's solidarity with the oppressed in self-emptying and self-giving, the gospel becomes impossible to believe. The kenosis of God in Jesus Christ cannot be believed unless it is experienced in the kenotic community. The mediating of this revelation can only be found in the concrete product of Christian living. As Moltmann writes:

> "The church is called to life through the gospel of Christ's self-giving. Hence it is fundamentally born out of the cross of Christ. At its centre is "the word of the cross" and the eucharist with which the death of Christ is proclaimed. It is from the cross of Christ that there develops the fellowship of the godless with God. What makes the church the church is the reconciliation "in the blood of Christ" and its own self-giving for the reconciliation of the world.
>
> The church of Christ is therefore at the same time the church under the cross. The fellowship of Christ is experienced in common resistance to idolatry and inhumanity, in common suffering over oppression and persecution. It is in this participation in the passion of Christ and in the passion of the people that the "life" of Christ and his liberty become visible in the church. Christian fellowship proves itself in temptation and resistance. /12/

A KENOTIC CHRISTOLOGY

The "remembering" of God's kenotic love for us in Jesus Christ is not and cannot be an empty return to the past; it is directed to the future and it demands action. The hoped-for redemption of the world from domination and alienation cannot be active except through an active solidarity with the oppressed and suffering.

"The Christian project of life," the idea revealed in the person of Jesus, the Christ, constitutes no threat to human authenticity. On the contrary, in our world where "small" must necessarily be beautiful, this Christian project constitutes our only real hope for survival. For the one area where Jesus reveals the fullness of human reality lies paradoxically in his self-emptying and his self-giving love. In the acceptance of the "other" as constitutive of himself, Jesus as the Christ, the revelation of who God is, does not simply present us with a static model of mature humanhood. There is an eschatological dimension of his revelation - a "not yet" that does not limit imitation to repetition nor restrict human development to a fixed pattern. We are yet to know what we are to become. The full depths of self-emptying are yet to be fully understood and realized. Our cultural and political situations are now demanding of us a global will for self-limitation.

CONCLUSION

NOTES

1. D. Tracy, Blessed Rage for Order, (New York: Seabury Press, 1975) p. 206.

2. Constitution "Church in the Modern World" in The Conciliar and Post-Conciliar Documents, A. Flanagan, ed. (Northport: Costello Publishing Co., 1975) p. 922, No. 22.

3. G. Baum, Man Becoming (New York: Herder & Herder, 1970) p. 37.

4. Cf. K. Rahner, "Is the Church Sent to Humanize the World?" Theological Digest (1973) p. 20.

5. Cf. Søren Kierkegaard, Works of Love, trans. Howard and Edna Hong, (New York: Harper & Row, 1962) p. 63.

6. Ibid., p. 79.

7. Ibid., p. 76.

8. G. Outka, Agape, An Ethical Analysis, (New Haven: Yale University Press, 1972) p. 11.

9. R. Niebuhr, op. cit., Vol. II, p. 72.

10. K. Rahner, op. cit., p. 20.

11. J. Moltmann, The Crucified God, (New York: Harper & Row, 1973) p. 97.

12. J. Moltmann, The Church in the Power of the Spirit, (New York: Harper & Row, 1975) p. 97.

AUTHOR INDEX

B. (Continued)

C.

D.

E.

AUTHOR INDEX

F.

G.

H.

H. (Continued)

I.

J.

K.

K. (Continued)

L.

M.

M. (Continued)

N.

O.

P.

AUTHOR INDEX

R.

S.

AUTHOR INDEX

T.

U.

V.

W.

SUBJECT INDEX

A.

B.

C.

E. (continued)

F.

G.

H.

H. (continued)

I.

J.

K.

K. (continued)

L.

M.

P. (continued)

Q.

R.

S.

About the Author

Lucien Richard, O.M.I., is a professor of systematic theology at Weston School of Theology in Cambridge, Massachusetts. His graduate work was done at Harvard University. In addition to various articles on Christology, he is the author of *The Spirituality of John Calvin*, John Knox Press, and *What Are They Saying about Christ and World Religions?* published earlier this year by Paulist Press.